COYOTES
AND
STARS

AMERICAN MOSAIC SERIES

For thirty-five years Free River Press has been developing a literary mosaic of America written by people from all walks of life. It is doing this through writing workshops that it conducts across the country in cities and rural hamlets, on farms and ranches. When complete, writings from these workshops will be anthologized in five volumes, collectively titled An American Mosaic. The first three volumes are published. The last two titles are in preparation.

An American Mosaic
Prose and Poetry by Everyday Folk

Heartland Portrait
Stories From the Rural Midwest

Rich Soil, River Soul
Stories from the Mississippi Delta

Coyotes and Stars
Stories from the American Southwest

Big City
Stories from New York and Chicago

COYOTES AND STARS

Stories from the American Southwest

Edited by

Robert Wolf

Illustrations by

Bonnie Koloc

Free River Press
Decorah, Iowa
2025

FREE RIVER PRESS

ISBN: 978-1-878781-20-8
1. American Studies .2 Southwest American Life 3. Cultural Anthropology

Free River Press
"Creating a Literary Mosaic of America"
1308 Laurel Drive 5
Decorah, IA 52101

In memory of Clyde Shepherd,
cowboy

CONTENTS

COWBOYS & COWGIRLS

HISPANIC VILLAGES

Work

Religion

Community

Characters

Misbehaving

Appreciation

THE PUEBLO OF POJOAQUE

ARIZONA

Douglas

Afterword

Acknowledgements

This book is the outcome of twelve years of effort by many people and organizations. The first workshop was organized by Lupita Martinez, former program manager at the Mary Esther Gonzales Senior Center in Santa Fe. Organizers for other workshops were Diane Armitage at the Center for Contemporary Arts; Vicki Watson, formerly of MesaLands Community College; and Reneé Rinestine with the Nara Visa Community Center.

Owen Lopez, former executive director of the McCune Foundation granted financial support.

A project of the scope of Coyotes and Stars relies upon the editorial and technical help of numerous people. Foremost among those who made publication possible is Tom St. Clair, whose software expertise and willingness to solve problems put this book into final form.Thanks are also due to copyeditors Kris Shanilec and Nancy St.Clair, and to proofreaders Karol Erdmann, Bonnie Koloc and Elisabeth Rosales.

General Introduction

Coyotes and Stars is a record of the Southwest focusing on those regional and local cultures—Hispanic, native American and Anglo— that have faded under the impress of modernity. It is a collection of stories and essays written for the most part by men and women without literary ambition, and developed in Free River Press writing workshops. The idea for the book came from my desire to get people from all regions of the country and as many occupations as possible to document their lives and work in an ongoing series of books. Coyotes and Stars is the second in a series of large regional anthologies.

It is an anthology of writings by everyday people from Arizona, New Mexico, and Texas. It is that region of the United States that I know and love best. These three states have given our country some of its most enduring legends, while providing us icons like the cowboy, the Plains Indian, bison, oil rigs, cattle ranches, longhorns, cattle drives, ancient pueblos, desert country, expansive skies and the open range. No matter that most of these icons have disappeared, they made an indelible imprint on the American mind, and consciously or not, impel many of our actions. The open range, the endless vistas, the cowboy, all of these feed into the American obsession with unlimited freedom: freedom from restraint by government and laws.

In my case these icons expressed themselves in a longing for the open road, fueling my own youthful search to explore America. I was in search of the American Soul, certain that I would find it by traveling widely enough, talking to hundreds of people, instinctively feeling that I would find it in those iconic Americans I had read so much about in the West, the Deep South and Midwest. I felt that America was still a land of untapped promise, and I expressed that in a one-paragraph paean to America which ended by calling her, "a giant of the morning." Many of my generation must have felt that, for many of us young men took to the open road, following Kerouac, and in my case, Sandburg, Vachel Lindsay, and others. The Vietnam War had not yet jaded us, and we who had grown up in affluent suburbs had felt nothing of the shocks of life. Everything seemed possible.

*

From at least the time of D.H. Lawrence and Mabel Dodge, disaffected urbanites have found refuge in what was once the primitive sanctuary of New Mexico. It is a stark land, best appreciated after driving, say, through Oklahoma and the Texas Panhandle. Eastern Oklahoma is almost Midwest—some parts green and rolling. But western Oklahoma with its flat land and sparse grass, mesquite and sage belongs to the Great Plains. The Texas Panhandle is more primitive, less cut to human scale or aspirations. Then comes New Mexico. Fifteen miles across the Texas line suddenly there are mesas, uprises of land flattened on top, dotting an almost empty landscape. The land seems flatter, longer, more primitive.

The ancient cultures here once seemed primitive, even at the turn of the last century when Lawrence and his friends, filled with the words of an exhausted civilization, arrived and found themselves renewed by the Other. One used to see the Otherness expressed in New Mexico mountain towns built of baked mud houses pitched on the sides of hills with their twisted, rutted streets. The people used to stare at you. And in their churches, the crucified Christs, not serene in death but tortured, gape in agony. I had seen the same Otherness in photographs of Penitente rites and processions in those villages, and in a small one-room Penitente building, a *morada*, into which I and a few others had been allowed to visit. Here was a room set aside for meditation and prayer once a year, during Easter week. No one knows how many males in each mountain village now belong to the Penitente Brotherhood. The Penitentes' rites in each town last from Lent through Easter Sunday. At night on Good Friday, the darkest day of the Christian calendar, the brothers used to proceed through their towns, shaking chains and chanting ancient modal hymns. They would flagellate themselves in a rite of purification. In former times the Penitentes crucified a man during Easter week. It was an honor to be chosen. If the crucified one died, his shoes were placed on the doorstep of his home.

I had experienced the Other outside one of the seven Hopi Pueblos in Arizona. Each of the seven pueblos was built atop a different mesa. I had driven to one of the mesas from Santa Fe all night to attend a dance the next day. I arrived before dawn, and at the base of a mesa, driving with windows down, I heard drumming. I drove to the base of the mesa, parked and climbed upwards. As I approached the ridge of the mesa and the drumming got louder, the sun rose, a great yellow half circle, its base the mesa itself, and into that half-circle stepped a man in buffalo headdress, singing, chanting, holding out a buffalo robe. I stood transfixed, hurled back untold years into that which lies beyond words.

It ended. I stepped behind a rock, but they had seen me, and another man, dressed in deer antlers and shaking rattles, came to exorcise my presence. I left.

I came to New Mexico, not to be immersed in the Other, but to find a culture and people that had not been standardized. For that reason people still come to Santa Fe, even though it is now changed into a stage set of its former self, and the newcomers, ironically, are themselves standardized.

My first experience of the West came in the summer of 1962 when I hitchhiked from New York to Pennsylvania, where I snagged a ride that swung southwest. My driver was a young, black-haired hotshot who said he was a journalist, and to prove that he had dangerous enemies, said, “I carry a gun just in case,” and opened his glove compartment to show it to me. He was on his way to Las Vegas to play the tables. He was a few years older than me and assumed the role of a life instructor informing the green kid (which I was) of the ways of the world. I didn’t like him but stuck with him as we headed west, connecting with Route 66 in Illinois and swinging southwest across the Mississippi River through the rolling Missouri countryside, into Kansas and Oklahoma flatlands, dipping further south into Amarillo and the Texas Panhandle.

In those days Route 66 was in many places a two-lane highway and in some places four lanes with a thirty-yard strip of land between east and west lanes. It rolled up and down over hills, a beautiful ride that took drivers through the main streets not only of towns, but of cities like St. Louis, Oklahoma City, Amarillo and Albuquerque. The efficiency of America had not grown enough to plow and dynamite through hills and cut around towns, creating an Interstate system that dried up hundreds of towns and killed the wonderful learning that came from experiencing towns and peoples of all types in America’s mosaic. Nowadays traveling on the Interstate is a soulless experience, one that I avoid when I can.

My driver wanted to detour and see Mexico, and I was game. When we came to Vaughn, New Mexico we cut south through hills dotted with jumpier and piñon, driving beside Southern Pacific tracks to the first town we came to, Duran. Duran was different, nothing like anything I had seen before except in photos of old frontier towns. It was small, a collection of wooden houses surrounded by dirt yards with wire fences, a Catholic church, a post office and a general store, all connected by dirt streets. I had fallen back in time.

My driver and I stepped inside the general store to consult a map. Hispanic men sat in a circle on old wooden chairs, smoking cigarettes and speaking Spanish. We looked at a road map and saw a long road leading from Vaughn south to Mexico. "It's too far," the driver said. He was in a hurry to get to Las Vegas, or else he hadn't intended to do more than push a toe across the border.

We bought Cokes and cigarettes and as I stood at the old iron cash register I saw that a forty-five hung by a nail on the wall. Underneath it was a sign that read, "Yessir, this ain't the gun that killed Billy the Kid." That decided me—as soon as I earned enough money back in Connecticut, I would return to Duran to rent a house and write.

I did just that. I worked that summer and fall and in February I took a train from New York to Chicago, and there boarded the Santa Fe Chief, which dropped me off at Vaughn. From there I hitchhiked to Duran and asked the general store owner if there was anything to rent. He said he had two shacks near the store and would rent one for $10 a month. It came with an outhouse. I went to one of the shacks. It was uninsulated with only one light bulb, a cook stove, a table and chair but no running water. I thought that was a great deal and moved in.

I don't remember how long I was able to stay there. The temperature fell below freezing every day. I scrounged for sticks and newspaper and made fires in the cook stove's narrow side chamber, but it was impossible to heat the ten-by-ten shack with a fire that quickly burned out. At night I slept fully clothed in my sleeping bag with all my other clothes stuffed inside, while during the days I sat in the shack and tried to write, looking at the steam that came from my mouth.

The young boys of the town began visiting me, standing about as I sat in the one chair, as curious about me as I was about them. Seeing how cold I was, they left and returned dragging limbs and branches of piñon and juniper, cut them into sizes for my stove and made a fire, not just in the narrow chamber but under the stove lids. But even with their wood, the room stayed too cold to sit and write, and for the next few days, after cooking breakfast, I walked to the general store where I would sit with the men and smoke. Out of courtesy they sometimes spoke English, but usually Spanglish, a mixture of Spanish and English.

But the nights were too cold and I wanted some place warm. But where? What was I to do? Manuel Chavez solved it. "You can stay with me."

Manuel was the man who had picked me up on my hitchhike from Vaughn right off the train. Now he was offering me a place to stay in his small trailer on the southern edge of town.

Manuel was part Apache, short with prominent front teeth and a bad limp, but had the purest heart I have ever known. I shared his narrow bed for almost two months and learned to cook a very simple meal of potatoes and onions and chile that we had almost every night. In years to come, I would return to Duran to see Manuel and sit on chairs outside his home (he had sold the trailer) and talk and smoke with the other men of the village, who sat with him every day in warm weather.

*

Three years later I was back in New Mexico as a student at St. John's College in Santa Fe. By the time I arrived in 1965, Canyon Road—the road lined with artists' studios—had just been paved the year before and otherwise was still looking as it had forty years earlier. Notable town characters were easily spotted on Santa Fe streets, and not just in the Canyon Road neighborhood. Indian artists and artisans sold their paintings, poetry and jewelry under the portal at the Palace of Governors. Hispanics and Anglos mixed at cantinas and restaurants and everyone mingled on the Plaza—hippies, cattlemen, artists, Indians, tourists, men and women scurrying back and forth to work. Santa Fe, "The City Different," was still different then.

For a young man who wanted to be a writer, Santa Fe was a great experience. I visited artists in their Canyon Road studios and spent evenings in bars, drove into the mountains to visit the old Hispanic villages with dirt streets and adobe homes where hostile eyes stared at strangers. But the life changing experience that summer began the morning I stepped into Hal West's studio. Hal was in his sixties, a western artist from Oklahoma who arrived in Santa Fe in the 1930s. I spent nearly every afternoon for two months in Hal's studio the summer of 1966, and it was in his studio and through our nightly bar crawls that I met men and women of all descriptions—lesbians, gays, cowhands, ranchers, newspaper reporters, editors, store clerks, and a gaggle of artists.

My experiences with the three cultures—Hispanic, Indian and Anglo—kept piling up over the years. During the next decade I taught junior high math to a predominantly Hispanic youth in Española, New Mexico, taught G.E.D. evenings at the state penitentiary, and spent much of one summer with an Apache and a Pueblo Indian, both my age, drinking and traveling the country.

Over the decades I have continued to return to the Southwest, making forays into Texas and Arizona. Like most of the stories and essays developed in writing workshops I direct for Free River Press, many of the writings in Coyotes and Stars describe vanishing regional cultures. In 1990, when I decided to create an American self-portrait through writing workshops, America still seemed a quiltwork of cultures that could be maintained. But now decades later, the quiltwork has vanished and can live only in the imagination.

COWBOYS AND COWGIRLS

Introduction

Like so many other iconic Americans, the cowboy is a vanishing breed. Gone are the days when the hired cowpuncher lived and worked on a ranch. Today, the cowboy drives his pickup and horse trailer to work, and then drives home. In fact, cowboying is now day work, with a job here and a job there. Cow punching was never high pay work, but the cowboy didn't do it for the pay, but for the life it afforded, a life out of doors under a seemingly endless sky, working with cattle and horses, a job with its own line of skills. Horse breaking. Or riding and roping. Skills you could display at a rodeo. Not an RCA rodeo, where the "cowboys" are professional athletes, not work-a-day cowhands. The working cowboys have their ranch rodeos, like the one I watched somewhere years ago on a back road in Utah, probably an Indian rodeo. No grandstand, no bleachers, just boards and poles marking off the area for the action, with people standing and leaning against the fence and shaded by cottonwoods.

When my friend Clyde Shepherd cowboyed in the 1950s through the1970s, cowboys rode out before dawn for spring and fall roundups, and camped overnight in bedrolls made out of a quilt and a sleeping bag and maybe a blanket, enough to keep them warm during prairie nights. In those days and earlier, the roundup crew included a chuck wagon run by the cook, who was number two on the crew. In winter, when they rode out to feed cattle, the hay or cake was hauled in wagons pulled by horses or mules. Today there's no chuck wagon, no camping out, and no wagon to haul feed. Today, cowboys use pickups.

Ranching and cowboying changed in other ways too. Once the railroads came to Texas in the late nineteenth century, there was no need for trail drives that herded cattle to Kansas railheads. With the demise of the trail drive, much of the romance of the cowboy went the way of the bison and the Plains Indian.

Consortiums of businessmen began buying up hundreds of square miles of range, beginning in the late nineteenth century. Now they are growing wheat for winter silage, and land that never should be plowed is being plowed again. Another Dust Bowl looms. Land with a mere three inches of sod with sand underneath—150,000 square miles of it—stretching from west Texas into New Mexico, Colorado, and Kansas— will once again become a land of dirt and dust.

The reality of the vanishing cowboy was driven home to me when I tried to sell my handmade, hand-tooled-in-Texas saddle to a saddlemaker in Clayton, New Mexico. The cowboys aren't buying, he told me. There's no work. Indeed, one cowboy I know, who once managed a ranch, now drives an 18-wheeler.

The romance of the cowboy lived in my imagination throughout the Sixties, and I was fortunate indeed to live out my dream on the ranch of one of Santa Fe's most colorful characters, a tall, lanky man with a craggy face, who could have gone to Hollywood, and in fact did play a villain in a Walt Disney western. He and his family were well known in the region, and he was a man who read Russian novels and loved bar fighting. In fact, bar fights are a cowboy sport. Even women can pitch in. Read Nelda Smith's story, "Feed Lot Life." I can attest it was still alive in the late Sixties when I and my opponent were both knocked unconscious as we squared off in a men's room by a man who wanted to keep the peace.

NELDA SMITH

Nelda Smith is a writer and visual artist now living in Amarillo and teaching at the Amarillo Art Institute.

MY LIFE AS A COWGIRL

My life as a cowgirl began as a young adult. I met my husband during my senior year in high school. My best girlfriend was dating his best friend. I fell under the spell of his cowboy charm. We married after my graduation and moved to the Mayer Ranch near Hardesty, Oklahoma, in the Oklahoma Panhandle. My first roundup was a series of cartoon-like blunderings of a city girl dressed up like a cowgirl.

This is one of those stories I don't tell very often because it isn't one of my bright and shining accomplishments. I was a naïve but willing cowgirl. For whatever reason, maybe the luck of the draw (or not), I was designated to ride Bandit. The cowboys assured me he was gentle. He was a beautiful chestnut quarter horse with a black mane and tail. However, they didn't tell me he didn't like being separated from his mares and that he was very insistent on having his own way. They also conveniently forgot to tell me that he was a stallion and had been moved from his brood of mares only three days earlier. At that time, I didn't know anything about the true nature of a stallion.

The brisk morning air caused him to feel frisky and fit. We started on our round-up at first light. I was given a spare pair of gloves that were several sizes too large. I was bundled up for the chill in such a way as to encumber me drastically. I was able to get on board without much ado and we left the corral as a unit.

I was riding along between the accomplished cowboys. My husband and the other cowboys took turns dismounting and opening the wire gates as we passed through several pastures getting to the herd of cows, the objects of our mission. As soon as we arrived inside the pasture, we headed straight away for the northernmost point and the cowboys then split up and galloped away in opposite directions, some going to the east and others to the west. My instructions were to follow the herd and keep any stragglers from turning back. They forgot to tell Bandit that this was our responsibility. I had become somewhat complacent and was setting there relaxed when he suddenly turned and began galloping straight for the open gates. He was determined to return to his girls. I hollered and pulled on the reins as much as I could with my right hand. He didn't respond to my yells or jerks on the reins. He sensed he had gained control of the situation. I was hanging onto the saddle horn with my left hand, which was slipping right out of the oversized glove. Suddenly my husband galloped up alongside us and cornered Bandit in the fence-line corner of the pasture, next to the gate. Bandit's sudden stop threw me out of the saddle. I grabbed his neck and mane and held on for dear life. I didn't exactly get thrown off but my dismount left much to be desired and gave the cowboys a hoot.

That durn horse was still going to show me who was boss and planted a hoof right on top of my foot. I smacked him upside the head with the reins and I removed my foot. After a few moments, I remounted Bandit, tightly gripping the reins with both hands. I was able to maintain a safe distance behind the herd, zigzagging so as not to lose any stragglers. I successfully stayed on board and the round-up concluded without further incident. I can say that I was greatly relieved when we arrived back at the corral.

Branding was a joint effort with neighboring ranches. Each person had specific tasks. The ropers and flankers brought the calves to the fire pit where the branding irons were hot and ready to sear the hides of the calves. Flankers usually were the cowboys or cowgirls who grabbed the flank quarters of the calf and held the back legs. The calves were wrestled to the ground by other cowboys or cowgirls and held while the foreman or owner stood ready to mark their ownership with the pre-heated branding irons. Castration was done only by the experienced cowhands and the entire branding process was done with precision and great teamwork. Since I couldn't rope and wasn't physically equipped to wrestle the calves, and certainly not strong enough to hold a thrashing, squirming calf down, I was delegated to the kitchen to feed the crew.

There was one young lady who was appropriately dressed in chaps, cowboy boots, spurs, and cowboy hat. She was muscular and had been around this process before. She could grab a calf, wrestle it to the ground, and hold it while they branded it. She could throw calves just like "one of the boys." I do recall that my husband and the other cowboys bragged on her expertise as a cowgirl. All 5'2" inches and 100 pounds of me vowed to learn to ride Bandit and throw a calf—the small ones anyway.

I felt totally inadequate, and I think this was the first hint that maybe being a cowgirl wasn't really my calling. I walked funny for several days after the round-up, but I did become the boss in my relationship with Bandit over the next several months. I could saddle him and ride him whenever the need arose.

On one occasion, while I was riding Bandit, I discovered an orphan antelope that was hidden in the rough terrain of a pasture. Her mother had been killed by coyotes and she was just hanging around her mother's lifeless body. I took her home and raised Skeeter until she needed to be set free. One day I was expecting the ladies from the home extension club and I knew she would cause problems so I locked her in the well house. This of course went against her nature and she broke the window in her attempt to escape. She cut her neck, which resulted in a permanent scar (a unique identifying mark). She would butt the doors of the house and demand I come out to play with her. So for her protection and my sanity, we moved her to the corral. I saw a buck circling the lot quite regularly and one morning I went out to feed her and she was gone. We concluded that he had enticed her to join his harem. Thereafter, I did recognize her amidst the herd when I rode the pastures, and sometimes she would hang back as though there was a flicker of remembrance.

My lessons as a ranch hand were many. I was dumb and foolish. Therefore, I fell into the trap of being the eager student. On one occasion, the ranch hands left the headquarters to go to the farm near Eva, Oklahoma, to plant wheat. One of my jobs was to put the orphan calves in with the milk cows to nurse twice daily. I had observed the process on several occasions and knew the routine. Well, when the calves had nursed for the allotted time, I was to move them back to their pen. The quirt was not available on this particular evening and so I decided I would improvise and do as my husband had done. I reared back to kick the calf in the belly (as I had seen others do) when the calf moved just enough so I kicked him in the hip instead and broke my toe. I tossed and turned all night trying to figure how I could explain this to my husband. When I went to the doctor, he was incredulous that I had broken my toe by kicking a calf (a first for him).

This same doctor was the one who rescued one of the prized registered quarter horses from a life-and-death situation. We were managing the ranch in the absence of Mr. Mayer and family. The horse got bit on the nose by a rattlesnake and was quickly becoming disoriented and losing his ability to breathe. We tried desperately to get hold of the veterinarian without success, as it was Sunday. I contacted a doctor to get some anti-venom and he agreed to give the horse a shot if we came to the back entrance of the clinic and parked the stock trailer a block away. The other stipulation was that we were not to tell *anyone* that he had doctored a horse. He is retired now, so I can tell this tale.

My husband broke horses professionally for the neighboring ranches. I was his partner, so it was my good fortune to have the assignment of riding the horses after he had decided they were broken. He figured if I could ride them, anyone could. In retrospect, I know that I had a guardian angel watching over me, as I was never bucked off or injured.

Another experience came about when the ranch hands were gone and the pump jack or something had come unbolted on the windmill. The owner's wife and I were given the task of repairing the windmill. (I don't know why we didn't get a windmill repairman.) Anyway, I was designated to climb to the second platform of the windmill and replace the broken bolt. I couldn't act scared because Mrs. Mayer had done it numerous times. I had to be at least as capable as she was. Thank goodness it was a day without high winds or blowing dust. As I climbed the twenty or so feet into the air on the wooden windmill, I was gripping the hand holds so tightly that my knuckles were turning white and my knees were shaking. I prayed a lot and I am sure I was holding my breath. I do remember the world looked much different from that height. Miraculously, I was able to replace the bolt without any complications. When I descended to the ground below I silently said a humongous "*Thank you, Lord.*"

When that marriage ended, his complaint at the divorce hearing was that I never learned to rope.

When I married my present husband, I stipulated that I wouldn't ride horses, milk cows, rope calves, or fix windmills. I can say truthfully in our thirty-five years of marriage these have not been a requirement for being his wife.

I am now an artist and paint pictures of cowgirls, expressing my respect for their talents.

SOPHIA JARAMILLO

Sophia Jaramillo was born in 1921 in Dawson, New Mexico.At age six her family moved to a large cattle ranch in Cimarron, New Mexico. Sophia, whose writings focused on her early life, self-published a nonfiction collection, Once upon a Time. *Free River Press published three of Sopjia's stories in two of its titles and a fourth story appeared in* La Herencia Magazine. *In 2002, Sophia was named a Santa Fe Living Treasure for her volunteer work with local charities. She passed away in 2006.*

POLITICS AT THE CORRAL

"Baaa, baaa!" This was the sound of a calf lassoed and brought to the ground and readied for branding! The next sound was that of a sizzling hot iron on its raw hide . . . and the whistling and yelling from the cowboys roosting at the top of the corral fence. A calf was brought up and the WS brand was distinctly imprinted on its left quadrant. Two expert hands made the calf into a steer with a simple operation. Rocky mountain oysters were collected for dinner, and the steer was set free in the corral to suffer its indignities.

This was branding time at the WS, an event where neighboring cowboys were invited to come give a hand. My father was manager, and he had invited cowboy friends from Raton, Las Vegas, Taos, Maxwell and Springer. They arrived before six that morning, dressed for work and ready to raise a little hell. They took turns roping, branding, and performing the operation.

While some worked, others took time to roost at the top of the corral fence and whoop it up. They whistled, they laughed and hollered, and made obnoxious statements. Cowboys are a brand all their own.

In between brandings the roosters at the top of the corral fence made their way to the north end, and there they formed a small circle where each brought out his own brand of whiskey, a bottle of Wild Turkey, Johnny Walker or whatever, and passed it around. This started another round of laughter, backslapping, whistling and wild noises. From where I sat on the bed of an empty wagon, all I could see in the circle were six or seven ten-gallon hats, worn out Levis, and dirty, messed up boots. They moved about like wild men. What I saw that day made me promise myself never to marry a cowboy.

I was about nine years old and had been given permission to stay home with my mother, and together we watched the branding. This was my first time, and would be my last! My mother and I slid our heads outside the lower boards of the corral, and for the most part watched from a distance.

"This is man's work and it must be done," Mama said.

"Mama, why did you give me permission to come to this horrible event?"

"I could not have stopped you if I hadn't," she said.

Branding time on the WS Ranch was as exciting as a Fourth of July rodeo. This particular day was not too accommodating for the cowboys wearing three-inch heels. It had intermittently rained and shined, and when the rain came, it played havoc in the corral grounds, creating a shitty mess with the mixture of rain and cow chips. However, this was a special occasion, and it was important that each cowboy have an hour of fame with a performance.

Sometime in the middle of the morning, when the rain had subsided, we saw a long black car slither into the driveway. It was no one we knew. As a man stepped out of the car, we could tell he was not dressed for the ranch. He wore a navy, blue pin-striped suit, a fancy white shirt with cufflinks and a red tie. He wore fancy leather shoes and a small hat; someone said it was a derby.

Someone sitting at the top of the corral fence said it was our senator, a Democrat, who was running for reelection. With an aggressive gait he came to the corral and introduced himself proudly: "I am your United States senator from New Mexico," and then asked who was the ranch manager. He was told it was Sandy, who was inside branding calves, and that he might have to wait a little while. Someone offered him a place to sit on top of the fence. Two of the cowboys lifted him up so he would not get his shoes in the unga.

The senator made himself at home, and at times hollered with the wild cowboys when another calf had been branded. My father, learning that a man was looking for him, came out from his post and greeted the visitor. I doubt very much if he knew who it was. You see, my father was a dyed-in-the-wool Republican, and did not give a damn who the man was.

The senator came down from the fence, offered his hand and introduced himself. "I was just going by for a rally to Raton, and I saw all the activity here among your cowboys. I wonder if you will allow me a little time to address them. I am running for reelection, and I need every vote I can get."

My father was kind and gracious. "Senator, we've got important work to do, and very little time for politics. So get started."

"Thank you, I will make it in a hurry."

The senator having moved back to his perch at the top of the corral, expounded on his virtues in Washington, D.C., and promised that if he were re-elected, he would see to it that New Mexico received all the water it needed, and sufficient rangeland to make ours the most lucrative ranch in the whole country. There was a lot of clapping and whistling for the senator, but from somewhere in the corral, someone yelled, "Unga."

The senator was not particularly perturbed.

My father thanked him for taking time to talk with "his boys," and explained that not too many politicians stopped by. He invited him to stay for the remainder of the branding and to come later in the evening to have some Rocky Mountain oysters for dinner.

The senator looked at his watch, and said he must leave but hoped to see them later that evening for the rocky mountain celebration!

Two of the cowboys helped him down from the fence, reminding him not to step on the unga.

As the senator drove away from the ranch, he saw a sign on the road which caught his eye: "YOU ARE NOW LEAVING CIMARRON, WHERE PAVEMENT ENDS AND HELL BEGINS.

P.S. I did not marry a cowboy!

CLYDE SHEPHERD

Born in 1927, Clyde worked two of the largest ranches in the Southwest, the J.A. and the Matador, and years later he managed a ranch in northeast New Mexico, where he and his wife, Beverly, raised two daughters, Cindy and Linda. In his last years he lived in Channing, in the northern Texas Panhandle.Clyde passed away in 2007.

Note: I came to know Clyde by pure chance. My wife and I had stopped for lunch at the café in Nara Visa, New Mexico. On our way out, my wife called my attention to a notice posted on the front door. It read, "Due to old age, the annual Matador Cowboy Reunion is canceled." It was signed "Clyde Shepherd" and gave his address and phone number. I copied the information, but it took me a year to muster the courage to call, thinking he wouldn't have time to waste on a writer. Instead, when I called, he was warm and invited me to stay with him on my way to Santa Fe. I did, and for the few years that I knew him, I stayed with Clyde, coming and going between New Mexico and Iowa. This interview was conducted in 2006. Clyde was a dear friend.

WHAT COWBOYING WAS LIKE

Starting off

RW. Why don't we just start when you were a young boy and how you started cowboying?

CS. I was born down there in Turkey, Texas, up northwest, down at the head of a little ole cedar canyon, in that ole bach [bachelor] shack, two room shack there. Mama says ever time it'd rain, she said they'd put a tarp on to keep us from drownin'. It leaked pretty bad.

I don't know how far they had to carry water to the house. I imagine it was about half a mile, or about that. They had to use wood for everything.

I don't know how old I was when I left there. We just moved around. We lived at Smith Camp for a while and a place called Hodge Camp.

RW. Was your father a cowboy?

CS. Yes, sir. Yeah, he had a little farm and run a few cattle too.

RW. Did he hire out?

CS. Sometimes. Sometimes he did. Most time he held his own. He made his first crop on a bunch of ole condemned horses. Broncs, you know. That and runaways. He'd just go out an borry [borrow] a few horses from some neighbors, you know, just about anything he thought could work.

My sister was born at Smith Camp.We moved from there to a place called Hodge Place. A feller come out there one day, comin' down there to Ox-Bow—Lewis's—to help 'em through brandin'. And he asked if I'd go with him. They let me go. I was about ten years old at that time there. That's when I started workin' on ranches, brandin' calves an' stuff. Then when I was fifteen I went back there [to Lewis's] an' then I went to the J.A.'s when I was sixteen, an' I had my seventeenth birthday there. I was breakin' horses there. Then I came up here an' started school. Went to school for a little while. My father said to quit an' go to work, so I've been kind of driftin' around a little bit ever since then.

I was back there at J.A.'s in '54. Broke horses again. That's where I meet my wife, down there. We got married and come up here an' worked a while, then I went to New Mexico and stayed out there about thirty-four years [managing Culverson's ranch.]

Winter

[*In this section, Clyde talks about the J.A. and the Matador. The J.A. was co-owned by legendary cattleman Charles Goodnight and John Adair, a wealthy Scot. The Matador was an 800,000 acre ranch in the Texas Panhandle, with more land in Montana and Canada At the Matador, the cowboys slept in the pastures from May until the end of November.*

CS. We'd get pretty cold by November. But they had a great tent, and they rigged up an old stove out of a barrel and put it in back. That helped keep you warm. Up at J.A.'s they had nothing but open flys. They had a side curtain; sometimes they'd put that up. It was either that or get in your teepee.

RW. How many guys might bunk in the tent?

CS. Maybe twenty, twenty-five. Once in a while there'd be some fellers there with teepees. At J.A.'s they'd sleep out in the wagon, or out in the open, or in them teepees. Once in a while there'd be some would sleep out in the open, but most of the time they got in the teepees. Gives you a little more wind break.

This is from when to when?

CS. They usually pulled out in May and they'd go until December. It'd be gettin' pretty cold by then. Lot of snow, sometimes.

We didn't have no clothes then like they got now. All I had was two shirts and an ole Levi jacket. That big ole black streak right around my waist, that's where that jacket didn't reach. It was just chapped and rough. That's the best we had.

Used tow sacks—feed sacks—for overshoes. We didn't have no good coats like you see now. Once in a while you'd see a feller with a pair of mittens, but a lot of 'em used them little ole leather gloves, little ole buckskin gloves. Them would freeze your hands off.

Then it got where once in a while you'd see a feller with a pair of them gloves and they'd put a pair of them little ole cotton jerseys on over it. That'd keep 'em a little bit warmer too.

That snow'd get pretty deep. It'd get cold. Man, it'd get cold.

And sometimes they would scatter them cowboys out; after that put 'em in the camps, help the campers feed [the cattle]. Each camper, you know, had a certain area of the country he'd feed and some of it was so big he couldn't feed [all the cattle].

RW. Were they feeding hay or cake?

CS. It was all cake.

RW. Was it hauled on wagons?

CS. Wagons. Mules and wagons. Other ranches fed cake and hay, feed an' stuff. Some of them big outfits didn't feed 'cause you couldn't get to them cattle. Too far apart. If you did [get to them], you had 'em all in one bunch, or just a few.

The whole country was rough! If the wind was up you couldn't hear anyone hollerin'.

RW. How late were they using wagons to feed?

CS. Sixties. I imagine some of 'em were still doing it in the sixties.

RW. Did you start working just about sunup?

CS. Oh, hell, we might start at two-thirty in the morning, dependin' on how far we were goin', what pasture we was workin'. Sometimes we'd ride a couple of hours or longer, and sometimes we set there another hour waitin' for it to get daylight. It was a different ballgame from what it is now.

RW. How often would you go to town?

CS. Oh, maybe once a month or somethin' like that. Wintertime you didn't hardly ever take a bath. Might go to an old camp somewhere and take an ole sponge bath. It was so dang cold you just as soon do that. I think about seventeen days was the longest longest I ever went without a bath. It was cold. Man, it was cold. Once in a while you could heat water in a tub, but you couldn't take a bath out in that wagon. Cooled off too quick.

RW. How many years did you live this life?

CS. Up until about ten years ago. I'm seventy-eight now. I got my back messed up, had to quit. Had to have surgery on it and then it messed my legs and feet up. I can't walk, have to keep them propped up all the time. They stay numb.

But I had a pretty good life. You sure didn't get rich [cowboying]; they didn't pay much.

*

I will never again meet a man like Clyde Shepherd. His was an open and welcoming nature that invited strangers into his life. On our second telephone conversation before we met, he invited me to stay overnight at his home. He was one of those country folk, now gone, that Sue West writes about in her story, "Before Santa Fe Bars."

IVAN CATES

Ivan and Judy Cates have been in the Texas Panhandle sixty years.

BIVINS XL RANCH

I left Foard County, Texas in late May 1963, intending to try my fortune on a ranch somewhere in New Mexico. My 1957 Chevy Coupe did not use much gas, but made up for it by burning oil. Thanks to STP, I made it to Amarillo. I had two brothers, already at the LX Ranch north of Amarillo, so I stayed a week or so with a brother. The LX did not need a hand, so I went to the Cold Water outfit at Bivins Ranch at Fritch, and they were not needing any hands either. Cold Water's general manager's son was going to work the summer before college, and was later dragged to death. I went out to the Bivins XL, north of Amarillo, and was lucky enough to get on there. The branding was just about over, but they needed some cleanup work.

I started at the XL as a single hand and of course stayed in the bunkhouse at the headquarters, where I made $150 a month. There were five of us in the bunkhouse, and the dinner bell rang at the cookhouse at 6:00 a.m. for breakfast, 12:00 noon for dinner, and 6:00 p.m. for supper. We would sit on the bunkhouse steps and listen to stories. I had an old cheap guitar as well. We would jingle the horses each morning, including Sundays, and get our orders for the day. Later on, the camp man left so another hand and I went to the camp and batched [were bachelors] for a spell.

The XL Bivens was fairly big, the best I remember about 150 sections. The Bivens families had ranches at Sunray, Fritch, Amarillo, Tascosa, and Channing, Texas and Portales, New Mexico. The XL ran cows and calves and several hundred yearlings. I remember that one shipping we penned 1200 yearlings in one fell swoop and didn't lose a head. Every cowboy was just at the right place at the right time.

In August of 1963, my wife, Judy, and I got married and we stayed at the River Camp. My wages increased to $160 a month. We did have a team of mules to feed the cattle and put out salt since the big boss did not furnish a pickup. My first experience with harnessing and handling a team was cause for wrecks of all sorts. A camp man's job was to look after three pastures, keep up the fences, check the windmills, feed cows in the winter, and plan the day's chores and, of course, go to the headquarters for shipping and branding. I would usually have a string of saddle horses, and one or two broncs to break. We had a milk cow and got our staple groceries and beef at the commissary at headquarters. So we had just about everything furnished other than personal items. Judy would ride horseback to help with chores until our first daughter came along. We depended on a generator for electricity until power was run to the camp.

My grandfather raised mules back in the Thirties and Forties. My older brothers helped break the mules along with my dad and granddad. I had never helped with the mules and was in for a learning experience. In the early sixties, the XL used mules for various chores, including bringing feed to the cattle in winter. The first team of mules I worked by myself was a team of little blue nose mules that had a real heavy britches harness with ornamental beads.

The feed wagon had 4' x 10' running gears and rubber tires. The wagon was pretty light and pulled real easy. I didn't realize that the right mule had to be in the right place, which caused problems. Besides, I got the collars mixed up right away and had what seemed to be countless straps. The first team was a little wild for me; if you just spit over the side, they'd go into a dead run. I traded the wild mules for a gentler team at headquarters. After I learned to handle the mules, I enjoyed working with them and it was a good experience. The foreman said that he would never catch a cowhand in town with a wagon and team. He was surely right!

My experience on the XL was a great part of learning the cowboy trade, plus getting to neighbor with some of the best cowmen and cowboys. I wouldn't trade anything for the experience I gained on the XL Ranch.

LISA HIGHT

Lisa Hight has lived in northeastern New Mexico for twenty-one years. She has four grown children. She and her cowboy/rancher husband and two boys ranch and raise Black Angus cattle. She is a homemaker and a substitute teacher, and loves to cook while listening to the Boston Pops. She draws, writes poetry and short stories and is musically inclined. She enjoys taking care of her herd of mischievous Boer goats and loves all little critters in her world.

FINDING MY WAY

My new husband brought me here to New Mexico in the early 1990s. It had been a good winter. A good winter means wet and heavy snows that stay on the ground for at least two days. It means moisture for flowers—globe mallows, sunflowers, Indian blankets, verbena, wild vinca, and purple asters that bloom in spring and early summer. In my mind I pictured a green valley. The old timers say it won't start raining here until you give up and think you can't stand the heat anymore. They tell stories about the time it rained so hard and the creek rose so quickly it flash flooded the highway. The rainy season brings rain and floods our two creeks. We don't cross until the waters recede. But our grandchildren make mud pies and our sons' water-soaked clothes are stained red with adobe mud after they fix the fences washed down by the torrent.

I have never gotten used to gazing for miles and miles on a land that never drops off, but keeps going. My husband, Gerald, has done his best to show me what he loves about this place. He's a rancher, and has a cow-calf operation because that is what his father had. Whenever I used to feed the cattle with him, I would usually feel somewhat queasy with our truck's starts and stops and the humps and curves of the feed road. Gerald has his own map of which road takes you to which trap, and which feed roads you have to avoid because the creek has eroded the ground underneath. The map is in his head.

I'd ask him, "Okay, which pasture is this? Shouldn't there be large neon signs with big red letters that read, 'Wayne pasture, go down road across big creek, turn right. Go to big silver gate.'"

"But you can't miss it," he'd say.

Gerald tried to show me the various traps, which we greenhorn folks call pastures, but my sense of direction has always been awful. Some of those traps are just an average of 320 acres. I confess that if I follow a fence line, I can eventually find a gate leading somewhere.

I can open metal gates, but not wire gates. Barbwire gates can be six or eight feet across with five strands of particularly evil whipping barbwire tied to a wooden post on one end and a stay—a small wooden limb—on the other. Each end of the stay has to be placed into a wire loop on the post. Wire gates can be the most frustrating contraption a range man ever invented, and unless I have a cheater (lever) I just can't do it. Stretching one ornery wire is difficult, especially if all the rest of the fence needs to be tightened. It has a high-pitched twang like the tightening of a bowstring and you know it's going to hurt if you let go. My arm is just not strong enough to get the top wire over the post.

In January in the late 1990s, when we actually could rely on getting a little moisture, Gerald was going to be gone for a few days and I offered to feed the cows. He said they would be all right, that I could drive out to look at them, if I wanted. We had a wet, heavy snow, and the wind had drifted the snow high in some places across the feed-road ruts. I drove through a few metal gates and was relieved to see the cows coming up from the creek. I counted the cows; they were all there. Then I clicked the feed out in five-pound piles for that many cows. The cattle can hear that click-click echo for miles and will come quickly from nowhere to crowd next to the truck or wait on the other side of a fence for their turn to be fed.

I found some bare spots where the snow had melted away and fed twenty cows there. Then I had to find the road again through the snow. I located and fed eighteen cows in another pasture, but there were supposed to be thirty. I found one metal gate that was very hard to open and when I finally opened it wide enough for the truck to go through, it actually came off its hinges.

"Well," I thought, "I'll just have to remind Gerald to look at it when he gets back."

I dragged it closed and wired it shut, so the older cows would not mix with the two-year-olds.

Something about driving way out in the flatlands, miles from the house, gives me an odd feeling, maybe because I don't do it that often. You hear nothing but the sound of the truck engine. And you are constantly jounced and jarred as you drive along.

When my husband got home, I told him that I had found and fed most of the cows. And I told him about the metal gate coming off its hinges. The next day he went to check the cattle. He came home late in the afternoon.

"What gate did you say you went through?" I couldn't tell him which pasture I'd been to, but he knew where else I had gone because my tire tracks showed where I had slid. I had done a few wheelies and had almost gotten stuck because of mud in the ruts. I had gone four wheeling across country in my husband's feed truck.

Spring finally sprung. March came; the snow melted and left everything fresh. Gerald came home from feeding and checking our pregnant cows to tell me he had actually found the silver gate whose hinges had come off and he hoisted the pegs back into the hinge. "I haven't been through that gate in years," he said. "That's not on my feed route."

LISA HIGHT

MAMA AND THE BULL

Drumming a beaten track around the circle of the corral was a very vigorous three-year-old Black Angus bull weighing about a ton. He had already escaped one corral, and having had the taste of freedom wanted more.... and he was mad.

Mama was distracting the bull while my step-dad bolted a new pine pole horizontally to the top of the vertical posts that made up the corral. The former one had cracked in two, right down the middle where it had been bolted. It had fallen sideways when the bull butted his head against it.

The bull was now circling the coral, looking for a weak place to make a break. Freight Train, aptly named by Hugh, came trotting around again with narrowed black, fiery eyes and lowered head, polled but deadly. This 2,000 pounds of bull, all muscle and sinew, was not happy. He shook his head and puffed out some steam. He was eyeing Mama. I don't think he knew what to make of the waving broom and fluttering lavender dress clinging to the side of the fence, but I knew he was breathing in her perfume.

Back then my parents didn't have a herd of cattle. My step-dad raised sheep, and shepherds worked sheep on the ground.

There was no need for horses. Instead, the shepherd almost always has working sheep dogs or Border collies to help sort or drive the flock. Hugh and Mama had recently purchased this bull to get pretty little calves dropped in the spring from our Brown Swiss milk cows.

"Mamma, oh Ma," I called. "Watch him!"

The bull made a low, savage bawl and came around at a brisk trot again, kicking up mud and manure and splattering Mama's town dress. Suddenly Mama jumped down from the fence and I thought, "She is going to get trampled." She waved her broom, placed her feet firmly in the mud and bent forward with a determined stare.

"Ma! I don't think he's gonna stop!" I waved my arms and growled, "HA! HA!" from across the pen.

Mama's face froze into a grimace. She stared Freight Train down like a Jedi knight in *Star Wars*. Freight Train lumbered forward as if in slow motion and I had this brief vision of a Spanish bullfighter. Mama didn't yell. She never yelled. She waved the broom frantically as the bull lumbered past her in slow motion.

Freight Train feinted right and Mama feinted left, smacking him on the hind end with the straw of the broom as he went past. Had he spun around he would have killed her, but the straw probably felt like an irritating gnat. Freight Train's hooves just missed her black pinned-up hair as he kicked up his hind legs.

Hugh finally bolted the log back in place and restrung the barbed wire over the top. He motioned with sign language, invented, I think, by sheep men and cowboy-ranchers to confuse their wives, indicating that he was done. Mama and I promptly opened the fence gate and slipped out. Hugh, Mama and I watched Freight Train for a minute. He stood heaving, white foam spilling down the sides of his jaw.

"He'll settle down," my step-dad said.

"A-huh," I thought, but I finally quit holding my breath.

JACK MCCARTY

Jack McCarty was born on February 19, 1935 and grew up on his father's ranch near Logan, New Mexico. He lived on the ranch all his life, except for five years in the army and four years on a ranch in Arkansas during the drought that lasted from 1953 through 1957. He and his wife were married forty-six years and raised two sons. They retired in 1998 and sold their ranch holdings in 2008.

THE CODE OF THE WEST

The "Code of the West" is a system of rules and regulations that a cowboy learns at an early age and lives by all his life. A few examples follow:

When a chuckwagon is set up to prepare meals, don't go between the cook and the cooking fire. If you need to get on the other side, go around outside the fly or tent.

Don't approach the wagon with the wind at your back, causing dust to blow into the cooking food. Go way around and come in from the other side, with the wind in your face.

Don't ride between a cowboy and the herd of cattle he is holding (restraining). Go around behind him to get to the other side.

Don't attempt to rope an animal that another cowboy is chasing.

Don't ride in front of another cowboy, unless his horse is bucking, and you are trying to help get him stopped.

Don't ride your horse into a chase after an animal, until the person chasing it has thrown the loop of his rope and missed.

If you want on the other side of a rider, you slow your horse and turn it behind the other horse, after he has passed. Don't ride in front of him.

Don’t cuss around the women folks.

Take your hat off when introduced to a lady.

Don't spit tobacco juice over a lady's shoulder when you two are on the dance floor.

Feed your horse, before you feed yourself.

*Breaking the Cod*e
Note: *Violating any one of these rules can get a cowboy chapped, which means he is hauled over a bedroll, with two cowboys holding his arms and another two holding his legs, while a fifth cowboy whips his butt with a pair of chaps. Any cowboy who does not help with the chapping, gets chapped.*

*

Clyde Shepherd was our next-door neighbor for thirty-four years, living just ten miles down the road from us. We would help him by trading out work in the spring and fall. We'd help him and then he'd come and help us. He would find people in town and bring them out to help him, providing them a bed and meals.

Clyde met a man named John, from England, who wanted to find out about cowboy life on a working ranch. John had a long braided pigtail down his back. Clyde came to help us brand and brought John with him. On our way to the pastures, where we were going to brand, the cowboys followed the boss in a customary pattern, with the first men going around the outside of the pasture, right after the boss, and everyone else taking their positions, depending on what part of the cattle drive they would cover. The cattle would be driven to a central point—a corral—and penned, with calves separated from their mommas. Then the calves would be branded for identification.

John wasn't happy with his position and continued to ride his horse in front of other cowboys to visit with someone. Clyde told him not to ride his horse in front of other cowboys. He told him that if he wanted on the other side, to slow down and let the other cowboy pass, then ride behind him to get where he wanted.

We branded until lunchtime, then came to our house and ate. Afterwards the men sat around under the trees to let their lunch settle before going back to work.

From the kitchen I heard this loud discussion and went around to see what was going on. The men were sitting in a circle, with a bedroll in the middle. A kangaroo court was in session. Cowboy poet R.W. Hampton was the MC, or judge. Each cowboy had a chance to testify that John had deliberately ridden his horse in front of him, breaking the Code of the West. The decision of the court was that each cowboy should administer one blow with a pair of chaps (cowboy's leather pants) to the defendant lying prostrate over the bedroll. (The chaps are folded together and held about midway up the leg, so as to give a good sting to the flesh and a loud report, but very little damage to the person. While John was over the bedroll Clyde took his knife and cut off that long ponytail. John said losing the hair hurt more than the chapping

*

Clyde's nephew has a chuck wagon down at Crowell, Texas, and cooks for the ranches in that part of the country. Clyde and I stopped to visit with him in 2004 when he was cooking for the Triangle ranch during branding. He invited us to go out with him at 3:00 a.m. to help feed the crew. The cowboys penned the cattle and we went up to watch them brand. There was a scuffle and a calf got up before the cowboy had branded him. The roper caught the calf and brought him back to the same set of flankers [who hold the calf down] to complete the branding. As soon as the calf was branded, the roper jumped off his horse and the crew spread those two flankers over a barrel and proceeded to chap them.

Because the man that was running a vaccination needle was standing back, the whole crew tackled him and chapped him for not helping to chap the other two. I asked one cowboy at lunch about what was going on, and he explained, “I didn’t want to get too close, 'cause they might not have finished chapping for the day and include me!"

NELDA L. SMITH

FEEDLOT LIFE

Life is a journey of changes and my life took a new path when I rerouted my career and began work in the feedlot industry in the early 1970s when feedlots were being built everywhere to fatten cattle for slaughter. It was a boom in the agriculture industry. The Texas Panhandle was the perfect location for the feedlots, as there were plenty of pasture cattle. Feedlots were advanced programs that caused cattle to gain weight quicker than if left to pasture. Thus, ranchers could get their beef to market in a more profitable way. These feedlots were the opportunity for investors to potentially gain many tax advantages, and people from the East were being enlisted. My adventures in the feedlot industry began when I was hired by Stratford of Texas. I was a single parent and this was an opportunity for me to earn a better income for my family. I began working in the headquarters in Stratford, Texas, a luxurious office building, newly built and decorated with authentic leather furniture and expensive western art. The offices were equipped with nice desks and spacious conference rooms in which we entertained the big city investors.

I was hired in the accounting division; specifically, I worked in the feed purchasing and billing department. We purchased the feed through numerous suppliers and had to purchase the feed required to fill rations prepared by nutritionists. It was our responsibility to buy at the best possible price and to project the needs of the six feedlots owned by Stratford of Texas. Every two weeks, we billed the pen owners for the feed consumed and any expenses incurred in that period of time. At that time, many persons were becoming millionaires in this industry.

Each industry has its own cultural environment and the feedlot industry certainly had its unique set of standards. I had to shift gears after working in a professional law office to working in an office where men and women both dressed in Levi's and boots. We had to present ourselves to the eastern investment clients as true cattle-savvy Westerners. We had to talk the right lingo and walk the walk.

For the first time in my life, I was living in a community where no one knew any of my family and background. I had to build a reputation from the ground up. No one knew that I was the daughter of Otis Longbrake or the younger sister of Ronald Longbrake. No one even cared that I had been state debate champion in high school or that I had won awards as a senior Girl Scout.

I worked in the headquarters for a total of three months before I was promoted to business manager for the recently constructed feedlot. This feedlot was located eighteen miles north of Dalhart. I was the first female business manager hired at any of their feedlots and that in itself required an adjustment for the cowboys and myself. I had to go through an initiation process whereby I had to stand up to the cowboys and yet I had to work amiably with each and every one of them. I had to set boundaries to what I considered acceptable, while they were setting theirs.

I bought a used mobile home and moved it and my three sons to the feedlot community located in the trailer park. Thus began the real adventure of living and working in the sometimes rowdy and always unexpected environment that is unique to the feedlot industry.

I am only now learning about some of the antics that my three sons got involved in. The boys are now grown and are confident that there won't be any repercussions for their mischievous deeds. The lifestyle of feedlot employees was a surprise to me. I tried to be protective and we didn't socialize a lot with the rowdies, but there were certainly some adventures that spilled over into our lives. One of the cowboy's sons was expelled from kindergarten school when he cussed the teacher out for trying to take his chewing tobacco away from him. Thankfully my boys weren't involved with either the chewing tobacco or the cussing.
The doctoring crew enlisted my three sons without consulting me. My boys were eight, seven and six years old at this time. I looked out the door of the office and saw two of the boys pushing cattle through the squeeze chute while the third handled the gate. Being the protective mom, I rushed out to see what in the heck was going on. The cowboys insisted they were perfectly safe and I was going to make sissies out of them if I didn't let them try their wings a little. Needless to say, they survived!

One of the feedlot cowboys was a professional bull rider. One day I looked out my office window to discover that they had one of my sons strapped onto one of the feedlot steers. That time I came unglued. I ran out to the pen and got right in the face of that cowboy! I emphatically and loudly told that rodeo cowboy that not all mothers wanted their sons to grow up to be bull riders! I believe I got my point across.

The manager of the feedlot considered himself a gift to the women of the Texas Panhandle. He had been raised in Austin, Texas, and was a city slicker. His feedlot experience was limited, as were his management skills. His path to the management office was aided by the fact that he knew the son of the corporation president. He was married, but that did not interfere any with his womanizing.

Many of his managerial decisions weren't based on anyone's abilities or qualifications, but rather on much more personal criteria. Luckily, I answered to the comptroller and because I had voiced my personal beliefs pretty firmly, he avoided me as much as possible. I didn't have much tolerance for his unprofessional conduct. I kept my job because he didn't know anything about the recordkeeping involved in running a feedlot. He was pretty much just the little man that sat behind the desk in the manager's office. I saved his hide on more than one occasion. He was short and stocky and had red hair and a fair complexion. He was a little man trying to act macho. He followed after the cowboys, trying to fit in and was definitely a misfit. He didn't know the front end of a steer from the backside.

The manager hired several girls with questionable work ethics as feed truck drivers. Their spare-time activities included visiting the local bars where they got involved in several barroom brawls—which of course, were never their fault—and getting arrested for drunk and disorderly conduct. Nearly every Monday morning I had to get them released from jail. This went on for about two months until the powers that be found out about this irregular behavior and insisted on their dismissal if their behavior didn't stop immediately.

This manager did get fired after about three years and was replaced by one of the cowboys from the doctoring crew. The feedlot was closed down soon after, due to the tremendous downturn of the cattle market and the economic backslide. There was a drastic cutback in employees, and I was part of that cutback.

VICKI WATSON
Vicki Watson was a product of the Texas and New Mexico high plains. A life on ranches and in rural communities shaped her view of the rest of the world. Long, caliche roads linked memories to ambitions. The benefits of such a life included a view from the back porch to welcome clouds and watch sunsets, a long marriage and a good life in New Mexico. Vicki passed away in 2021.

BUILDING CASTLES

The whole world looks very different from the top of a haystack.

*

Living thirty miles from the nearest town—a very small one at that—creates a separate sensibility for a seventeen-year-old girl. Teenage dreams are reserved for the night, but during the day I was my dad's only son. That meant summers spent as a ranch hand, complete with boots, chaps and sweat stained hat. Oversized gloves protected those “girly” hands from barbed wire, mesquite thorns and rope burns.

Dad was a hired hand. Stubborn, worked too hard, talked too little, drank too much. But no one ever had a stronger work ethic. His Oklahoma cowboy upbringing during the 1920s and 1930s taught him the codes of self-reliance and honesty. While he may never have known what to do with a daughter, he was a man of nature, who took his role as its guardian very seriously. It was hard for him to take orders, and although he always respected the boss, he was often looking for a new job. There always seemed to be one more rancher who appreciated Dad's direct eye contact and firm handshake. There was always one more move, one more isolated ranch that appealed to this man with the spirit of the 1840s, who was caught in the clamor of the 1960s.

So what was the daughter of such a man to do in such remote surroundings? How was the daughter of such a man to relate to his solitary, removed character? The "Rebel Daughter" often struck back, defending against his harsh criticism and unpredictable mood reversals. The "Good Daughter" tried to learn more, work a little harder, and complain less. The reward was in knowing that every day would reveal new opportunities to examine problems and find creative solutions, the cowboy way.

Solitary days on horseback—riding fence, checking water tanks and looking for sick cattle—created the perfect environment to develop the art of thinking. Keen sensibilities are required for these simple assignments. You notice coyote tracks, sagging fence lines, spent rifle shells and signs of unwelcome visitors. The report taken home must be accurate. Great strength comes from the act of doing a job well.

The summer could drag on with these duties.

Occasionally, mom, dad and I would huddle in the front of the pickup and head to town. There was no radio, so mom and I often sang the latest Hank Snow or Patsy Cline tunes. The windows were down and the wind whipped my hair into my eyes. It didn't take long to feel stuck to the seat cover and realize my freshly ironed blouse was soaked with sweat. Sitting in the middle made it difficult to see out the narrow windshield. The view from the side-mounted mirrors gave a sense of being tied to what was past, with no promise of what might be ahead.

Once in town, the necessary chores were completed. TG&Y held all the treats of an old-fashioned five-and-dime store. Buying barrettes or hand lotion could remind me I really was a girl! Mom often picked up a mail order at the Montgomery Ward's catalog store. Sometimes that would be a dress for me to hoard away until school started. She liked stripes and large flowers and chartreuse and orange. My sense of style came from old black and white movies, so bright colors did not suit me. Our big treat was a visit to the library. You could depend on the library being air-conditioned. Of course, there was a stop at the liquor store, and then we headed back home.

*

Even when the days were long and hot and exhausting, the evenings did not always bring relief. Trying to fall asleep in the night heat was impossible. With the windows wide open, the steady breeze only blew more heat into the room. The heavy air was filled with the familiar smells of livestock and feed, mingled with the scent of wildflowers. If the wind was from the right direction, it might bring the sweet smell of alfalfa. The sounds of moths bouncing against the windowpane were unrelenting! Staring at the ceiling became intolerable.

When sleep doesn't come, there is no escape into dreams. The Rebel Daughter had to seek a solution to the problem!

*

There's really no need to tiptoe out the door. Still, when slipping off to one's special place, a hint of secrecy seems required. The darkness offers an escape from much more than the heat. Adventures await!

And, oh, those midnight adventures! White nightgown fluttering around my legs, I climb to the top of the haystack. Perched there, on the highest point of my sanctuary tower, I can sense all of my fellow night creatures around me. The comforting sounds of locusts, owls, and even coyotes are background music for my private reverie. Bare feet sink into the straw. The breeze now soothes as it pushes damp hair away from my face.

*

Hay bales can become magic flying carpets at that time of night. They lift you to just the right height to take in all the sky from horizon to horizon. The enormity of the blue-black sky is enough to awaken first time questions, the kinds of questions you may never really want answered, just contemplated. Starlight offers a sense of security, as though the firmament is looking down to protect the flying carpet. This mystical stage is set for me to envision my life's story and to imagine things beyond my life's reality. This stage is offered as a place of dreams, plans and fulfillment. This flying carpet will take me to all that is possible.

There among the stars I learned the difference between loneliness and being alone. Being alone on a haystack is the springboard to that canopy of stars. This "aloneness" has a power of its own. It is also where a rebel daughter realizes that her dad's connection to the land and reverence for nature may have begun on another haystack, back in Oklahoma, decades before.

The whole world looks different from the top of a haystack.

JACK McCARTY

A FEW WRECKS

When I was sixteen, I went to Dalhart with my Dad to buy a palomino horse. I asked the trader if the horse was gentle. He said, "Sure!! My sixteen-year-old son rides him," which sounded good. I found out later his sixteen-year-old son was the top bronc rider in three states!

We started out to gather a pasture in the spring and brand. I was riding my new palomino, Blonde. He bucked me off right in front of the house! And with ten other riders cheering him on! They brought the horse back to me, and we went on to brand.

I rode him ten out of the twelve tries in the twelve days that he bucked with me. After that, he quit bucking. When the rodeo came to Dalhart in August, one of the younger cowboys convinced me to enter the bronc riding in the rodeo.

“Those horses don't buck any harder than the one you rode all spring,” he claimed.

We got there too late to enter the rodeo, and after watching those other horses buck, I was never so proud to be late in my life.

At sixteen I had a little black horse named Indian that would buck in the corral every time he was saddled. He bucked around the pen, and as I started to get on him one of our cowboys (an Indian from Oklahoma) said, "Let me have him for a moment.” He stepped into the left stirrup, and instead of swinging on over him with his right foot, he kicked him in the belly three times with his right foot, then stepped off and said, "Now try him. I've got his attention off bucking. " That was the first time I'd ever seen that done.

I never got over the fear of getting bucked off. I took Blonde down to our south camp and was going to check the wells. I rode him three miles to a gate and shook so bad that I rode him back to the house, then turned him back into the remuda [string of horses] for someone else to ride. I was the only one around for twenty miles and didn't want to walk home.

It's not unusual for a horse to buck when he has been running loose for a while. I was going to ride a three-year-old horse that we started in the summer. This was a cold day in November with ice about an inch thick on top of the water trough. I held the corral gate open so the other cowboys could come through, then closed it and stepped up on my horse, Biscuits. He dropped his head and went to bucking back towards the gate, and since there wasn't room for him to go ahead, he jumped into the water trough while bucking. I turned loose and fell into the trough!

Do you know how cold that water was? Every now and then some of those old cowboys would ask, "How cold was that water?" Since I wasn't hurt, they all got a laugh out of it. Anyway, I turned my horse loose and went to the house for some more clothes. I rode the pickup the rest of the day.

We started to gather a pasture to start our fall roundup, hauled our horses about four miles, unloaded and rode together about a mile to the backside of the pasture. Then the crew divided, with me riding Hardtimes. He decided that he didn't want to leave the other horses, dropped his head and planted his front feet in his first jump, which shook me loose. As I was sailing right towards a yucca with my arms outstretched to land on it, face first, he made another jump and his head came up under my belt buckle and turned me a complete flip and I landed on the other side of the yucca without a sticker. One of the cowboys saw the whole thing and caught my horse and brought him back to me, then tied my left rein up close on his saddle horn and said, "Go to kicking, hitting him with your spur every time his feet hit the ground." We loped for a ways, and the bucking discontinued after a few licks. I rode him to finish gathering the cows and drove them to our shipping pasture, but I was laid up with bruises for a couple of weeks.

JACK McCARTY

SHEEP HERDERS

My dad was Sam Houston McCarty, Jr. He came to the Nara Visa area in 1923, wanting to live in town and have a ranch close to town. While looking around, he found that everyone in town had that same idea, all wanting to grow their operations larger. Since he wasn't going to be able to expand there, he went back to work in the oil fields to accumulate some more money to buy land.

He spent a winter or longer on a ranch in North Dakota and found that they cut and put up hay all summer long, then hauled it out to feed the cattle all winter. The hay sleds were pulled by two large Percheron horses, willing to work regardless of how cold it was outside.

He came back to Nara Visa in 1927 with his mother and baby sister and her husband, Brian, and bought land twenty miles west of Nara Visa where he could grow and expand, which he did. For several years he owned and leased over a 150 square miles of land. Dad enlarged the size of the ranch when he got into cattle in a big way. One part of the ranch he bought in '39 and another in '41. When he first bought land it was four dollars an acre; in 1962 it was $100 an acre. He had about 80,000 acres, including 150 sections that he leased.

One of his younger brothers, along with his college teacher and college buddies, built a house on the edge of a hill, six miles east of the old headquarters. The cement footings of several houses and the rubble of a sheep shearing shed, are still there.

The house at the old headquarters was infested with bed bugs, and the men would sleep in bedrolls outside on the ground. The greyhound dogs were sleeping there also, and if you got cold, you just pulled up another greyhound for warmth. One warm night a wool buyer spent the night and put his head to the north. They advised him to turn his bedroll around, but their advice was ignored and they all snickered when the cold wind switched out of the north at about 3:00 a.m. No one got up to help him get his blankets back down out of the wind.

I was told recently that one man soaked the bed and table and walls of the old headquarters with kerosene and went to bed, and the fumes blistered him so bad that they had to help him get around the next day. My mother told me that the old house was burned to get rid of the bedbugs, and a new one built after she and my dad married in 1931.

My older brother was born in January 1932, and I was born in 1935. I have a photo of us that was taken when I was about two, in front of the house with sheep in the background.

Dad started with sheep and cows, with fewer cows than sheep. Dad wasn't the only one in the country raising sheep. All the big ranchers raised sheep because they could run more sheep than they could cattle, and they could get a quicker return on their money because the sheep matured faster.

The sheep were moved to the mountains around Bernalillo, New Mexico when everything dried up during the Dirty Thirties. My dad went ahead of the sheep to let the landowners know they were coming in case there was a fee for crossing. One rancher, two miles north of Logan, met them with rifles and didn't want those stinking sheep on his property. My dad went back to the herders and told them to bed them down, as they had come a long way that day and they'd have to go around this ranch tomorrow. By sunup the next morning, the sheep were ten miles south of Logan. I guess the riflemen went to bed that night and didn't post a guard.

Ferd Fort, a neighbor, told me that my Uncle Brian once took a load of supplies over to the sheepherders in the mountains in a truck. When he got back, my dad asked how everything was over there.

"You took supplies."

"Yes."

"How about meat?"

"They had plenty, and boy, it was good!! Everything is going well."

When he got back, after the next load, he was mad. "I'm not going back over there."

"What's wrong?"

"Those damn guys are eating burros!"

So my Dad asked Ferd if he'd hire out to haul water and supplies over to the sheep and the herders for the rest of the summer.

*

Three sheepherder wagons with their wheels removed were parked in a "T" shape, with a porch built over them and enclosed with a door and windows for a bunk house. It had three private rooms and three folding cots on the porch for the single cowboys. We had four cow camps and, besides the bunkhouse, three married quarters at headquarters. Each camp was outfitted with a four-wheel wagon and a team of mules plus five or so cow horses. The wagon was used to haul salt and mineral and cottonseed cake (cow feed) to the feed grounds, which were usually located close to the windmills in each pasture.

*

My dad always told me, "If you are going to buy a pistol, be sure it is a .45." He told the story of the day he was checking on his shepherds in the mountains around Bernalillo during the Dust Bowl days. He drove a Model A roadster, with a small trailer behind loaded with tents, camping supplies, and groceries for the sheepherders. One herder asked where he and the missus were going to spend the night. Dad said there was a clearing down by the road, about a half-mile from there. The herder told him not to stay there that night, but to go on down about two miles to another clearing, which he did. He came back by the first light the next morning. There had been a fight there the night before. There was a gringo—a white man—there with three .22 bullet holes in him, and three dead Mexicans lying there with a .45 slug in each one. So if you want a pistol for protection, be sure it is a .45!

*

I met a man in the barber shop in Tucumcari, New Mexico who told me that he had herded sheep for my dad years ago. He said that during the Depression, my dad would bring a case of sardines and a case of crackers out to feed the sheepherders and that this man was always be grateful to him because it was all they had to eat. He said my dad came to them and said that he was going to get rid of the sheep, as they could work for the WPA and make more money and stay home at night with their families, instead of out in the pastures with the sheep.

SUE EMORY

Sue Emory grew up in a ranching family in Colorado. She and her husband, John, raised two boys and a girl. She has fond memories of early ranch life.

THE RANCHING INDUSTRY

The ranching industry has changed so much and not for the better. Cowboys like what they do and take pride in their work. They have to have several skills, which is why they like it. It is not like assembly line monotony. New problems arise and need to be solved. Changes in weather must be dealt with. Cowboys learn most of what they know by experience. Experience can't be taught, you have to earn it the hard way. They not only practice their skills, such as roping and training young horses, they learn how animals think and work with that, making the work easier for themselves and the animals as well. It saves time and effort. Ranchers often comment that they cannot pay cowboys enough for all they do, and for their loyalty and time they give to their work. Ranchers had a saying, “When you think you know it all, something new comes up to remind you that you don’t know it all.”

The ranchers now are mostly those who got wealthy in some other industry. They seem to think of owning a ranch as a status symbol. They hire educated people who are into management, finances, proper feed. All well and good, but they have no experience with the actual work, or how to get the work done. They don’t ask a cowboy anything. He is just there to do as he is told. They know nothing of his pride in his ability to do the work, and they care less. He hasn’t been to college, so he doesn’t know anything, so they think. Work then is like making a mountain out of a molehill. What could have been a simple job is usually an exercise in futility. It doesn’t occur to the new ranch owners that livestock have a mind of their own. Understanding that would make work easier. The new ranchers are always in a hurry, which complicates what could be done easily. When you get in a hurry, livestock get mad, which adds to the problem.

A friend of mine was on a ranch during branding, and said that once the calves were branded, they turned the cows and calves out of the corral into a large pen. It was getting late, growing dark. The rancher asked the cowboys to bring their pickups to the fence outside the pen, and turn on their headlights, so they could see. The cows and calves were running and bawling. Sand churned up into a dense cloud in the pen. Cows and calves were getting more anxious and stressed out. It was after midnight. I asked what was he trying to do? “He was trying to Mammy up the calves with their mothers. I thought everybody knew that cows and calves went back to the last place they had sucked. All he had to do was open the gate and let them out."

One young cowboy took a job on a ranch near Vega. The ranch was bought by a rancher who was buying up several ranches. The cowboy said he had worked on big ranches and was given a certain amount of territory to take care of—check windmills so the cattle had plenty of water; keep up fences, ride through the cattle, counting them to know they are all there; look for sick ones, and so on. Then he was told to go to headquarters every morning for his orders for the day –a thirty mile trip. He was usually sent to other places and on the road most of the time, eating meals in cafe's when he could find one. The work he should have been doing, what he thought he was hired on for, was not what he was doing. He finally quit in disgust. There didn't seem to be any order or method, or any certain routine in their idea of work.

One young cowboy gave up trying to work on ranches. He took time out to go to school to be a brand inspector. He is called out to ranches that are shipping cattle out, or receiving them. He said, "I go out to the ranches and I'm glad that I'm not working on those places. It's usually a wreck. They can't pen the cattle, cattle won't go in the gate –and are running all over the place, in all directions. Cowboys spurring their horses, cussing a blue streak. I don't envy them a bit."

One of my friends worked at a big feedlot as a maintenance man, keeping the water system going. They had a lot of moisture, and the cattle being unloaded were very muddy. The office boys decided to build a ramp to unload cattle into the feedlot. They came and asked him to look at it. The cattle would have to turn into a gate at one side. He told them if the cattle couldn't see a gate in front of them, they would turn back and climb over the cattle behind them. The office boys were shocked. "Well, how could we get them to see the gate?" "I guess you could paint some arrow to show them where to go." He laughed and said, "I had them believing it for a couple of hours!"

My husband was foreman on a ranch in New Mexico. The rancher asked me, "How does John know all these things? He never went to college." I told him, "Over forty years of experience should teach a lot of things. They say experience is the best teacher. You get the test first and the lesson after." The rancher was amazed. He would say, "John has a way with cattle."

In John's early cowboy days, you never talked while you were moving a herd. If you did, you were fired. Everyone knew what to do and did it. Most people think cowboys have an unusual freedom. There are more unwritten rules than you can imagine and every cowboy had to know them. The rules all had a reason. The work was organized, well organized. Most of the cattle on big ranches were on the wild side. Anything that was unusual would startle them. You didn't risk a stampede. John was always shocked when men talked loudly, let alone whoop and yell on a drive. The whole purpose was to keep it calm and quiet to make the animals easier to handle. You certainly did not drive cattle at a high trot, especially in hot weather. Not only does it take the weight off them, some might die of heat exhaustion. As one cowboy described it, "You don't get any money for the dead ones."

So many of the ranches do not correct their mistakes. Hotshots, a cattle prod that gives the animal a jolt of electricity, are one of the problems in penning cattle. Cattle do have some memory and know when they go into the pens what will happen. So they try anything to avoid going inside for more of the same. The old ranchers and cowboys never thought it necessary to use hotshots and disdained the idea. It seemed to cause more problems than it solved, so why bother to go to the trouble and expense?

John told me about a situation where three of four heifers calved about the same time. Two calves were not breathing. Two cowboys were slapping one on the back and trying anything they could think of. John went to the other calf, found a straw and tickled the calf's nose with the straw. The calf reacted, twitching his nose, and inhaled a deep breath.

The first rule on any ranch was well known. Anyone who abused an animal was *fired.* His reputation for cruelty to animals went with him, wherever he went.

They also had a saying, "You can get land poor." When you have more than you can take care of, when you have to fly or go all over the country to tend to your business, sooner or later you have to rob Peter to pay Paul. You are land poor. They watched several entrepreneurs getting themselves into that situation. The old ranchers preferred a steady, well-organized business that produced something, paid its own way. Ranching itself is gamble enough.

HISPANIC VILLAGES

Introduction

The writings in this section were developed in Free River Press writing workshops in New Mexico beginning in 2006. I lived in Iowa then, but Santa Fe had been a second home for decades. I had lived there in the 1960s and 1970s and had known a wide range of people—Hispanic, Native American, and Anglo—from artists and teachers, to tradesmen and ranchers.

By the time I returned to Santa Fe in 2006, I had already published *Heartland Portrait*, a large collection of stories from the rural Midwest.The goal I set for Free River Press was to develop and publish three large anthologies from regional cultures. New Mexico was the natural choice to begin a second regional anthology. I still had numerous friends in the city, friends I could stay with while exploring workshop possibilities. Someone suggested that the Mary Esther Gonzales Senior Center would be the perfect place to host the workshop. It is a gathering spot for Hispanics and Anglos, both mornings and afternoons, and especially during lunch. Because it was the largest and best known of Santa Fe's five senior centers, it drew the people with the stories I wanted.

Hispanics are proud of their four-hundred-year-old New Mexico culture and when I proposed a workshop to the center director, she and her staff were enthusiastic. They publicized the workshop and twenty-five people signed up, despite the fact that the workshop would run for five consecutive days, from 9:00 a.m. to 4:00 p.m., with a forty-five minute break for lunch. In fact, almost all the participants returned for subsequent workshops over the next five years. We had dinners together and our first book, *Ayr y Ahora: Yesterday and Today*, won the New Mexico Heritage Preservation Award for Publication from the State of New Mexico. Today, many of us remain in contact through emails and phone calls, and even letters. One of the workshop members, Andres Romero (who contributed to this volume), was a member of the Free River Board of Directors until his passing.

Two of the first workshop participants I knew from the 1960s. One was Tom Hamel, a tall, imposing artist with a bass voice who had arrived from New Hampshire decades earlier. In those days we were both habitués of Claude's, the legendary watering hole for the bohemian colony in the Canyon Road neighborhood. The other acquaintance I knew, Priscilla Hoback, was an artist and native Santa Fean.

The other participants were new to me. Some lived in Santa Fe, others in nearby towns. The workshop was pretty evenly divided between Anglos and Hispanics. The Anglos had Santa Fe stories from the 1960s and early 1970s when the town was still wonderfully off-kilter, filled with eccentrics and others who charted their own course. The Hispanics, however, whose forebears had settled New Mexico centuries before, wrote stories of the life and culture in agricultural mountain villages where their forebears had lived since the villages were first established.

Lydia Lopez, for example, described her father's flour mill and the techniques and practices that marked rural Hispanic life. Mercedes Roybal wrote about herding goats and Saturday night village dances. But there were comic stories too, such as the Romero family's descriptions of their encounters with l*a vicina mala*, a crazy Anglo neighbor.

What became clear to me after assembling this collection of stories was the depth to which their religious life permeated their daily lives and shaped their culture. Catholicism was not something added onto daily life: it helped to coalesce family units, knit community, and provide a moral compass, as all religions do. These villages were among the last traditional communities in the United States and bear witness to what we have lost through modernity.

Hispanic roots in New Mexico go back to 1598, when Juan de Oñate led an expedition out of New Spain (Mexico) across the Rio Grande to explore and colonize the new lands. Oñate's cruelty to the Pueblo Indians as well as the colonists is legendary, and in 1606 he was recalled to Mexico. In 1598, the year he arrived, Oñate established a town, *SanJuan de los Cabalelleros*, which was capital of the province until 1610. The succeeding viceroy established *La Villa Real de la Santa Fe de San Francisco de Assisi* (City of the Holy Faith of Saint Francis of Assisi), which became the capital of *Nuevo Mexico*. In succeeding years the Spanish crown granted large tracts of land to members of New Spain's ruling class. But it took over a century before colonists moved out of the safety of Santa Fe to the north, where they established outlying villages. Taos, ninety miles north of Santa Fe, was established in 1650, close to the ancient pueblo that gave the village its name. Las Trampas was founded in 1751, El Rito in 1807, and Truchas in 1754. These and other villages, some of them on dirt roads in remote mountain regions, remained isolated from the world until the mid-twentieth century. Their culture was intact, and with limited access to the outside world, they were closed to Anglo outsiders.

Soon after arriving in Santa for the first time, I heard people say of these villages, "They're in the mountains," or "They're very old," and "Their people don't like outsiders."

Hearing these stories meant I had to visit these towns. I'm not sure which of the villages I saw first. But it seemed to be a collection of mud huts ready to slide off the mountainside. The villagers stared at us. True or not, we had heard that these towns were rumored to be unsafe for Anglos and we did not stop.

I did not visit any of the towns again until the day I was married in Truchas, a village sitting on top of the world at 8,000 feet, a place where you might expect to see Tibetan prayer flags flying. I was engaged to a woman who, for some reason, thought it would be the coolest thing in the world to be married in Truchas. Not only that, but to be married by a primitive artist named Bill Tate, who was also a justice of the peace. I think Tate was the only Anglo then living in Truchas. He wore an old sports jacket, but we saw the forty-five strapped to his hip. "I wear it," he said, "because the people here want to kill me." I didn't believe it. As I found out, Bill was a teller of tall tales.

He was one of the first Anglos to move into one of the old villages. It has taken perhaps four to five decades—even after the mountain road to Truchas was paved in the early 1970—for the Anglos to begin a slow invasion. As of this writing, the internet lists fourteen vacation rentals in Truchas and the nearby area.

Whatever finally becomes of these villages, we have in *Coyotes and Stars* a record of traditional life as it was lived in northern New Mexico.

WORK

LYDIA LOPEZ

Lydia Lopez, wife and mother of seven, grandmother of twelve, great-grandmother of two, served as a substitute teacher in her spare time. Twelve generations of her family were raised in the beautiful Española Valley of northern New Mexico. Her grandfather was a trustee of the Santa Cruz land grant, her great-grandfather went on the Santa Fe Trail to bring supplies to the colonists before the railroad came to this region. Lydia has always been a writer. These writing workshops have served as an opportunity to write her childhood memories for her children and grandchildren so that they will know their roots.

EL MOLINO DE JUAN (JOHN'S FLOUR MILL)

This crisp October morning Juan rose quickly, putting on his favorite *pecheras* (bib overalls) grabbing a quick breakfast of scrambled eggs wrapped in a warm tortilla prepared by Lucia, his young wife, who had risen early to prepare this hearty meal! Off he rushed to begin his daily routine of checking his monstrous engine, filling first the tank with gasoline, then filling the water tank that would cool the huge motor, checking the belts, and finally cranking the machine to life. The noisy contraption came alive!

The whole village was awakened by the deafening sound. Everyone in Santo Niño heard the noise. Juan's *molino* (mill) was bustling with frantic activity as he went about the business of checking the grinding stones and the sifters that separated the crushed grains into flour and bran, filtering them into aluminum tubs holding the flour, switching the full ones and setting the empty ones in place, filling the chute with grain again and again. Running, changing, filling, emptying, people waiting, people bringing sacks of wheat to be ground, unloading, loading, Juan looking more and more like a white ghost, even his eyelashes covered by the flour dust that rose up throughout the mill!

Juanito, his eldest son, would help customers with the orders of wheat to be ground. They arrived in wagons pulled by teams of horses, some coming from as far as Truchas in the high mountains twelve or more miles away! They came prepared to spend the night, sleeping under their wagons, feeding and watering their horses, tending to a common fire where they warmed their meals. Juan worked tediously without stopping, the engine chugging away furiously, crushing and sifting endlessly!

At lunchtime Lucia would send her eight-year-old daughter, Eloise, with a lard bucket full of tortillas, folded and filled with meat and *chili verde (*green chili), a large jar of cold water for thirsty Juan and Juanito, which was consumed in no time! The engine working through the night, lit by a single battery lamp! Juan would hand Eloise a bucket to fetch water from a well in the center of the hacienda-shaped compound. Eloise slowly lowered the bucket into the deep well, let it fill with water, poured the water into her father's bucket, proceeded to the mill, and with each heavy step tried not to spill a precious drop. Eloise handed the bucket to her father to feed the thirsty tank that cooled the huge engine. The noise was deafening, but the bucket handed back to Eloise had a silent message: "Bring me some more water, *mi hita!"* (my little one).

The earth shattering noise awoke the cows, pigs, and chickens as well. Lucia's Holstein cow, Bossy, had been milked and turned into the grazing pasture to eat the last green blades of grass that fall morning. But Bossy smelled a familiar smell in the air, so she followed the scent of sweet bran fed to her the previous day and broke through the fence, headed in the direction of the flour mill. Juan readied a large wooden box, filled with bran for Bossy. After having her fill, Juan tied a rope around her neck, handed it to the water bearer/lunch carrier/now cow shepherd . . . me, Eloise!

LYDIA LOPEZ

PAPA QUITO'S WELL

As a very young child I was sent to stay with *Pápa* Quito and *Mí* Valencia, my grandfather and grandmother, to wean me from the breast when I was two years old. They lived a couple of miles away, across the Santa Cruz River that separated the villages of Sombrillo and Santo Niño. I spent two weeks with them before I was sent home to my parents again. My mother, Lucía, told me that when I was finally brought back home my father, Juan, asked me, "*¿Que té dan para comér tus abuelos, mí hijita*?" (What did they feed you at your grandparents, my little one?) In my limited vocabulary, I replied, "*Frijoles! Frijoles! Frijoles*!" ("Beans! Beans! Beans!") much to the amusement of my older brothers and sisters.

But my earliest memory of *Pápa* Quito is sitting on his ample lap when I was five years old. He was sipping hot *átole*, a type of gruel made from blue corn meal, which MíValencia had prepared for him.

My grandfather's real name was Francisco Montoya, and he was my mother's father. He was a tall, stocky, well-built, and hard-working man. As a child lovingly raised by his aunt and uncle, who had no children of their own, Francisco grew up strong, yet gentle. We never knew his exact origins; we only knew that he had relatives we never met that lived on the other side of the Sangre de Cristos, the area now called Rociada, east of Las Vegas. If we travel to that area today, it will take us maybe two hours by car, but the only means of transportation at that time was by horseback, horse and buggy, or a four-horse-drawn wagon, and it would probably take at least four or five days to get there, in good weather. Pápa Quito remained close to his relatives in

Rociada and they helped each other in times of need. Francisco grew into a young man who affectionately cared for his *tíos* (uncles) until they passed away.

My grandmother was named Teodocía Valencía, but as a sign of respect we were taught to address our elders by their relationship to us, as well as by their last names rather than by their given names; hence we called her *Mí* Valencía. *Mí* Valencía lived close to where my grandfather grew up in Santo Niño, the small close-knit community where I was born. Santo Niño was a village near Santa Cruz de La Cañada, which was established in 1695, and was larger than the earlier settled Villa de Santa Fé, which was settled in 1610. Francisco married my grandmother in the 1870's. Their children were my *Tías (*aunts) Elena and Lorencita, my mother, Lucía, my *Tío* Eútimio, and *Tía* Antoñia (the youngest), all dearly loved by my grandparents.

A few years later my grandparents beain their quest to improve the property they now owned. The property was on the side of a hill, called a *ladera*. Pápa Quito laboriously leveled this property into terraces, using his horse, a scoop and a shovel. Now he was ready to dig his well. Oh, how I wish I had a real picture of this marvelous sight! He labored long and hard, physically and mentally, to achieve this miracle.

The well, to my young age of seven or eight, seemed so deep I imagined that you could get to China at its bottom! I had never seen anything so cavernous before. Francisco had lowered himself on a rope with a sturdy platform to support the heavy *rondañilla* (wheel) where the rope attachment was held fast. I am wondering how this feat could take place! He must have lowered himself tied to a rope, along with a pick, a shovel, a bucket and a determination to overcome any obstacle that he might encounter. Bucket after bucket of dirt came rising out of the well. Did my tiny grandmother help him? I was too small to ponder what immense labor this project would entail.

My uncle was too young to be of any help, as he was younger than my own mother; maybe Pápa Quito's tío was his helper! Eventually Francisco hit pay dirt. Water! Muddy at first, then clear and clean. That must have been a great relief for both my grandparents. What a monumental task this must have been. Precious water! No longer must they boil water from the *acequia* (water ditch) or make a long trip to the river at the bottom of his property, where at times of flooding, the river covered the lower portion of his land.

The last remembrance of my beloved Pápa Quito was at his death. His strong arms lying peacefully on his robust chest, this vital human being lay on Mí Valencía's beautiful dining table (awaiting the construction of his coffin which was taking place on his immaculately swept patio.) (The same table where we grandchildren had played post office, pretending the narrow, spindled legs supporting the table were the grills of the post office window.) As we watched, bewildered by this somber experience, we wondered if his body would disappear up to Heaven, just like the dead bird whose funeral we had held months before. We had wrapped the bird in tissue, placed it in a grave we dug with a large spoon, covered it with dirt, and planted a cross made out of Popsicle sticks at the head of the little grave, returning the following day, digging the dirt off, to see if the little bird had really gone to heaven as we had been told! What a great miracle! Surely it had! The belief we held was that our dear pápa would also go straight to heaven! I am of the belief that this strong, generous, gentle giant of a man surely earned his eternal reward, for he left a legacy of strength, integrity, and moral values instilled in his children, that told us that if you work hard for the benefit of many, the reward continues to bear fruit! Dear pápa, may you rest in peace!

LYDIA LOPEZ

RISTRAS

As a young girl I lived in the small village of Santo Niño, near Santa Cruz de la Cañada, the village where the Spanish colonists settled after the Pueblo Revolt of 1680. Families lived close to each other and helped each other—making *matanzas* (killings), building with adobes, plastering with mud, making coffins, lending a hand in any emergency.

Everyone in my village spoke Spanish. My first language was Spanish. My parents farmed about ten acres and grew an enormous garden. They grew chili and corn (sweet, blue, and white), peas, green beans, zucchini, juicy cantaloupes, huge watermelons, peaches (my favorite fruit), apples (Red Delicious), cherries, apricots and nice plump plums.

When harvest time came, my older sisters and I would help our mother pick bushel after bushel of ripe red chili pods and haul each bushel to a trailer my father had made for this purpose. He would hitch it up to the tractor and let me drive it ever so slowly to our house a short distance away. My two older sisters, being stronger than I, would carry the colorful bushels of chiles into one of our bedrooms, which had been emptied of furniture.

The chile picking had to be done either before going to school, bright and early, or after school, as our parents made our education a priority. On weekends our cousins would come to help, as chile does not ripen all at once. Thank goodness!

Lucia, my mother, was in charge of making the beautiful fragrant *ristras (*strings of dried chilies tied together). It was a tedious job. She first sorted the red chiles by size—the nicest in one pile, the crooked in another pile, the orange colored, not-quite-ripe in another.

Mother would send me to our neighbor Magdalena's home to ask her to come and help with the rest of ristra making. Magdalena was a strong but gentle woman in her late forties with milk white skin and dark curly hair, who had been crippled either by birth, or through some accident.

Mother and Magdalena would first tie three chiles together with string and take three more and tie them to the same string, and three more, until they had a three or four foot string of chiles. Mother would measure her height with a length of heavy twine and start weaving the chile strings around the twine. The ristra tying would last until midnight. When my sisters and I awoke the next morning, the room would be filled with all the ristras lying lengthwise on the floor! They were ready to be hung up by my father, as they were heavy. He climbed the ladder and hung each ristra outside on a *viga (*eam) to dry in the warm sun. After all these trips up the ladder with ristras, he must have been as tired as mother.

What a colorful sight greeted us when we returned from school! The outside walls of our house had turned bright rich red. All that hard work so we could enjoy the savory, fragrant, hot red chile our mother would fix for us with warm soft tortillas, or in a steaming bowl of *posole (*hominy).

Magdalena would return to help us set our room back in order and mother would pay her and send her home with her arms full of whatever we had to share.

MERCEDES ROYBAL

Mercedes Roybal lived in Santa Fe with her husband, George. They had five children and nine grandchildren. Mercedes was born and raised in Pecos, New Mexico and taught school for twenty-one years. She passed away in 2019.

TRANQUILINO GONZALES, MY DAD

My dad, Tranquilino Gonzales, was born and raised in La Cueva, a small community near Pecos, in San Miguel County. His ancestors had homesteaded the lands in El Macho, La Cueva, La Joya, and Rowe Mesa. His parents and grandparents were large landowners who depended largely on sheep for their livelihood. While they owned a lot of land and a large number of sheep, they were ordinary ranchers, *una gente buena y muy humilde* (just good humble people) who lived simple, honest and unassuming lives. As their families grew and lifestyles changed, the flocks of sheep dwindled and their wealth shrank and they had to work hard like everyone else. As a young man, my dad did own a fancy vehicle and he was proud of that. But in later years that fancy car broke down and just sat in the yard, and little by little was vandalized and destroyed.

Don Tranquilino was tall and slender, charismatic and quiet. He was real. Don Tranquilino never complained about work or his life. During the shearing of the sheep, the castration and marking of the lambs, he was there among the workers, doing his share and making sure that *sus trabajadores* (his workers) and his children were taken care of and fed first.

Many tasks were not pleasant: many were just plain hard work. But in the midst of the daily grind, my dad saw the beauty of his surroundings. He loved the sunsets and the blue skies. He described his ranch up in Rowe Mesa and his home in La Cueva as peaceful places where you could raise your family and live *muy agusto* (very comfortably). *"Ya mejor lugar no encuentra uno."* ("You can't find a better place.") He constantly gave thanks to God for his many blessings.

When he took his sheep up to the Pecos Wilderness in the summertime, he took his time. He was in awe of his *alrededores* (surroundings). He had help in taking the sheep to summer pasture. Mom, my older sister, and my younger brother sometimes accompanied him. I never did, but when they returned there was a certain amount of excitement and many stories to share.

I recall that when he came home after a hard day's work, he'd drive up in his old, black pickup truck, slowly get out and very calmly walk in the house and greet us. He would slowly sit down, sigh and request: *"Trai me un vaso de agua y el platon para lavar me las manos."* ("Bring me a glass of water and a wash basin to wash my hands.") He would slowly remove his hat, pull out his red handkerchief, wipe the perspiration from his forehead and from his hat. Next, he slowly drank his glass of water, then wasedh his hands and face. He would briefly tell us about his day. I recall him talking of his horses. Those horses that had once served him quite well and had been strong and healthy were now old and slow. *"Pobrecitos, son una pachora para todo pero me han servido muy bien."* ("Poor things, they're slow as molasses, but have served me well.") He loved his horses and his livelihood depended on them. They helped him get to areas that you couldn't get to in a vehicle.

My dad's sheep were his pride and joy. They were special to him. He always spoke about how many sheep his ancestors had owned. He reminisced about the grasslands that had existed. *"Mas antes habia sufiiciente pasto para todos los animals." (*"Years ago there were plenty of grasslands for all the animals.") Now the pasture was very sparse, overgrazed or controlled by the federal government. He wasn't bitter. That's the way things were and somehow he would survive.

Another favorite topic of his was the weather. His excitement over the fact that rain clouds were gathering was contagious. *"Hay vienen las nubes y hay viene la lluvia, gracias a Dios."* ("There come the clouds and there comes the rain, thanks be to God.") He would get so excited when it looked like it would rain. There was gusto in his anticipation of rain. He actually rejoiced when it rained. Thunder and lightning fascinated him. He had many tales of many people that had been struck by lightning. He would explain excitedly how you had to take shelter under a tree or in a *chosa,* which was a shelter built during a previous storm. If it didn't rain and there was a drought, then it was drastic. We would pray for rain and take the *santos* (the statues of saints) in procession through the plowed fields and pray and sing *alabados* (hymns). This was all very exciting and special because we knew how important the rain was for the ranch and the livestock. Dad called it *una bendicion de Dios* (a blessing from God). We were a close family and we shared both blessings and worries.

There were times when I would accompany him on his daily rounds, and I look back at those special times and remember them vividly. On our way home to La Cueva from Rowe Mesa he would stop at Padilla's Liquor and Grocery Store in Rowe for a shot of whiskey for himself and some candy for me. He would chat with the owner, el Senor Padilla, drink his shot of whiskey and then hurry home. These contacts with the Spanish-speaking populace kept my dad content and grateful. They were short stops and after a hard day's work, quite innocent and well deserved. However, if my mother found out that he had stopped at "La Cantina," the bar in Rowe, my dad would catch hell. I actually considered these stops exciting and quite harmless. He had earned this short respite.

I recall his constant reference to God. For example, *"Si Dios es servido*" or *"Si Dios quiere.*" ("If God's will is done" or "If God wills it.") Every morning and every evening he would make the sign of the cross on his forehead, his lips, and over his heart and accompany that action with the prayer, *Por la Senal de la Santa Cruz (*For the path of the Holy Cross). I can't recall him saying lengthy prayers—well, the rosary once in a while. He usually attended Mass on Sundays. Before Mass all the men would gather outside St. Anthony's Church to chat. The women and children would hurry in and start praying early. Tranquilino paid homage to his Creator but he also cherished his *amigos*. He enjoyed greeting them before and after Mass.

I knew how hard he toiled, and I also knew that he relished his work and loved his animals and his ranch. He didn't seem to mind the tedious work. Actually, he never complained about this drudgery. His daily statement was *"hay poco a poquito voy a hacer lo que tengo que hacer"* ("Little by little I will get things done"). I looked forward to his coming home. I knew he loved us because he showed it by his actions. I loved him dearly and he knew it. He made me feel as if I was his favorite, and he had special greetings for me, *"Como esta mi Grillito Negro?*" "How is my little Black Cricket?" Other terms of endearment were *"mi ayudanta, mi Mercy, mi hijita, mi cocinera"* ("my helper, my Mercy, my daughter, my cook.") He followed his expressions of affection with a big hug or a pat on my head.

My dad wanted all of us with him at Rowe Mesa to help at the ranch. He needed help and he valued earning a living. The ranch was his livelihood and that is what mattered to him. When he stayed alone up at Rowe Mesa, he lived in a tent and *"y a el le gustaba pastorear a sus ovejas."* (He loved to take his sheep out to different pastures.) When school was out, we joined him, and we would stay in this old, long ranch house that originally belonged to his grandparents and in later years to his parents. This was just an old, simple place, nothing fancy, just a big stove in the middle of the room and a corner fireplace, beds, a table and benches, just essentials, but it served us well. We enjoyed going there and we thought it was a nice ranch with the corrals and everything that you needed.

My dad helped many friends and relatives by gathering and bringing firewood for them. He loved helping and he loved sharing. He shared many lambs and young goats. Since we didn't have refrigeration, we had to share the butchered lambs or goats with our relatives and friends and they shared with us when they butchered their animals. The whole process of butchering is still vivid for me. I can still see my dad hanging the young goat or lamb and then quickly killing him and then opening it and removing the insides. Next he removed the outer skin by first using a knife and next his fist. Looking back, it was such a normal thing to do. We didn't waste any of it, including the blood. Mom made a tasty blood pudding out of it and the intestines were cleaned thoroughly and baked and enjoyed as a meal. Even the head was baked and eaten. We made use of almost everything.

I have great memories of his lovable presence. I admire him, miss him and think about him even more now that I'm getting closer to the age he was when he passed away. I ask myself, "What would I tell him if I saw him now?" I think I would say, "I think you were absolutely right, this is a downright beautiful, peaceful place and I thank you for your love, your guidance and your inspiration. *Mil gracias, Don Tranquilino Gonzales.* I love you dearly, I admire you and I miss you."

MERCEDES ROYBAL

THE LITTLE GOAT GIRL

I was born in a quiet, picturesque community right outside of Pecos. My parents were humble farmers who owned sheep, goats, chickens, horses and a few cattle. I never considered our family poor. I thought we were regular people, proud of our heritage and culture. I remember mom and dad telling us how important it was to never depend on welfare. They wanted us to be honest about our language and our roots, and proud of our humble beginnings. Telling this story is perhaps a way to comply with their wishes. I'm the "Little Goat Girl "from Pecos, and I'm proud of it. It was an honest living and a grand childhood.

Perhaps I was a little haughty, at least that is how I remember those days. My many feisty cousins lived all around us, and I don't remember any of them having to take care of goats. We were a proud bunch.

My husband tells me that he thought I was a snob. He said he was afraid to talk to me. I was from west Pecos and he was from east Pecos, on the other side of the river. The west Pecos kids considered the east Pecos kids to be from Timbuktu. I felt he was a *morodo*. He tells me I was a know-it-all.

My parents had to work hard, and they did have hired help to assist with the sheep and other large animals. We kept a few goats close to home for the milk, cheese and the *cabritos (*goats) that when butchered and roasted were very tasty. I thought goats were for poor, needy people, but we were not needy or poor, yet my parents insisted on keeping these stinky goats. Yet these frisky, smelly goats were special. They were like pets and we even had special names for them. I was the lucky, or at times unlucky, one who had to look after them in the summer, on weekends, and, during the school year, after classes. I was the designated goat girl.

I would take the small group of goats and their babies out to pasture; it was a necessary chore, but in certain ways a pleasure. I was supposed to take them out to the nearby fields and forest and it was not a big deal for me, if I could just keep it a secret.

I was like some of the characters in the children's stories I loved to read, about girls like Heidi who took care of goats. I loved these animals, and I loved the long leisurely walks. I thought I was blessed and thinking back, I was. Then why did I insist on keeping it a secret? Because goats don't have the prestige that cattle do and this proud young girl didn't want to be teased. In elementary school boys love to tease and tease me they would. I can still hear the Ortiz boys from Pecos and the Ruiz boys from Rowe chasing me and pulling my braids and calling me *cabrera,* or little goat girl. I look back now and I think surely they had a crush on me and that was their way of showing it.

I can still hear my parents' voices: "Goats are good, goats are necessary, and we need them."

RELIGION

AURORA G. SALAZAR

Aurora G. Salazar was born and raised in Wagon Mound, New Mexico. She was married to Max J. Salazar. They had four children, Connie and Yolanda, and two that died in infancy, Eugene and Wilma. She taught school in Wagon Mound for seventeen- and-a-half years. The family moved to Santa Fe where Aurora taught for fifteen years. After retirement, she was active in several organizations and did volunteer work for a number of community programs. Aurora died in 2011.

LA SEMANA SANTA

My parents and grandparents owned a large ranch which they had homesteaded, about eighteen miles from Wagon Mound, a small community in northeastern Mora County. We spent most of the time there.

My grandfather was a member of the *Hermanos de Jesus Cristo*—the Brothers of Jesus Christ—a large fraternal Catholic men's organization that had its roots in Spain. The *morada* was on his property. It was a one room adobe structure nestled close to the ground on the grassy hillside.

The *Semana Santa* (Hoy Week) rituals and ceremonies that took place at that time are among the happiest and most vivid memories of my earliest childhood.

In the context of the times, and because of geographical isolation, the *hermandad* (brotherhood]) fulfilled the spiritual, worldly, and even the judicial needs of the people. They adhered to a very rigid code of ethics based on Christian principles. Because their rules were so strict and harsh, my grandfather would not allow his son, my uncle, to become a member.

Semana Santa was the last week of Lent. It was totally dedicated to spiritual services. The preparations for this holy time were made many days beforehand. The local ranch hands and the men in the family cleaned the grounds, outbuildings and all the surrounding area. All the hermanos and their families from the nearby ranches came to congregate and worship at the morada. They all stayed at the ranch. There were horses to be fed and watered, as well as people to be lodged and nourished. They chopped huge, monstrous piles of firewood to be used for heating and cooking. No heavy manual labor or extraneous activities were permitted during the holy days—Wednesday, Thursday and Friday—before Easter. There would be no music, singing or dancing.

My mother and her cousins would construct an altar in the corner of the long, wide dining room. It had been stripped of all furniture except chairs and *tarimas* (benches) that were placed around the room. The altar walls and the altar were covered with pristine white cloths. A large primitive, hand carved crucifix was hung on one side and framed pictures of saints were placed on the other.

Tall, dark wooden candle holders were placed on the altar. The perimeter of the area was decorated with colorful crepe paper flowers that we had made. At the end of the celebration they were carefully stored, to be used again from year to year.

The women would prepare huge quantities of food—*posole,* (hominy) *chico*s (corn kernels) beans, dried *quelites* (young, tender plants) and *rueditas* (pasta wheels). It was a time of abstinence, no meat. They baked dozens of beautiful golden loaves of bread, fragrant spicy pies made of dried apples, apricots, peaches and prunes, as well as huge mounds of delicious anise flavored *biscochitos* (cookies) baked in the *horno* (oven), the outdoor adobe oven.

One by one the horse drawn wagons and buggies arrived. There were people of all ages, old people, young children and even infants. They were laden with clothes, bedding, "goodies," and provisions. How excited and happy we all were! There were hugs and kisses and joyful words of welcome. My sister and I were so happy and eager to have the younger children because we rarely had playmates.

When all had finally arrived and got settled, the men retreated to the morada for the duration of the celebration. The women and children remained in the house to do the cooking and cleaning, and to prepare the house for the *visitas* (visitors) and *velorios* (wakes) that were held nightly. Food was prepared and sent to the men at the morada for each meal. We children were given daily chores. We brought in the wood, water from the well, fed the chickens and gathered the eggs. It was such fun to go into the chicken coop, barns and the hayloft. We laughed and shouted, "Look how many I found!" when we had found a nest. We were assigned to the large attic room above the first story main rooms. It was now covered with wall-to-wall mattresses, bed rolls and warm, cozy blankets. What fun we had, being careful to stifle our laughter, for we had to be quiet. We built tents, turned somersaults on the cushy floor, played "statue" and other games.

Once a day the hermanos came to pray at the altar. At home, we watched the procession as they came from the morada. They came slowly across the rough, barren ground. At times, one or two brothers would carry a large, heavy wooden *madero* made of thick logs. On occasion, they were accompanied by a few flagellants—men with black shrouds that covered their heads, and stripped to the waist, flogging themselves with long *disciplinas* made of rope. They walked slowly to the rhythm of the whips, with the red blood streaming down their backs. They entered the room and shut the door to conduct their own private rituals. We children would stealthily creep up the stairs to the attic room. Being curious and inquisitive, as children are, we would softly creep to our "secret" viewing place a small knot hole on the floor, which was the ceiling of the altar room. We would take turns viewing the scene below. I shudder to think what horrendous punishment would have been meted to us if we had been discovered.

The hermanos were strict disciplinarians. Woe unto anyone who had to answer for his misdeeds. At one time my young uncle and his cousin were sent to deliver a large wooden trunk-like chest from the house to the morada. Boys being boys, they thought they would play a joke on them. There were some skeleton remains of animals here and there on the pasture land. They gathered them and put them inside the chest and slowly trekked their way to the morada, carrying the heavy chest. They knocked on the door, left the chest, and ran all the way home, laughing and chuckling, as they imagined how horrified the brothers would be when they opened the door. But their glee was short-lived. The very next day my grandfather sent word to my grandmother to send the boys to the morada. The two culprits went, dragging their feet. They presented themselves, quaking with fear, dreading the punishment they would get. They tearfully confessed and asked to be forgiven. For their penance they were given a large pail. They were ordered to fill it with the gravelly sand from the ant hills that were in the area. Then they had to make two crosses on the ground with the gravel. They had to roll up their pants' legs, bare their knees, kneel on the rough sand, and stretch out their arms. A heavy rock was placed on each hand. They knelt, painfully shifting from one knee to the other, tears streaming down their faces. After a while they were released and sent home and admonished to behave themselves.

Sometimes we could see from our house past the *acequia* (water ditch), a penitente on the rocky hillside slowly walking back and forth, flagellating himself. It was said that some did it as a sacrifice, as a prayer, in atonement, or in punishment.

There would be *velorios* at the house in the evenings. These were held to pray devoutly. They would also sing *alabados,* mournful hymns of the Passion. The *Rezador* (leader of prayers) would lead the congregation in prayer. Sometimes my grandfather, who was proud that I could read Spanish, would have me read aloud some of the prayers. I must have been about seven years old. I felt so proud and important!

On Good Friday afternoon we would all go to pray the Stations of the Cross. They had been laid out on the ground near the morada, each station marked with a short wooden cross.

A penitente carried a heavy cross on his back. Some of them with shrouded heads and stripped to the waist, whipped themselves, first across one shoulder and then the other, as they walked along. Once I loudly asked my grandmother, "Who washes their bloody hips and clothes?" She promptly pinched my arm and hushed me.

That night there would be a velorio and *tinieblas* (penitente ritual devotion), the *Tenebrae* (religious service during the three days preceding Easter.). It was a solemn somber service simulating the darkness, the quaking of the earth and the thunderous tumult that occurred when Christ died. All the lamps and candles were extinguished. Then the brothers chanted prayers moaningly, the *matracas* (wooden noisemakers) were whirled, making their clackety noises. Large, heavy metal chains were pounded and thumped noisily on the floor, again and again; the chanting and moaning went on and on. Children were not allowed to attend this ceremony, for it was too eerie and frightening.

The next day everyone packed their belongings, harnessed their horses, and loaded their wagons. There were a lot of heart-felt and tearful good-byes. We all hugged and waved, saying, "*Adios*," "*Vuelvan pronto*," "*Vayan con Dios*,"—"Goodbye," "Come back soon," "May God go with you." My sister and I were sad, we would miss our friends and the good times we had enjoyed. My folks, I'm sure, would breathe sighs of relief as they went back to work and got things back to normal.

FLORA LEYBA

Flora Leyba was born in Chimayo, New Mexico in 1930. In 1950 Flora moved to Los Alamos where she worked in the University of California's accounting department. In 1951 she married Walter Leyba and in 1953 they moved to Santa Fe. Flora worked in financial services from 1978 until 2010. Walter and Flora had one son and one adopted daughter, twelve grandchildren and nine great-grandchildren.

PENITENTE JUAN M. SANDOVAL

Chimayo, New Mexico was my home for twenty years. I was raised by a Catholic family right next to the famous *Santuario de Chimayo*. In the early years of my childhood, we said the rosary every evening at home. In the month of May, the recitation of the rosary was done at the Santuario. My Aunt Eduvijen would climb a couple of long ladders to reach the tower of the church bell in order to ring it with a couple of rocks and call the faithful to gather for the rosary. The fragrance of lilac flowers as we walked past these bushes into the church still lingers in my mind.

Throughout northern New Mexico and perhaps southern Colorado, where the Spaniards settled, the Penitente order was supreme. From the early nineteenth century until today, the Penitente brothers in local moradas have practiced the charity of St. Francis and observed the Passion of Jesus Christ.

The burial and resurrection of our Lord Jesus Christ was of singular importance to our family. My father, Juan M. Sandoval, belonged to the Penitente brotherhood. He was at one point in time *el hereon mayor*, head of the brotherhood. Mr. Martinez and my father led the recitation of the rosary and my father was the lead singer of the choruses.

My father was gone from home for all of Easter week. We, his children, took turns bringing his meals to him at la morada, where he was staying. La morada is a structure where the Penitentes meet and supposedly scourge themselves, using the tail of a cow or horse to scatter the blood from their wounds. They also sleep on the bare mud floors in order to do penance.

Two or three times a week we would see and hear them approaching the Santuario. A set time day or night was never planned, so their visit to the Santuario was always a surprise, with their lanterns flickering in the darkness and their chains and *matrahas* (rattles) sounding. The choruses they were singing could hardly be heard because of the spooky noise. Before they entered the Santuario, my oldest brother, Apolonio, would join my father as well as my *Tio* (uncle) Antonio, and all together they would recite the rosary. Two *faroles* (lanterns) and five candles were all the light they had.

Whenever the Penitentes chose to visit the Santuario, especially if it was late at night, my mother felt obligated to wake us children to witness their approach. Not totally understanding all that the Penitentes did, fear set in. Clinging around my mother Chonita, we held tight to her hands and legs, begging her to take us back into the house and tuck us in bed. She obliged and we felt more secure within those adobe walls.

As the rosary was said, one candle was extinguished as each mystery—ten beads each—was recited. Soon it was very dark in there. After the rosary, a refrain was said in unison: "*Vivos y defunctos que vivan todos juntos*." (The living and the dead shall live in union.) These moments were very frightening for my brother, Apolonio, and to make matters worse, my Tio Antonio would squeeze his leg just over the knee to scare him. Apolonio could hardly wait to get out of there!

The old morada was built next to an arroyo. It was flooded, collapsed, and washed down the river. Apolonio, my father, and my uncles Antonio, Benjamin, Emiliano, and Julian—and no doubt other members of the Penitentes—gathered to salvage what they could. Not too far from the original morada they built a new one, in Los Ranchos, that stands to this day.

SOPHIA JARAMILLO

VIERNES SANTO AT THE SANTUARIO de NUESTRO SEÑOR de ESQUIPULAS

It was 5:30 in the morning of one Good Friday of Lent when I awakened. It was cold outside, so I dressed warmly and donned my best pair of walking shoes. I was going to make the pilgrimage to the Chapel of E*l Santuario de Nuestro Señor de Esquipulas*, known to most of us as *El Santuario de Chimay*o. I was anxious to learn what is it that brings not only pilgrims to make this spiritual trek to the old shrine from as far away as Albuquerque and other New Mexico towns, but tourists from other parts of the world.

The Santuario is an old Spanish pueblo church, built sometime between 1812 and 1816. My husband had dropped me and my two friends off at the bridge at Nambé, some eleven miles from Chimayo. Hundreds more pilgrims joined us from Santa Fe, some carrying heavy crosses, some praying their rosaries, others singing psalms in Spanish.

For the first hour or so, between 7:00 and 8:00 a.m., it was bitter cold. By 10:00 a.m. the sun came down with a vengeance. Some cars sped by. Another hour went by and the sky had become worrisome. I wrapped my jacket about me and increased my pace. My face was so cold. I ran my gloved hands over my ears to warm them. Then came a flicker of sleet, then snow, and then rain. I could hardly see the person ahead of me! There were others, more cheerful than I, singing "Oh, Maria, Madre Mia." After a while their singing got under my skin.

More people carrying heavy crosses passed us, some praying the rosary aloud while others sang. Still others had come strictly for a joy walk, and talked and gossiped; others griped about the weather. Some tourists accompanying us thought this was a high price to pay for coming to see people smear mud on their faces! I assured them that they were talking about the *posito* (little hole) and the sand at the Santuario, which believers rub on a disabled area of their body for a miraculous cure. We disregarded their remarks.

After six or seven hours of walking, we came to that last bend on the road. Below us was the village of Chimayo, and in its midst was the Santuario. Soon we were there and so were a few other thousand ahead of us. There was no way we could all fit into the small chapel, so instead we dropped wearily on the ground of the churchyard.

After an hour or so the crowd dissipated, and we were finally able to enter the Santuario. The service was over, but a nice man at the entrance greeted us and invited us to come inside. We had many questions to ask, especially about the name "*Santuario de Nuestro Señor de Esquipulas*," and the legends about the church. It appears that the area where the church is built was the site of an Indian shrine. Our guide said that it is believed that Chimayo once had been a place where fire and hot water had developed under the earth, forming something like a geyser, which eventually burst forth, forming a sacred pool. Like so many other storics which arc woven into *S*antuario legend, this may be just another one to add to the many told by the people of this community. There are enough stories to fill a library about the healing powers of the dirt in the posito and about how the church was built.

We eventually entered the tiny chapel and marched toward a tiny altar guarded by a tiny wooden rail, its paint now faded, weakened by the hundreds of clasped hands that had come for prayer or communion. On either side of the middle aisle the chapel was furnished with rough wooden pews, the benches as old as the building itself. The blue paint had peeled off, exposing some splintering. For a minute we sat on *bancos* (wooden benches) which wobbled unsteadily from the uneven dirt floor

Because the floors are of native dirt, I could smell the odor of earth after a rainstorm. It was a smell of promise. To our left we perceived two wooden confessionals set obtrusively against the wall, the fronts covered with a burlap-like cloth, which for years had been pulled back and forth by sinners making their confessions.

As we reached the altar, we saw the five *reredos*, a series of sacred paintings done by early members of the church. Behind the main altar was one painted by Molleno, nicknamed "The chile painter." His painting depicts a heart with four wounds, a stalk of wheat, symbolizing bread of life, and grapes, the symbol of wine or the blood of Christ.

To the right of the altar is a *bulto* (carving) of a man on horseback, representing St. James, better known as El Senor Santiago, the patron of Spain who helped fight the invading Moors.

To the left of the altar is a small opening. I shall always remember the door because even the shortest of us had to bend down to enter. Visitors were still there looking at the crutches which lined the walls. Notes and stories were pinned to the walls, some telling of healings, others asking Jesus to pray for them. To the right of this room was a tiny alcove, and in it a small table with many lighted candles. The smell of balsam permeated the area. Just below the table is the posito, exposing sand or maybe dry dirt, which is called "blessed earth." Some people were still there lighting candles and filling small containers with the sand, which is said to be everlasting. I know it is not so, but I want people to keep on believing, if this is part of their culture and heritage. They have the right to do what they want, if it gives them faith.

SOPHIA JARAMILLO

WHEN CHRISTMAS WAS CHRISTMAS IN NORTHERN NEW MEXICO

Christmas Eve 1919 brought special rejoicing and spiritual renewal to northern New Mexico. Church bells had been ringing for the last three weeks in the villages of Santa Fe and Chimayo. World War I was over, and village sons were returning home. A three-year drought was coming to an end. The influenza, which had infested many New Mexico villages, was over. Husbands had cut and stored wood for traditional *farolitos* (lanterns) after three years without them. *La Misa del Gallo* (Midnight Mass) would again be celebrated, and weeks of prayer services and confessions prepared villagers for a spiritual renewal.

The afternoon sun was fading. Children were excited about the celebrations ahead, but also knew the time for atonement was but minutes away. Soon *el abuelo malo, t*he dreaded old grandfather with his ugly mask and substantial switch, would knock at the door, looking for them. He would use his leather switch on those who had committed serious sins. This was a time to atone.

The masked *abuelo* would appear again Christmas day in a mock fight with *el toro* the bull, in the dance of the *Matachines*.

In every home, parents had gathered their children, ages four to twelve in a back bedroom. Children had to remember and tell el abuelo all their sins of the past year, and get ready to accept penance for their atonement.

Mario had the most to fear. His sins could be considered more serious because he was the eldest. Disrespect to adults was the worst sin a child could commit. Stealing was a close second. Hopefully, the smaller sins would be gently forgiven.

Early afternoon of Christmas eve the dreaded knock came to the Martinez home. Full of awe and fear, their eyes round with expectation, the youngest children clung to each other for support as the parents ushered *el abuel*o into the room.

"Well, well, what have we here? What is your name?" he said, pointing to the tallest boy.

"Mario, señor abuelo."

"And tell me what sins have you committed that disappointed your parents or others, especially your elders?"

"Señor abuelo, I smoked a cigarette in the corral. It belonged to my father."

"Aha, you smoked and you stole!"

"Si, señor Abuelo."

"And, do you expect to do this again?"

"No, senor. The cigarette made me very sick, and I am sorry to my father for taking it without his permission."

El abuelo took his switch and gave him several smart swats on the back.

Mario got on his knees to pray ten Our Fathers and ten Hail Marys.

The younger children were so afraid.

"Ooooooooooohhhhhh," they said in a small voice. "That was a great many swats and prayers, especially since he said he was sorry."

. Then one by one, the rest of the children confessed their sins and were given a proper lecture. They were told to say one "Our Father" and to pray for an hour.

El abuelo left for the next house, but not before collecting his *oremos*—a glass of red wine and a *bizcochito* (cookie).

The children were happy to see him go, but one hour is a long time to be on their knees.

"I wish mama would let us go early because if we are too late there might not be any *oremos* left for us".

Parents were strict disciplinarians.

An oremos is a traditional begging of gifts from the neighbors at their door. The neighbors were happy to receive the children and had prepared gifts of simple handmade socks, caps and scarves; candies and cookies; dolls for the girls and sling shots for the boys.

When the hour was over, mama opened the bedroom door softly and said they could go out for *oremos*, but they must be back by ten o'clock to prepare for La Misa del Gallo. "Be nice to the neighbors," she cautioned.

Upon reaching the first neighbor, the Martinez children chanted their little poem:

"Oremos, oremos,
angelitos semos d'el cielo venimos
a pedir oremos
si no nos dan,
puertas y ventanas quebraremos."

("Oremos, oremos, we are little angels coming from the sky to ask for gifts. If they are not given, doors and windows will be broken.")

While the children were seeking oremos, fathers, brothers, and returned soldiers built and lighted luminarias. These are cheerful and appropriate bonfires built of pitchy, resinous sticks of wood laid log-cabin fashion. Luminarias signify the Christ child's footsteps and way back to earth. These bonfires lit up the village, and filled the frosty air with tangy smoke and the spirit of Christmas. This year men again passed the traditional bottles of whisky back and forth. There was much dancing and rejoicing in the streets, and some men played their guitars and sang, never mind how cold it was outside.

The children were all home by ten o'clock and were dressed in their best Sunday clothes and warm coats and heavy shoes for their trek to the church. Parents and grandparents clothed themselves in long coats, hats, gloves and high top shoes. Tradition has it that *gallo*, the rooster, crows at midnight to celebrate the Lord's birthday. Although roosters don't really crow until daylight, midnight signifies the beginning of this new important day.

They arrived at the church where all the village was congregating, expecting the volley of shots fired into the sky at the designated hour. Meanwhile, the churchgoers prayed and sang *Noche Buena* (Silent Night) in the cold of the night. The priest came to the door, ready to usher them in at the sound of the twelfth blast. The first blast went off, then the second, and last the twelfth.

La Misa del Gallo was two and a half hours long. It was the frosting on the cake. The entire neighborhood had gone to confession and now received communion, some perhaps only this one time in the year. Children who had made their first communion went first, followed by all the elders.

By the time the priest gave the Christmas blessing, it was nearly two-thirty in the morning. Everyone was very happy and very hungry. Priests were invited to all homes but the Archbishop had said they must stay sober, especially if they had Mass scheduled Christmas morning.

Every home in the village had made preparations for the Christmas Eve celebrations and all were invited. The women had cooked and now served posole, tamales, chiile, and bizchochitos. So that everyone could visit every home, the invitation extended from after La Misa d'el Gallo throughout the night and continued all Christmas Day.

Children sat on the floor and counted their oremos.

. Returning sons ate their fill of *menudo* (tripe) and posole, "the breakfast of champions," and those who had had too much to drink ate a bowl of *principe,* which means "the final send off." This dish is made of boiled beef, onions and raisins. It is supposed to be very good as a restorative for excessive drinking or overeating.

Christmas Eve 1919 was one never to be forgotten. True to tradition, the rooster crowed for all of those who walked home after a full night and day of celebrations.

The morning after Christmas Day everyone went back to work, thankful that the earth was back in the hands of the Lord, for the rains had come and the sons of northern New Mexico were home again.

COMMUNITY

MERCEDES ROYBAL

THE SATURDAY NIGHT DANCE

The big shindig that we all enjoyed was the Saturday night dance, either at Glorieta or Pecos. Besides these dances, others were held to celebrate feast days, weddings, fiestas, and other special occasions. For wedding dances the musicians played all afternoon and way into the night. Everybody danced; yes, everybody danced. I always felt such happiness when I knew that there would be a dance. It was a special celebration. I remember praying to St. Anthony of Padua (patron saint of lost items) asking him to help me find a wonderful dancing partner. Not just an ordinary dancing partner, but a good looking one.

I felt that it was absolutely necessary to dance all night. The dance was where all the action was; it was where you saw all your friends and cousins and the place to wear your new outfit or you new shoes. The community dance was a super special social.

Early Saturday we did any necessary work, such as cleaning and baking. We behaved like angels because we needed to be on good terms with mom and dad. First, you did all your work and then you got ready. You curled your hair and next you had to convince your parents that it was terribly important for you to attend. The whole world was going to be there.

Your parents had to take you because you were not allowed to go alone. However, they might let you go with some responsible adult, like a cousin or a neighbor. If your parents were upset with you, they would not allow you to go to the dance. That was real punishment, that hurt.

About a hundred or more attended the dances. These included adults, who also enjoyed dancing but didn't relish it like we did. The whole family attended wedding dances. Some couples even took their young baby in a small basket and shoved the basket with the sleeping child under the bench while they enjoyed a dance. The adults would entertain us with some old fashioned dances like the *el valse* (waltz), *las cuadrillas* or *el baile del pano* (handkerchief dance) and many more. It was entertaining and absolutely great.

The custom of the regular dance was for young girls to sit in a half circle around the dance floor and for the boys or young men to stand in a space behind them. When the music started the young men would come and ask the girls to dance.

The women could not or should not refuse the request. It was considered very bad manners. That was called *"el desigre,"* or the refusal, and you just didn't do that. During intermission several friendly dance hall personnel would come around and collect the ten cent fee from the male partner. That interval provided you with enough time to chat or flirt with your partner.

You might even check out who was wearing what and who had been lucky enough to be asked to dance. If you weren't asked out to dance you sat there and pretended that you didn't care. The idea was to get the attention of some young man so that he would notice you and ask you to dance the next time. If you were popular, you would dance all night and that was terrific. I must have been popular because I remember dancing all night and I loved that.

On Monday morning when we went back to school, that's all you talked about, and boy did we exaggerate about how we had danced all night. *"Algunas pobres solamente habian bailado los ojos."* (Some poor souls had only danced their eyes.)

"Hay Chihuahua!" Those were memorable good old days!

FLORA LEYBA

RELATIONSHIPS AT EL POTERO

I grew up in Chimayo, in the section known as *El Potero* (the pasture), right next to the Sanctuario where the holy dirt is located and tourists from all over the world come to visit. The house where I was born is now the religious articles store.

Growing up, I was most fortunate to have had very industrious parents. We had a garden and grew chili, tomatoes, radishes, zucchini, onions, and corn, enough for a family of ten—my father Juan, my mother Juanita, four brothers and four sisters.

My family was close-knit. We always had our meals together. The menu was the same every day—beans, potatoes, chili, tortillas, eggs and oatmeal. Meat occasionally.

Normally we kids got up very early in the morning around 6:00 a.m. and immediately were taken to the field to plant, irrigate or hoe and, later in the year, to harvest. The day got very hot by 11:00 a.m.; therefore, starting early in the morning gave us an opportunity to get the job done early. My mother would have fresh tortillas, scrambled eggs and oatmeal ready for us when we returned home. Just the aroma of the food gave us an extra surge of energy. I am indeed thankful to the Lord for His bounty unto us!

In the spring we planted wheat up at Truchas and harvested it in the fall. The crop was called "*La Temporada* planting" because our Lord watered it, and it did not need any more attention. Our family made only two trips to Truchas, a seven-mile journey uphill from Chimayo. My father and mother would prepare for this journey for days. We had to have plenty of food, as well as bedding, clothes, seeds and tools. The horses had to be shod.

We had a *fuerte*, a log cabin,on the property, built out of materials that were locally available. A blend of dirt, water, sand and straw formed the mortar that was applied between the logs to seal out the elements. The roof was slightly slanted to keep the snow from building up.

After a hard day's work, we were privileged to go for a swim in the *tanke,* a pond. Mealtime was especially welcome, and the food had an exceptional taste up at Truchas.

*

What other foods we needed we purchased from Donna Alfonsa Ortega-Vigil, who owned the original Vigil Store right in the middle of El Potero. We purchased a small quantity of food there. Fifteen cents worth of sugar, ten cents worth of salt. We traded our chili or whatever fruit or produce we had for potatoes and beans.

Our *mantanzas*—hog butcherings—at different households were indeed celebrations. There were thirteen families living around the *placita*. Sharing *chicharrones* (chittlings) and a small amount of meat with each other was a pleasure.

If the Lord should will it, I will build a fuerte in Chimayo and be able to pass these stories on to my children, twelve grandchildren, and five great-grandchildren.

DELORES SUAZO GRIEGO

Dolores was born in 1920 in Taos where she attended local schools. She worked thirty years for Mountain Bell in Santa Fe and was married to Gilbert Griego for fifty-three years. Dolores was active in her church and sang in the choir. She passed away in 2020.

LA ESCUELA

Formation

My parents were our first teachers. Our learning center was a solid rectangular wooden table with two drawers underneath where the important documents and other mementos were kept under lock and key. The table was made to order by my father's brother, Nasario, who was an excellent carpenter and cabinet maker. It was around this solid, polished kitchen table that my two brothers and I were fed— body, soul, and mind. We were taught responsibility, honesty, commitment and integrity.

We were taught to respect not only the elderly but all others. We were advised to be friendly and to choose our friends wisely. They would say,“Tell me who you hang out with and I'll tell you who you are.”

It was at the table that we would sit around during the long winter nights to learn about our parents and what it was like when they were growing up. We also learned about our grandparents—Mama and Papa Grande—and our ancestors.

We learned the satisfaction of hard work, the value of money, and to make do or do without.

We were taught how to pray, and would not jump into bed before we knelt and recited our nightly prayers. We addressed the Holy and Blessed Angel of Guardia, asking for protection in the night. We would then remain kneeling to receive the blessing of our father and mother.

Aunt Aurelia

Sometimes Aunt Aurelia, dad’s sister, would spend a couple of days with us . She would walk five or six miles from Canon to Ranchito where we lived. I will always remember her as a kind and gentle woman about five feet three inches tall with olive skin, brown eyes, and long gray hair parted in the middle and wrapped in a bun on the back of her head. She wore narrow, gold-rim glasses and dressed in long, dark dresses and wore a hat when she went to church or to visit, as was the custom.

As soon as we recognized her coming down the path we would go to meet her. She would take us by the hand all the way home. She was an amazing and wonderful storyteller. In the evenings my brothers, two or three of my cousins, and I would gather around her, making ourselves comfortable as we listened attentively while she told us children's stories in Spanish.

Some, like "Snow White," "Cinderella," and "Hansel and Gretel," I later saw in books, but many I have not seen in print. Once in a while she would stop to take a couple of puffs from her "roll your own" cigarette that she made with very thin paper. She would kind of curl it and pour Golden Grain tobacco in it. She would barely moisten the edge of the paper, close one end, tap it gently and light it.

We could hardly wait for her to continue or begin another story. When she stopped to take a breath my brother would tell her, "*Sigale, sigal*e." (Don't stop, continue, continue.) We could hardly wait to hear what happened next.

When she told stories she didn't use gestures. The stories came alive by the way she described events and characters and the enthusiasm in her voice.

She sang beautiful old Spanish hymns that had been passed from generation to generation, hymns we still sing.

She didn't have any children of her own, but everywhere she went the children flocked around her.

Nurtured

We had a very loving and secure childhood, which was the foundation of our learning. As long as our parents were there, I felt that nothing and no one would harm us. My happiest childhood memories are in the 300-year-old adobe house where we were surrounded by their unconditional love. They taught us through stories that had a moral but, more important, by their example

CHARACTERS

MATILDA ROMERO

Matilda Romero is a life-long resident of the Española Valley, where she graduated from Santa Cruz High School. After raising six sons, she attended Highlands University where she received a degree in Early Childhood Education. She was a Head Start teacher for eighteen years and is now retired. At present she is writing her memoirs, primarily for her grandchildren. She occupies much of her time creating in straw applique, a traditional New Mexico Spanish-colonial art form.

THE CASE OF THE CUT PERCHA IN KANGAROO COURT

(El Cerco, La Percha, y La Vecina Mala)
(The fence, the clothesline, and the bad neighbor)

One day I decided to transplant a silver lace vine against the fence in my backyard. With the help of my children, I dug up the vine from its old location and moved it to a spot where I thought it would look best from my kitchen window. The three of us positioned the plant in the hole, filled it with soil, watered it, and guided some of the vines up the fence. After completing our gardening project, we stood back to admire the pretty green vines clinging to the fence wires. I visualized the day when it would fill the whole back fence with pretty white blooms.

Suddenly *La Vecina* (neighbor) came running from her house about one hundred feet away. As she approached, we heard her yelling: "Get away from my fence! Get away from my fence!" The children and I looked at each other, somewhat puzzled, then looked at La Vecina. She was yelling at the top of her voice, claiming that the fence was hers and warned us not to touch it. She yelled at us, saying that the fence belonged to her and that we were trespassing if we touched it.

I stayed calm, explaining to her that the fence was ours since my grandfather had put it up many, many years ago. I continued to explain that according to local tradition, if the posts were on my side of the property, then the barbed wire would be nailed to the side of the fence closest to her property. Traditionally, that is how one can tell which property owner originally built the fence. I remember my grandfather cut the posts from trees growing along la acequia that ran through his property. My grandfather, a real traditionalist, had explained this custom to me when I was a little girl.

I figured that because she had moved here from the East Coast she didn't know much about fences here in the Southwest. My attempt to educate La Vecina about local customs regarding fence ownership did not go over very well.

Next thing we knew, she pulled the green leaves from the vines, threw them on the ground and stomped on them. She was yelling and pulling and stomping . . . yelling, pulling and stomping the beautiful vines that my children and I had just planted!!!

El Vecino (her husband) heard her screaming, as did everyone else in the neighborhood. He came running, grabbed his wife by the arm and pulled her away from the fence. La Vecina continued to scream "It's my fence! It's my fence!" till she was out of sight.

My children were shocked by her temper tantrum; they were shaken by all the screaming and antics of La Vecina. My children said that she looked like a *gallina culeca* (cuckoo hen) as she paced back and forth, screaming at us and yelling obscenities and threats. After this incident, my children referred to the neighbor lady as "La Vecina Mala" and sometimes as "La Vecina Loca."

My children and I looked at the torn leaves and destroyed vines sprawled on the ground on the other side of the fence. It made us very sad to see our work destroyed. My sons asked me why La Vecina was acting that way since they had never witnessed that kind of behavior before. For lack of a better explanation I answered: "Guess La Vecina wasn't feeling very well today." We left the shredded plant and walked away slowly and quietly.

Having put the incident aside, I proceeded with my usual chores. About thirty minutes later, I finished a load of laundry and hung my wash out to dry on *la percha* (clothesline). La percha just happened to be tied to one of the fence posts near the wilting silver lace vine. The clothes were flapping gently back and forth in the summer breeze when all of a sudden along comes La Vecina Mala again, running back to the fence. She took out a pair of wire cutters from her apron pocket and proceeded to cut la percha from the fence post. She worked very fast and before I knew it, she managed to cut down la percha. All my laundry came tumbling down. When I looked out I saw my freshly laundered towels and sheets laid out on the ground, still attached to la percha. That was the second time in one day that La Vecina had destroyed my day's work.

When I went out to see what all the commotion was again, La Vecina Mala was standing at the fence yelling profanities and proclaiming that the fence posts and fence belonged to her. El Vecino came out again and hauled her away again as she continued to yell at the top of her lungs, claiming ownership of the fence. Once again my children were puzzled by such bizarre behavior. We were very sad to see such a disturbed and agitated person. I just shook my head and we all went back into the house. The children asked if they should pick up the clothes from the grounded percha.

Luckily I had a Polaroid camera. I took pictures of the cut percha and my laundry lying on the ground. The next day my husband and I drove to the county courthouse and filed a complaint against La Vecina in magistrate court. On the day of the hearing, La Vecina showed up late. When she did arrive, she made such a grand entrance into the courtroom that it took her what seemed like a lifetime to approach her seat at the front. She was dressed in her Sunday best.

She walked through the door assisted by a walking cane and her husband, who accompanied her at every step. Based on La Vecina's appearance, the impression she was attempting to make for the benefit of the judge was that of an innocent, frail little old lady who was too weak to do the things we said she had done. If this was the judge's initial impression, it did not last long. The judge (a justice of the peace) would soon get a taste of her medicine.

He started by asking her why she had cut la percha. Her answer was because the clothes line was tied to her fence post. After more deliberations and photo proof of La Vecina's actions, the judge found her guilty of destroying property and imposed a fine.

At that point La Vecina Mala proceeded to proclaim the judge's decision invalid. After the judge asked her to conduct herself in a respectful manner, she yelled out that she was not going to adhere to any decision made in a kangaroo court. Startled by her behavior, one of my sons asked, "What is a kangaroo court?"

At the judge's request, La Vecina Mala's husband quickly escorted her out of the court. This time it took her only a fraction of the time to walk the length of the courtroom. Needless to say, the interest generated by her entrance did not compare to the excitement she generated by her exit. Her accusations of being tried in a kangaroo court could be heard throughout the whole courthouse. As my husband, children, and I left the courtroom, I looked over to one side. I saw La Vecina's walking cane lying on the floor. I thought about my percha.

JOE E. ROMERO

Joe E. Romero, a New Mexico native and World War II veteran, is a retired business agent, Painters Local Union 869 in Santa Fe. He served as Labor Representative to the New Mexico District Council #63 in Albuquerque for over twenty-five years. Joe participates in various community activities and projects. Of noteworthy mention is his fifty years of dedicated service to the local community acequia/ditch association. His hobbies include wood carving, gardening, and volunteering for the Santa Cruz Senior Center.

LA VECINA MALA (THE MEAN NEIGHBOR)

Episode I: "Ain't Got No Chicken Feed!!"

It was just another day, but the need to go to the grocery store arose and off I went without a care in the world. I felt relaxed, confident and in fact, cheerful. Never had I dreamed about what was about to happen to me.

As I walked down the aisle in pursuit of my designated purpose, I was stunned to hear what I thought was a gentle and inquiring voice asking if I was "Joe," and without thinking, I replied, "Yes, I am." As I turned around to face the person, I was surprised to recognize La Vecina. All hell seemed to break loose.

She started ranting and raving, pointing her fingers and moving in all directions, hollering at the top of her voice: "YOU are the one that has been stealing my chicken feed!"

I was completely dumbfounded and amazed at such an accusation. I tried to reason with her. I told her I didn't even have chickens and had no need for chicken feed and that perhaps she was in error.

She wasn't about to listen to what I had to say, but she continued from aisle to aisle, gesturing and hollering and repeating her accusations. I had never felt so embarrassed in my whole life. I left my shopping cart and walked to my vehicle to regain my composure and to assess my situation, as I was shaking and shivering. I finally drove home, told my wife all that had happened *and without the groceries!*

Episode II: Gun Wielding Neighbor—La Pistolera

There would be other incidents involving La Vecina, as her property was serviced by the community ditch, of which she was a member.

Community ditches (*acequias*) have a long history of being the lifeblood of the community, providing water for the purpose of growing agricultural products.

Community ditches for years have established easements or right of ways through the properties it services in accordance with state laws. The governing body of the ditch system is composed of three commissioners and one *mayordomo* (ditch boss), elected by the participants and landowners. The mayordomo is executive officer of the ditch and is in charge of the distribution of the water.

Early one morning the mayordomo knocked at my door all shook up and quite agitated, *"Vamos con migo, esa vieja cabrona no me deja echar el agua."* He was telling me "that old lady didn't let him turn the water on". He went on further as to what was happening and I suggested that perhaps we should invite another neighbor and landowner as a witness in case La Vecina decided to make good on her threats to the *mayordomo.*

The next door neighbor was more than glad to accompany the two of us. As we approached the main gate at the ditch, we could hear La Vecina yelling and making motions with her arms. We ignored her and continued with our assignment. The neighbor and I stood by while the mayordomo proceeded to open the head gate

It didn't take long before La Vecina with pistol in hand, accompanied by her husband, approached us at the head gate. The mayordomo was still in the process of securing the head gate when two shots rang out and the bullets hit the water right in front of the mayordomo.

The mayordomo was a gutsy middle-aged man and wanted to take them on. I suggested that this was a case for the law to handle. They both agreed and we headed to the county courthouse in Santa Fe to file a complaint. Her day in court was a loss to her and her appeals were denied.

Episode III: The Ditch Witch

We thought that perhaps La Vecina had learned her lesson on that encounter, though she had gotten off easy. It wasn't long before we were faced with a similar problem involving the ditch on her property. As it happened, La Vecina in prior years had covered the whole ditch area with boards and the boards were now rotting and breaking away, causing the water in the ditch to overflow. The only solution was to open the ditch channel to remove the obstructions and repair the area. La Vecina would have nothing of that and told us that we were trespassing, that she had covered the ditch and that it was *her* ditch. This time we got the community involved. We thought that perhaps La Vecina would listen to other members of the community in trying to resolve the problem, but to no avail. We chose a day for the neighborhood to get together. We notified the sheriff's department and they came on that day and the job got done over the objections of La Vecina Mala.

RON ROMERO

Ron Romero is a recently retired public health dentist. Ron served as New Mexico's Dental Health Director focusing on improving the oral health status of New Mexicans through the provision of dental care to the state's underserved populations. Dr. Romero continues to be active in dental public health through the American Public Health Association.

HALLOWEEN WITH LA VECINA MALA

The month of October was the longest month of the year. I would count the number of days leading up to what I felt was the most important day of the year—Halloween. I would stare at the old Rexall calendar hanging on the kitchen wall next to where we kept the house keys, as if to encourage time to move faster. Instead, it seemed to move slower. In my mind I crossed off each day, memorizing horoscopes, the daily weather, and all other information on the old drug store calendar. Day by day went by. Dad's birthday was in mid-October andin mine was on November 1, the day after Halloween and All Saints Day. I looked forward to my birthday but Halloween came first. These two events seemed to help me get through the month. I remember hearing my brothers exclaim, " You should have been born on Halloween, instead of All Saints Day."

On this particular Halloween I was more excited than other years. Instead of the usual home-made outfit, I received a hand-me-down, store-bought costume from a relative who was now too old for Trick-or-Treating. I proudly wore my new-to-me skeleton costume to school for the Halloween party but did not tell anyone that it was a hand-me-down; instead I said I got it at the local J.W. Owens 5 & 10 Store. Don't know if my classmates believed me because much of the silver glitter which formed the bones of the skeleton had fallen off. I didn't care if they didn't believe me or not. A store bought costume was a real treat in those days.

On Halloween night the neighborhood kids, my brothers and I would meet across the street at the local motel, which had a trailer park adjacent to it. This was a good place to start, and depending on how it went, we would know how many other houses we needed to go to—to fill up our bags with candy.

Not having such a good year, the gang said, "Let's go over to La Vecina's house." Instinctively, my brothers immediately yelled out, " NO WAY!" Unfairly speaking for me, my brothers told the neighborhood kids to go ahead and go, but we could not go. My brothers said that we would wait for them and repeatedly told them that we were not allowed to go to La Vecina Mala's house. Kids being what they are, they wanted us to join them. They convinced us that La Vecina would not be able to tell who we were because we all were wearing masks and costumes. "Besides that," they said, "she usually gives out a lot of candy." That made for a convincing argument for an eight year old. Reluctantly, giving in to group pressure, we decided to give it a try. What the heck, it couldn't hurt.

The gang of kids went to the door and rang the bell. The porch light went on and La Vecina walked out. We shouted out the usual Halloween chant, "TRICK-OR-TREAT." La Vecina was surprised to see such a large group, about ten of us. She invited us to step onto her porch where she could get a better look. We did, and she then proceeded to ask each of us, one by one, to remove his mask and asked who we were. As this was going on, my brothers and I slowly inched our way to the back of the crowd. She allowed each child to step into her house after identifying him. I'm not sure why we just didn't turn around and leave before she got to us. I suppose we were caught by surprise. I remember being so scared that I couldn't move from hiding behind my two older brothers. When she got to us, hindsight should have told us to make up names, but the good children that we were, we told her that we were the neighbor kids and pointed to our house. La Vecina's whole attitude changed immediately. She told us to wait outside and slammed the door in our faces. It took a while for her to come back. When she did, she opened the door and threw one apple into each of our bags with such an angry force that I thought she was going to tear my brown paper bag and my candy would fall to the floor. I was not fast enough to get it out of the way—the apple flew into my bag as she yelled out to us, "The nerve of you kids coming here. Don't you ever come back again!" The door slammed once more. As we left, the other kids were still inside La Vecina Mala's house and I thought of Hansel and Gretel's fate. Low and behold that did not happen. They came out with big smiles on their faces, boasting that La Vecina had filled their bags with lots of candy—no apples. At this young age, I was not yet prepared for life's lessons.

MISBEHAVING

GEORGE TELESFOR ROYBAL

George T. Roybal born in Pecos, New Mexico in 1933. His parents were Telesfor and Luisita Roybal. George was educated in the Pecos school system and graduated from the College of Santa Fe in 1959 with a degree in Business Administration. He retired from city and state government in 1986. After retiring he went into real estate sales and construction as a general contractor. He married his high school sweetheart, Mercy, in 1952. They has five children: three boys and two girls

EL JORGE, EL CONSENTIDO (The Spoiled One)

At an early age I was assigned certain chores and one of my favorites was to feed the chickens. My creative skills turned this chore into lively entertainment. I would place a bucket in front of myself and place chicken feed in front of the bucket. When the chickens came to eat and were close enough to the bucket, I would flip the bucket and trap a chicken inside it. The chicken would twirl inside the bucket until she would somehow free herself and come out in a stupor. I thoroughly enjoyed this prank and laughed every time I repeated this cruel act, until my mother finally took note of my behavior and put a stop to it.

Our family always kept a dog. To amuse myself I would place a rope around our dog Dewey's neck, then tie a bucket or can to the rope and push the object toward Dewey, which would scare him. Naturally he would run all over the yard, thinking that something was chasing him. I would bend over laughing. My mother would finally come out to see what was happening and when she opened the door, the frightened dog would dash inside and knock down chairs and anything that got in his way. This would upset her terribly and she would go after me.

Looking back, it seems that I always got away with a lot of mischief. One day I was home with my younger sisters and, as usual, we were playing. We concluded that a large holy picture of the Sacred Heart of Jesus was looking at us disapprovingly. Everywhere we turned, Jesus kept looking at us, so I took a broom stick and broke the framed Sacred Heart. When my mom and dad got home, we just invented a story and both parents believed us.

My carefree childhood quite often got me in trouble. My dad, who was a disciplinarian, firmly believed in spanking his kids to teach them what was right and wrong. However, he would have to catch me if he was going to punish me, and that was always a challenge for him, since he was thirty years older than I and couldn't run as fast as I could.

Quite often my mother would get so frustrated with my behavior that the only alternative she had was to threaten me by telling my dad of my behavior when he got home on Fridays from his job in Los Alamos. She kept a long list of my misdeeds and would pour out her frustrations to him in hopes that he would do his duty and punish me. One weekend, after hearing all about my mischief, he was determined that I would not go unpunished. So he went out and locked the back gate and waited until I got home, then went and secured the front gate. Once he secured both gates with wires he figured I couldn't possibly escape. As soon as I got home and inside the house, he took after me, but I ran out of the house, first running to the back gate, which I found locked. I then ran to the front gate and found that one was also secured. I had no choice but to outrun my dad and went around the house a second time and back to the front gate where I climbed it like a cat, jumped over, landed on my back and started crying. My dad knew how much it must have hurt, but he admired my tenacity to do whatever was necessary to avoid a spanking. He laughed but at the same time told me that he would catch me sooner or later.

In 1946, when I was around fourteen years old, I learned to drive my dad's truck. It wouldn't go faster than thirty-five miles per hour and when you went at that speed it seemed as if it was traveling at a 100. While learning to drive, I occasionally borrowed the truck to go and get the mail from the post office. In order to show off my driving skills, I would invite my cousin, Isidro, to go with me. After picking up the mail, I would drive towards Rowe, which is about five miles south of Pecos. On the way there, I would go the maximum speed of thirty-five miles per hour, which made it appear as if the old truck was flying. Because of the rackety sounds Isidro would get so scared that he would be near tears and beg me to please stop or slow down. I somehow enjoyed that.

Early in my life, when I was about five or six years old, I had seen this beautiful young girl in church. We both sat in the small pew section, which the church provided for youngsters, and it was here that we began to exchange glances and smiles with each other. I thought that she was beautiful, and I had a crush on her. I even admired her pretty clothes and knew her name was Annabelle Byrd. Several years later, on a sunny Sunday afternoon, I was out riding my horse near the Pecos River and noticed her with her parents driving by in their fancy car. I followed their car on my horse to get her attention, and since this was a dirt road, cars created a lot of dust. My horse was momentarily blinded by the dust and ended up getting too close to the car, and I crashed into it. The horse climbed the side of the car, almost knocked me off, but I managed to stay on. That incident almost killed me, and as a result I lost all interest in getting Annabelle's attention. I ended up with a severely scraped leg and a ruined pair of pants and shoes. Her parents, Mr. and Mrs. Byrd, concerned about what had happened, drove to my parents' home to explain the incident to them. After they left, I recall my parents questioning me and saying, "Are you crazy or what?"

One time, Isidoro Vigil's mother brought Isidoro to my mother's house to show my mother what I had done to her son. What I had done was hit Isidoro with a rock on the head and given him a good size bump. After they left, my mother tried to catch me to punish me. I slid underneath a twin bed and clung onto the bed springs as my mother moved the bed back and forth, until she finally grew tired and decided my dad would deal with me later.

Religion was important in the Roybal family. My parents encouraged me to become an altar server. I received my training from the nuns at St. Anthony's Church. In those days the Mass was in Latin. The training was brief and in a short time I was an altar boy. However, I never learned the Latin responses completely, and what I would do was mumble words that were as close as possible to the Latin. On certain occasions altar boys were required to place incense in the thurible (the sensor). We would light the incense and gently swing the thurible back and forth by a short chain that was attached to it. I loved this responsibility and used the opportunity to entertain myself and the other altar boys. I would swing the thurible as high as I could without making a complete circle. The nuns, who were also our teachers, would observe my misbehavior and attempt to make me stop it, but I pretended not to see them. I would later on receive a stern warning and would promise not do it again.

My growing up years in this charming adobe village were fascinating. I recall many incidents where I was just plain mischievous. One time, my friend, Octaviano Segura, was walking across a wooden *canova* (water trough), when for no reason at all I picked up a rock, took aim and hit him right on his chest. Octaviano chased me all the way home to where my dad was watering the alfalfa. I informed my dad that Octaviano wanted to hurt me for no reason. My dad chased Octaviano and I was spared.

As a young boy my dad had to take care of goats and thoroughly disliked that task. He was determined that his children would never have to take care of goats. I really didn't want to take care of goats either, but I did want the companionship of my young buddies. My dad did have a cow and I would take it out to pasture when my friends took their family's animals out. My mom would pack me a sack lunch and I would spend the day with my young comrades in the national forest grazing our animals.

On another occasion, Lorenzo Vigil, one of the local boys, who also took care of goats, somehow was able to get a bottle of wine and took it with him to an area where all the boys gathered. Before long we were all taking turns drinking the wine. Lorenzo drank more than the rest of us and got sick. He had eaten noodles the night before and when he started to throw up, Lorenzo thought his intestines were coming out and began to cry out loud, "I am dying! Look! Those are my intestines that I am regurgitating!" We were all dead scared because it did look like they were his intestines and that he was really dying. We were all frightened, but the following day Lorenzo showed up quite healthy. This episode became a laughing matter for all the youthful shepherds.

On one summer morning my friend, Alfonso, and I were taking care of his goats and I was taking care of our cow, and I found a .22 caliber bullet shell and took it with me. Within a short distance from home, I took out the shell, placed it on a flat rock and began dropping good-sized rocks on it. After repeating this action several times with no results, I thought it was a dud. I knelt down, grabbed another, smaller, rock and began to hammer the shell with it. After hitting it several times the shell finally exploded and frightened the goats who took off running in all directions. Alfonso and I couldn't hear a thing for several hours. After a while we realized that the goats and cow had taken off and we began to look for them. After looking all day long we went home and concocted a story that coyotes had chased and scattered the animals.

When we came home, we told my parents the coyote story. My dad knew I wasn't exactly George Washington when it came to telling the truth and questioned me as to what actually had happened and to describe the kind of coyotes we had encountered. I began by telling him that one coyote was pink, one was blue, and another yellow. Right away he knew I was lying and demanded that I tell exactly what had happened. Finally, I told the truth. He wasn't happy to hear it and gave me a good lecture. The next day the goats finally came home.

One Sunday afternoon Macario and Isidoro were sharing secrets inside an outhouse and wouldn't allow me and some of the other boys to come in and be a part of what they were planning. I didn't like it and to get back at them I found a hole on the side of the outhouse and proceeded to urinate on Isidoro's pants. Isidoro wasn't aware of what I had done, and as soon as they came out of the outhouse, I let him know that I had peed on him and started teasing him. Macario took note of what I had done to Isidoro and took after me to avenge his friend. He chased me all the way home, determined to catch and whip me. I ran as fast as I could with Macario right on my heels all the way into my house. While Macario was chasing me, I remembered that my parents weren't home, so by the time I realized that, both of us were inside the house and Macario was about to start to beat me. I quickly pretended that my parents were home and started hollering for my dad to come to my rescue. "Dad! Come and help me! Macario is going to beat me up!" Macario believed that my dad was home and turned around and ran out of the house as if he had wings on his feet. My siblings and I were utterly amused and laughed so hard that we rolled on the kitchen floor.

One another Sunday afternoon my friends, Macario and Carlos, and I decided we wanted to have our own rodeo. We spotted Happy Ley's pony in a pasture, so we went and captured him and proceeded to take him to East Pecos to enjoy a nice private rodeo. It didn't take long for Happy Ley to realize what these young rustlers were doing and he gave chase on his horse. Within a few hundred yards he caught up with me and made me give him the names of my friends. He told all three of us to report to the post office the following day. The next day at the post office he proceeded to lecture us about stealing and showed us wanted posters of horse thieves. After that he released the young rascals to their parents. That was a lesson we never forgot, and now we admire Mr. Ley's deed.

In junior high I had a friend named Nash, who also loved playing tricks on other kids. One dark Halloween night, both of us methodically arranged an old spring mattress on the side of the road near a bridge. We attached wires and sheets and other things so that when we pulled the mattress, it would appear as if a genuine moving ghost was on it. That night we waited until two youngsters were walking up the street. The youths were discussing a recent accident in which a man had been killed at that location. As the kids approached the bridge, Nash and I slowly pulled the spring across the road while making spooky, weird noises. The youngsters were so terrified that as they attempted to turn around and run home, they kept colliding with each other. Finally, they got their direction straight and ran home as fast as they could. Nash and I could hardly contain our laughter, and for years we enjoyed recalling and laughing as we relived that silly prank.

APPRECIATION

JUDY GOLDERBERG

After nearly five decades, Judy Goldberg continues to work within northern New Mexico communities to build connections through educational, cultural and creative programs, inspired by the wisdom and experiences of local residents. Judy has served as an independent radio producer and host of Back Roads Radio. She founded and directed the nonprofit Youth Media Project and facilitated numerous community programs - through museums and schools - in curricular development, story-making and listening events to capture and celebrate our humanity and collective history.

THROUGH THE LENS

After attending the Anthropology Film Center in Santa Fe, Jeff, a wild-eyed, hard-driving thirty-something hired me for a one-day shoot as an assistant in the production of a thirty-second TV spot about senior citizens having to choose between heat and food. Government assistance for the elderly was threatened and images of an empty refrigerator with a pack of bologna and an old man with a crocheted blanket over his shoulders were to deliver the message of need and response. After a successful day's work, I was asked if I wanted a job in Las Trampas, a village in the mountains of northern New Mexico—and my life took a dramatic and lasting turn.

It was spring 1979 and I was hired to make documentary videos about traditional life, self-reliance and community survival. I worked with three other fellows—Jeff, the fast-brained hippie from Los Angeles; Juan, a Las Trampas native; and Chris, a young, bright, yet floundering guy from New Jersey.

Jeff spearheaded the Self Reliance Foundation with the explicit purpose of developing a TV series on traditional ways of life, coupled with modern appropriate technology, like solar food dryers and passive solar homes. As a Beverly Hills export, Jeff had lived in Las Trampas since the late Sixties. He had been attracted to New Mexico by national news about Reyes Tijerina and the Courthouse Raid in Tierra Amarilla.

"It was a time when locals still took the law into their own hands," he would say, "proving the West was still alive." This single event attracted Jeff to New Mexico. Along with other urban youth of the Sixties, Jeff found his way to the isolated communes and eventually to Las Trampas. He bought land and built an adobe home with the help of Juan's father, Tranquilino Lopez, and other villagers. Having come from fast-paced, over-populated Los

Angeles, Jeff wanted—as we all did—to communicate how time-honored customs, sweat equity, and neighbors helping neighbors could be a model, if not a movement, for revitalizing villages and urban centers, alike. Each of us had seen how the degradation of small town, rural life was on the rise.

Just like everywhere else in the country, the younger people in northern New Mexico villages were abandoning their towns. Jobs, education, opportunity, and money had lured away those who left. Change for the villages had been taking place for some time, but in the late Seventies and early Eighties there were still remnants of the old ways and we were heart bent on capturing the images, the observations from the ancianos and the wisdom inherent in lives of hard work, devotion and real-to-goodness, living-and-breathing, family values.

My days at the foundation were filled with researching and writing grants, writing scripts, shooting and logging footage and editing shows. I need to admit I had mixed feelings in me about our work.

The Lopez family seemed supportive of our efforts to preserve culture and perpetuate a way of life that was dying, but others perceived us as exploiters—assuming that if we had cameras and recorders we were from Hollywood, therefore making a lot of money. My short-term CETA position of $5.50 an hour was something, but making a killing—I don't think so. Yet, the act of capturing images and sound bites put us on the outside of the real work. So, as much as possible, I would jump in and do the real work—turning the soil, irrigating crops, harvesting fruit, shucking corn, making tortillas, peeling roasted chilies, mixing mud for plastering the church, chopping wood, feeding chickens and the like. To be solely the observer, the image gatherer, felt empty. I, too, wanted to contribute to the necessary work.

The opportunity arrived when I could merge desire to help and document this way of life. We stood in the fields taping a horse drawn plow turn the earth. We documented the whole process of making *chicos*, a traditional way of preserving corn.

We taped Tranquilino as his eighty-year-old cracked and bent thumb punctured the white kernels of corn on the stalk. If milk spurted from the broken kernel casing, the corn was ready for picking. Repositioning the camera, we panned as Tranquilino; his wife, Filia; his daughter, Priscilla,; and his nephew, Timmy, filled the sacks and lugged them from the *milpa* (cornfield) to the bank of the acequia beside the *horno (*oven)) In somewhat frantic, yet well-practiced rhythm, the team of hands wet down the corn, scooping buckets of water from the acequia. Juan scraped out the last shards of hot coals from the horno before the one-take-only action began. In rapid fire the green-sheathed cornhusks were whirled into the horno and the wooden door was securely sealed into place with wet mud slapped around the edges of the door. Priscilla inserted the designated rock into the smoke hole and the horno was set to do its job. Overnight the corn steamed and cooked.

In the brisk early morning light, with the majestic Sangre de Cristo peaks in the distance, we set up the camera to capture Tranquilino, hoe in hand, as he pried open the mud encased door off of the horno. As he peeled back the horno's mudded door, we were engulfed with the wood-smoked aroma of fresh baked corn. One by one the oven-baked cornhusks were peeled back and tossed to the side, until only a few leaves were attached to the cob. The leaves were braided into *ristras* (strings) of chiles with five or six exposed ears dangling like jewels. The chains of ristras hung on the wire fence to dry. Every once in a while we would snag a fresh ear and chomp down on the steamy, moist, and buttery kernels.

Having the opportunity to live in Las Trampas, to get to know my neighbors, to help them in small ways and to document a life that has all but slipped away was personally invaluable. Nearly thirty years later, I'm still championing the voices and stories of those of humble means and remarkable and bountiful spirit.

THE PUEBLO OF POJOAQUE

Introduction

New Mexico is home to nineteen pueblos, all of them located in the northern portion of the state. The Pueblo of Pojoaque, located about fourteen miles north of Santa Fe, has been undergoing a cultural and economic upsurge in recent decades, thanks to its casino (which supplied funds for pueblo businesses) and above all, to a succession of inspired Governors. The pueblo's cultural growth is evidenced in the Poeh Arts Center, a place where tribal members can study various disciplines—sculpture, pottery, jewelry—and in so doing contribute to the preservation of their Tewa culture. The pueblo's recent history is remarkable, considering its difficult past.

The Pueblo of Pojoaque can be dated to at least 150 C C.E., but its history has not been continuous. The pueblo was abandoned twice. Between the Pueblo Revolt of 1680 and the reconquest of New Mexico by De Vargas in1692, the pueblo was slowly abandoned. It was repopulated in 1706, but in the late 1800s a smallpox epidemic and a drought attacked the tribe, and its members scattered once again. In 1934 the Commissioner for Indian Affairs placed an article in various Southwestern newspapers, calling for José Antonio Tapia, the former governor, to reclaim tribal land, or lose it. Cordie Gomez, whose family was one of those who resettled the pueblo in 1934, said in an interview with me, "My grandfather was asked to get fifteen people, Indian or non-Indian, age didn't matter, in order to re-establish the Pueblo. My grandpa had to go to the pueblos to find fifteen tribal members of Pojoaque. He got thirteen and was allowed to go with that. This was through the B.I.A., the Bureau of Indian Affairs. So that's how the Pueblo of Pojoaque was [re]born."

Cordie's sister, Phoebe, wrote in a story printed here, "I am both Spanish and Indian. My dad was Spanish and spoke nothing but Spanish. My mom was from the tribe, Pojoaque Pueblo. My parents, Fermin and Feliciana Tapia Viarrial, along with my grandfather, José Antonio Tapia, reestablished our pueblo. They wanted to come back to the pueblo because it was abandoned and because my grandpa read in the paper that the land was going to be given away."

Prior to re-establishing the pueblo, Cordoe and Phoebe's parents lived in Colorado. During that time, they were visiting a friend in Abiquiu, New Mexico when their father happened to read in *The New Mexican* that the B.I.A. was attempting to locate the last governor of the Pueblo of Pojoaque. Cordie said that her father asked his friend, "What's his [the governor's] name?" and the friend said, "José Antonio Tapia." Cordie's father replied, "That's my father-in-law."

Cordie said that her father, his brother and father-in-law loaded up covered wagons with "bedding and clothes, chickens, goats, and a little pig," and headed south with their family over dirt roads. They arrived at the abandoned pueblo after a week and a half's journey.

From that re-founding, the pueblo has grown to a population of nearly 2,300, with thriving businesses, two casinos and a hotel. The driving force behind this growth was Governor Jake Viareal, who died in 2004. Governor Viareal wanted to build a casino. Former tribal Governor George Rivera wrote that "the State of New Mexico did not allow for Indian gaming. . . Indian gaming was a monster political issue that was fought hard. It took all nineteen pueblos and three tribes uniting to legalize gaming in New Mexico. Governor Jake had been leader in the fight locally and nationally. The tribes wanted a change in state politics and helped oust three-time New Mexico Governor Bruce King." King's successor, Gary Johnson, had run with a pledge to approve an Indian gaming compact, and in 1994 followed through on his pledge. But in 1997, a U.S. Appeals Court declared that Johnson lacked the authority to sign the compact.

Governor Viareal solved the problem with a brilliant pubic relations move. Since US-84 W/US-285a passes through pueblo land, Viareal, along with two relatives and casino security, stood on the highway, stopping cars and handing out leaflets stating that the tribe needed funds, and if gaming was not an option, they would raise funds either by leasing tribal land for nuclear waste storage, or setting up toll booths on the highway. A gaming compact was approved, naturally.

Rebuilding the pueblo's Tewa culture has meant, among other things, relearning the Tewa language and Tewa dances. The stories in this section are a tribute to the pueblo's resilience and to the basic human need to find one's place within community and within the natural world.

DANIEL MOYA

Daniel is a sculptor, painter and potter whose work has won numerous awards, including a 2009 Artist Fellowship from the Southwestern Association for Indian Arts. Daniel studied fine arts and anthropology at the University of New Mexico and has traveled in Europe, South America and Asia. He now lives at the Pueblo of Pojoaque.

ME, MYSELF, AND US

On the evening of November 2, 1966, I was born into a family of about eleven siblings. I say "about" because there always seemed to be more people in that house than actually lived there. Whenever there was some poor soul down on their life and luck, they seemed to find a place in our home for a day, a week or a month. I learned that life on the rez is for giving and forgiving. Anyway, I am third to the youngest and for as long as I could remember, poverty was all we knew. Mother, stepfather, and about eleven hungry kids filled a two-room, half-adobe, half-pumice block, but all-rundown house. Even our dogs were rundown. We survived off of beans, potatoes, tortillas, more beans and the once-a-month enchilada dinner when the long anticipated collection of food stamps arrived.

For each family meal, we were seated at an uneven and unsanded long and dark hardwood table. Each plate filled with food had to be strategically placed atop that plank so as not to spill over with the lumps in the wood. The seating arrangement consisted of a collection of unmatching chairs on three sides and a bench on the fourth. The bench appeared to be made of the same uncomfortable materials as the table itself. Being poor was never as it is seen in Hollywood movies. Isolation only added to the despair, as did the ridicule, embarrassment and shame which the school bus rides provided on a daily basis.

Memories of our house are still fresh in my mind and on my skin. Even to this day I am still not sure who built that shanty, but it seems to have served its principle purpose, as all but one of its crew are alive to talk about our journey. I was taught to love and hate in that house, but I also was taught to eat all your food, drink all your water, and never make a pan full of hot cereal unless there is sugar, because you might be forced to sit and eat it all by yourself. I can still taste the lumps.

Not properly insulated, a green wool, military blanket covered the bathroom entrance. Our humble home's interior was something like a soldier's quarters, as it was small, cramped, filled with bunk beds from corner to corner and complete with a small black and white television to provide evening entertainment.

Looking back, I do not recall any form of art or objects even resembling art hung from the walls or placed over the multicolored works of unmatching furniture. Old dark bed sheets covered our windows, which were tightly knotted to the upper corners of the window frames, with nails holding them securely into place.

With gaps in all corners, our house created a musical composition: the slightest wind would play the song of the poor. The slow rise of a well-scaled, whistled tune provided by the numerous cracks in the window panes was always present. Somehow, as if not wanting to be left out nor outdone, a subtle type of competition would begin within the house. The front and back doors frantically inserted a well-patterned snare drum beat in some sort of strange melodic fashion. Awakened by these shifting and sporadic rhythms, the old dark bed sheets, which covered our windows, dramatically flew into a frenzy of dance routines, refusing to give way until the gale force had passed. The floor and walls also added to the songs with their cracks and creaeks, as if the house might blow into the next county.

Desperately wanting to keep to code within this multi-talented structure, the roof was just as seasonally entertaining and structurally unsound as the other parts of our home. Following each downpour and snow thaw, it was our duty to spring into action and fill the floor with dozens of finely tuned water-catching vessels. Had it not been for all those garage sale pots, pans and bowls, we might have been the next version of Noah's Ark. I can still remember those tattered vessels by tune, and how I was required to place them strategically into position so as to not have our already warped and tainted wooden floors discolored. When the pling, pling and plop, plop changes to splat, splat and flop flop, a motherly yelp from behind the drape-hidden toilet would yell, "Someone change those damn things before they get everything wet." So, if the storm and season was well placed in time and space, the windows, doors, drapes, floors, walls and water vessels brought to life a true symphony of life on the rez.

*

The rivers chilled and the trees fell to sleep as the autumn winds welcomed another time of change. As all kids in all types of communities around America, every Halloween was a welcomed day for our entire mob. With no money reserved for any sort of just designed, homemade costumes, Dora's mob ran about the neighborhood dressed as "ourselves," carrying old dirty flower sacks in the hope of hoarding as much local candy as humanly possible. Even now I am not too sure which was more entertaining on those evenings of rampage. Was it the fact that we were so poor and had not a care in the world or was it the look on the faces of the people who were unlucky enough to open the door to find a family of poor, not-Indian-and-not-Hispanic kids that could empty a treater's bowl in a single stop.

*

Having been requested to join the lucky club of writers and storytellers, I opened my book of memories. Looking back at all the now-faded photographs taken with someone's outdated Polaroid camera, I am led to believe there was actually no type of hair brush in any house able to tame my hair. It appears that my curly hair was wet down in the direction it was molded into over the evening.

Accustomed to surviving on quite a wild imagination in those years, I made bottles, rocks and sticks my materials of warfare, and the hordes of stray dogs and cats, prairie dogs and jackrabbits my enemy.

The family members I grew closest to at the time were my two older brothers, Jimmy and George; we did so much together in those tough times. From dawn to well after sunset, we used the highway as our field for target practice. With an endless supply of cars, we had so many clueless drivers believing they came in contact with a gaping pot hole or had somehow lost their headlamp, muffler, or engine when a well placed dirt clod made contact. Those were some of the perks of having a major motorway as your front yard.

After several weeks of wrestling each other in the dirt and playing with lizards, ants and grasshoppers, my two older brothers and I were usually lined with dirt and who knows what from head to toe. Well, if you have ever heard the saying, "Don't throw the baby out with the bath water," well, that was all about us. Somehow, tucked away in an unknown crevice of the house, stood a low-to-the-ground fifty-gallon container, and once a month it was unveiled as water was heated atop the butane stove for our monthly form of sanitation. As always, when it was my turn to bathe, the water looked like a cross between mushroom gravy and onion soup.

We loved it when the commonly lost and confused strangers would trickle by our fortress for help or directions. These visitors were always respectful as they walked past or over our shabby pets and somehow delivered an ever-so-gentle knock as to not remove the life-beaten doors from their hinges. Following the knocks and unnoticed at first, they were automatically and systematically greeted by dozens of eyes peering through the holes in thc window sheets and the gaps lining the sides of the door frames. Once aware of, and as if somewhat startled by our bizarre security system, the strangers always gave a surprisingly odd stare and took a step back as they sometimes were unsure of what precautionary measure that they might need to take.

Parked in front of the fortress sat a faded green two-door Dodge Duster. I believe we could pile more family members and friends into that vehicle for an outing than most college students could in a similar car for fun. I never really minded the trips as I sat among six to eight people in the back seat, because somehow I was able to be stacked atop the lap of someone who was probably stacked atop someone else's lap. Had there been seat belt laws at that time, we never would have made it out of the driveway. Once or twice a summer we would gather neighboring kids and all head to the drive-in movies at the Star Lighter, at five dollars a carload. We all got our money’s worth and the ticket agents always looked at us as if they were somehow being cheated, and they were! During those evenings, we were all bitten a hundred times by the hordes of mammoth mosquitoes which lived nearby, but there was a playground, one box of popcorn and one fountain drink for all to share during the show, and life was in full swing. Besides, we had snuck in bread and potted meat.

Twice a year, until I was about seven or eight years old, I would be given an entirely new set of clothes; well, in a manner of speaking, that is. When I say new set of clothes, I now know they were obviously someone else's hand-me-downs that were obviously someone else's hand-me-downs. Fortunately, to cover my young and growing feet, all my wardrobes were somehow always completed with at least a single pair of matching socks to cover the hole-filled BIA and garage sale shoes we received. It is quite funny talking about the BIA shoes. As if somehow raised in social ranking for a few days, and all at once, every rez kid in the valley sported a new pair of orange or green canvas Hi-Top Converse. In a manner of speaking, this was an easy way to help us define us from them.

Like clockwork, life continued on the same path for a few more years, through blazing summers, blistering winters and someone else's hand-me-downs . . . until my Aunt Josie and Uncle Manuel arrived for an unlikely series of visits which helped change the way I now see things. We always knew our aunt was super strict and really hated it when we had food in our teeth, drank water too fast, or ran around the house and yard like a pack of wild Indians. Uncle Manuel, on the other hand, was mellow and loved to laugh with us, or maybe it was at us; nonetheless, he was neat and I miss his comical humor. I was attending school overseas when he passed. I remember my uncle and aunt walking about the house as if to carefully inspect our living quarters. I think they were somewhat amused or possibly astonished at what they saw and perhaps even more so by what they did not see. Well, to make things short, they took George to live with them and the three mighty Musketeers fell to two. Trying to recall the moments of that visit, it seems as if there was a fresh litter of pups and my uncle and aunt were given the lucky chance to take the one of their choosing. Anyway, we all said our goodbyes to George and he hoped we could stop in and see him as his tears fell on his way out the door. Jimmy and I took a few days to shake off the shock, but there were still things to be broken, tempers to flare, and animals to terrorize, so off to work we went as we split the stuff George left behind.

Upon our initial visit with George, I was in absolute and total amazement as to what was before my eyes. Aunt Josie and Uncle Manuel's house had a finely cleaned carpet of one color, a large color television, a matching sofa set, walls all one color of paint and a bedroom furnished just for George. George now wore his hair short and parted to the side, his clothes were clean and nicely pressed, and he was never dusty. The outside of their house appeared to be just as strange. As I looked around, I saw no old abandoned cars to throw rocks at or play in and no hills to roam, but there were other areas for imaginative play. Aunt Josie and

Uncle Manuel's yard had fruit trees and a square unfinished blockhouse to climb on and, best of all, a cool ditch to swim in.

Years passed and several of my siblings moved on into other parts of their lives, and two other new ones moved in. Spring was nearing and another school year was coming to its end as I went to visit my grandparents. As always, we piled into whatever vehicle we had at the time and rumbled up through the washboard roads that led to our grandparents' house a few miles away on the hill. Those trips were always fun, as we seemed to drive those old folks crazy. I can still hear my grandmother yell, "And remember, no mischief." If something was broken, which something always was, grandpa always seemed to say, "Oh, goddamn it, oh no primo, look you broke the whole works. Ah shit!"

Grandma Feliciana and Grandpa Fermin were farmers who earned their stripes from life. Over their lifetimes they grew large fields of crops, raised a big family, fertilized a new generation of thinkers, and plowed a better future for us all. Only through their pain-filled stories was I better able to understand how we almost never happened. During the days and nights when I was brought up to date with their stories, my grandmother would light a Raleigh cigarette that never left her mouth as she ate through mounds of pinon nuts. The ash would almost run the length of the cigarette as it would twist and bend until it dropped off into one of her open apron pockets. In most cases, the ash would fall because my grandmother would have to stop and yell at my grandfather for telling me some strange story about her. I can still hear her say, "Eeeee, that damn man loves to lie. You can never believe anything he says, and don't give him any more beer." Grandfather was not a raging alcoholic, but he did love his evening and weekend swig; more so, he loved to tell the grandkids stories about our grandmother that made her yell and made him smile. My grandma told me stories of when she was younger and how she used to drink. She told me nothing good ever comes from drinking, so she stopped. Grandma came to hate drinking so much she made my grandpa buy his own refrigerator and keep it outside the house. She would talk of her torturous times at the Santa Fe Indian School. I'm sorry for your pain, which was our gain, my blessed grandma. I will always love what you and grandpa did for me and for us.

After third grade, during my summer vacation, my mom once again dropped me off with my grandparents because it was time to finish planting. Grandpa explained to me that he had already finished two acres and only needed another ten or twelve to go. At that time, ten or twelve meant nothing to me. A few days later, I quickly learned the size of an acre, the time it took to do everything by hand and then to multiply that by ten or twelve. For a child from the lower dust bowl section of Pojoaque, ten or twelve was a big step into the unwanted.

Over the next few weeks, I began to spend even more time with my grandparents, until the day I never went back to the musical house of pumice and mud. I became a resident with my grandparents and those living on the hill. I was now given three great meals a day, two snacks, a box from the local drugstore for my plaid clothes, and all the Lawrence Welk I could watch. This was a life unknown to me, for now I was always eating and working with my grandparents, quite a different tale from the years at the shack, where there was nothing or very little to choose from.

As mentioned, for a kid from the dust bowl, the springs and summers were a very hard pill to swallow. Between the crops, the farm animals and all the woodcutting, I was provided with small periods in which to play, but never any real time for friends. On weekends, my grandpa cleaned up around Al's Drug Store. It was not a big shop, but it did manage to supply local families with essentials between trips into Santa Fe and Española. Al and Trinny Romero were not from our village, but they treated my grandparents like gold, and to this day, our families are still close friends. While cleaning Al's and doing other odd jobs in the valley, grandpa and I rode around in this 1950s pickup with chipped orange and brown body paint. In order to keep the boxes and trash from escaping during our trip to the dump, grandpa designed a garbage rack from the parts of an old rusted bed frame. Had it not been for those adventures at the dump, my toys would have been limited to seasoned farm tools. The man who worked the dump was always fun to look at too.

Every morning before we left home on the way to Al's, grandma always told me to let her know if I had seen my grandfather drink. Once we arrived at Al's, Grandpa would head inside for the local gossip, as the local crew on duty tossed down a few miniatures. Making sure I stayed quiet as to what I was seeing, Grandpa always threw in a few candies and quarters my way. Those tokens were always good enough to buy my silence.

During all of those weekends I spent with grandpa cleaning up around Al's Drug Store, I met several of grandpa's friends, and still to this day, even though several have since passed on and moved on, Grandpa's friends, their children and now grandchildren have remained lifelong friends of mine. I see them every now and then and with a well-placed handshake or a hug from these now gray haired people, memories of my youth come back to me with a smile and "How's the family?"

During our down time in the evenings, after all the television shows had ended, my grandfather taught me how to light a cigarette, open and pour a good glass of beer, cheat at cards and lose at checkers. Other nights you could find grandpa at the table playing solitaire as grandma read through her TV Guide magazine. I was so freaked out when I stared at my grandmother the first time she talked to me without her teeth. What the hell just happened?

On weekends, I had other special times after my long week of work. Grandma controlled the television and she would allow me to watch the National Geographic programs and Mutual of Omaha's Wild Kingdom. This was my chance to watch television because these shows started before her favorite shows like *Starsky and Hutch, Beretta, Mannix* and some news program. During the news programs, the news anchor was always talking about the cosmonauts and the Russian space program. We three sat in front of the tube as white rockets with the red letters CCCP were shot into space. I can still hear my grandfather say, ". . . those damn Russians are sure smart!" Next time on the news, it was all about China. Sure enough, I can still hear my grandfather say, ". . . those damn Chinas are sure smart!"

Had it not been for the great programs on Public Television Station Channel 5, I might still be wondering what I am to do with my life. National Geographic and Wild Kingdom were then my only windows to the world outside Pojoaque. For two hours a week, I could travel across the world, seeing people, places, and things and hearing ideas, which filled the dreams of every young person. One week it was Africa, then China, then Mexico and Russia. Would I hunt big game, climb a pyramid, or simply tangle with a man-eating fish next week? These were the adventures to look forward to, and for a child of my age and location, having no real person to play with, the television people were my imaginary playmates for the next few years. My wife still catches me talking to myself.

During that time, I went to the theater a few times for a new space movie, Star Wars. Before that, it was a movie about a big fish in a movie called Jaws. The small ditch running through my grandparents' land was the perfect place to find a fish of that size and bigger. When the ditch was low, I found other places to explore.

First of all, in order to save the universe as the characters in Star Wars had, I needed a strong base to initiate my defense from the aerial attacks from outer space, and the apple tree seemed to do the trick. Now, the ditch was great, but when the water was low, I would need another place to dive and the garden in full growth was perfect. Through these space movie characters, I could now save the universe from atop the apple tree just as I made the oceans safe for all when I swam through the danger-infested rows of healthy garden growth. These were the times when I was in complete control and the hero for every citizen and screaming baby around the universe. There was never a better equipped or faster spaceship than the one placed within the upper reaches of the apple tree and never a braver swimmer than I when I was among the dangerous corral depths of the corn, beans, chili and squash.

My mind was slowly beginning to expand as I passed time with my grandparents. Trips around the country and to Mexico were the reason for my better appreciation of life and natural beauty. My introduction to family in Colorado was great, but the time my grandmother and I were driven in the blue VW Beatle by my Uncle Jake all the way to Washington was what changed my life forever. My cousin Samuel Fletcher lived in Aberdeen, not too far outside of Seattle. That drive took us past dozens of our relatives in Colorado and Idaho. Wow! The cornfields were longer and wider than the acres grandpa and I had grown. For several miles I was thinking about the poor kids who had to plant all those rows, never really knowing large scale farming had been going on long before I was around.

Once we hit Samuel's house, pictures were taken and stories were exchanged for hours. Somehow, Uncle Jake received information about an exhibit at one of the local museums and he was able to get us all tickets. He told me how important this show was and how it was one of the greatest archaeological finds in the world. Thinking back to my weekend shows from home, I had some idea as to the importance. Anyway, I thought I had an idea. Was I so wrong!

Well, the show we adventured through was that of the great Egyptian pharaoh, Tutankhamun. Before every child, janitor, and teacher in my school, rich and poor both, I had the chance. I was face to face with a true king from across the sea, even if he was dead. My little headset walked me through the exhibit and taught me about the king who would change the world of art and history forever. Even though I was only about nine years old on that summer trip to Washington (and many would find my trip unbelievable), it nonetheless laid the groundwork for my new dreams for the future. Once wanting to be a part of the United Nations program and live around the world, I found new dreams as an artist, art historian, and anthropologist.

Since that summer of dreams, I have been blessed with the chance to visit numerous parts of the world, both above and below the ground and above and below the ocean. Although I no longer fly about in my ship atop the apple tree, nor swim through my grandparents' garden, I am still blessed with the chance to continue to live a little of all my dreams. I may not work for the United Nations, but I do partake in the lives of dozens of government and non-government officials from around the world by working at the Poeh Cultural Center. I also work to influence the lives of each Pojoaque tribal member by explaining the trail of education from my life history—failures and successes.

*

As father sun set on another beautiful and rather glorious day in Pojoaque, I pass the home of my now departed and very well appreciated grandparents. Looking toward the grand orchard where my youth was shaped and heart was fed, I rapidly rode over the now accepted asphalt street which covers our humble washboard road of generations past. I glanced toward the orchard below and quietly noticed and broken heartedly observed the dried hollowed trunk of the once massive apple tree which embraced my quests high atop the earth. Even as I write about the legend of that great tree of life, I am filled with hurt, for my mighty companion has since come crashing down to lay twisted and broken upon the earth. Itv is now but a shadow of her once proud and fruit-bearing hideaway to a happy child of the pueblo past. No longer do the birds, insects and children seek her foliage and fruit for snack, shelter, shade and play, but she is rather a reminder of the cycle of life, here and gone. A few days later, I once again passed my grandparents' home to dream upon the apple tree's memory as my eyes were drawn toward the area where their garden once stood—my grandparents' years of labor. Somehow, the new caretakers of the "field of dreams" seemed to neglect their responsibilities of their traditional youth and now sow only weeds.

In closing, most of us here in Pojoaque have defeated the odds just by still being alive to tell our story. Today, all my dreams have come to life because my grandparents cared enough to give me the chance to explore, as they helped to remove me from the chains of poverty and ignorance. I am not the same person I was before my children were born, and I am nowhere near the person I thought I would be. My family has elevated me higher than I ever imagined I would be. Now as a father, husband, uncle, brother, cousin, and devoted member and follower of our tribe, my goals have changed slightly, but the changes will always involve the love instilled within me by my people, from past and present. We are of the blood of the ancient people of Po' Suwae Geh Owingeh; we are the Water Drinking People of the fertile Rio Grande Valley. As Tewa people, our lands are for educating our youth as we continue our tradition of existence. We must learn to mold the clay, weave the willow, and grow and harvest the fields. We must learn, then teach. So, until I pass on, and it becomes my time to paint the sky, blow with the wind, and fall with the rain alongside my ancestors, I am alive to retrieve, revive, and redistribute the Tewa realm with our young. It is also my responsibility to fight for our sovereignty, as well as our dignity and to diligently work toward making a difference.

I am Tewa, and more so, I am alive to tell you so.

MICHAEL LOPEZ

Michael Lopez is a member of the Pueblo of Pojoaque. He holds a B.A. in political science, and for several years was a member of New Mexico Senator Tom Udall's staff. In 2009, Michael was awarded the New Mexico TRIO Achiever of the Year. He currently works for the Golden Spread Council Boy Scouts of America, where he serves as the Golden Eagle Senior District Executive. He has three adult children (Athena, Abagale, and Michael); a grandson, Landen; and a life partner Shaleigh.

THINKING BACK TO WHEN I WAS YOUNG

Although it has been almost two years since his death, my Uncle Jake haunts me very often. Now I'm not talking about sheets with the eyes cut out, or some image making the "ooooh" sound that gives people the chills. This is the kind of haunting that really scares people. This is a haunting that stays with a person but will never be turned into this season's scariest movie. I'm talking about living up to one's potential.

My Uncle Jake always encouraged me to do something good with my life, as he had lived many lives himself. Uncle Jake was a Vietnam veteran turned homeless drug addict who made tomato soup from fast food restaurant catsup and pepper packages. He was a martyr, a politician, and he was the greatest man I ever knew. From him I received my first pair of moccasins on a cold October evening. He was the person I always tried to impress with my accomplishments.

Uncle Jake was a very particular kind of person. Five feet and about seven inches separated the top of his head from the ground. He wore a pot belly that got in the way whenever I tried to hug him. He probably had the messiest curly hair anyone had ever seen. Uncle Jake would show his smile through his beard. Sinus problems often plagued him, and he had a nervous twitch that always caused his left arm and shoulder to twitch the way a person with Parkinson's disease twitches. It was really a rough looking thing that would command a person's attention upon introduction. Since I was used to it, the twitch never bothered me, but I remember it scared a friend of mine. Kyle was my college roommate. One weekend I brought him home with me to Pojoaque. While we were sitting around the table where Uncle Jake always did business, Kyle kept twitching every time my Uncle Jake twitched. It was a subtle thing, but my Uncle Jake picked up on it. So he turned to Kyle and explained, "I have a nervous twitch." Kyle sat silently, not really responding. Then Uncle Jake joked, "Don't let it scare you. I don't let it scare me."

Before the night's end, Uncle Jake held true to fashion and once again showed that his generosity was only shadowed by his heart. I almost began to dislike it. Uncle Jake bought us dinner, gave Kyle a piece of pottery and money to me. Whether or not I needed money, Uncle Jake always gave it to me. I mean the man wouldn't let you buy your own candy bar. The generosity he showed almost bothered me because I wanted my Uncle Jake to know that I was self-sufficient. I would go by his house to visit and it would happen every time.

"Mike," he would say in his friendly voice, "can I talk to you in the other room?" That was Uncle Jake's thing: talking to people in the other room. So we would walk along the white walls and over the carpeted hallway of the adobe house into his bedroom. This is where it would happen.

"Mike, do you need anything?" he would ask.

I always tried different responses, but none of them could get him to stop giving me money. Not that he was a millionaire or anything, but he would give me what he had in his pocket, even if it was just five dollars.

"I'm fine, Uncle Jake. My mom gave me some money," or "I've got money, Uncle Jake," or "My scholarship money comes in today, Uncle Jake." I was lucky to have someone love me so much.

When I was about fourteen years old, my Uncle Jake called and asked me what I was doing that night.

"Nothing," I responded.

"Mike," he said, "I was wondering." It always took Uncle Jake a little bit of time to get a sentence out as he twitched and grunted between parts of his sentence. "I was wondering if you wouldn't mind coming over for a while and staying with grandpa while I go to the office to finish up some things."

"Sure," I said, and with that we made arrangements for him to pick me up and take me to his house. At the end of the night he took me home and tried to give me twenty bucks, but I refused it, because all I did was make grandpa a cup of coffee and watch television while he slept. Besides, he was my grandpa. This may have been the end of the night, but it was the beginning of a chapter in my life.

*

Uncle Jake gave me a red 1989 Mazda B2200 truck with a white camper shell. This was my first vehicle. A lot of my life's firsts were the result of Uncle Jake's efforts.

"Mike," he said, "I think I'm going to go ahead and give you the truck."

"Really? Wow, Uncle Jake. Thank you very much," I exclaimed excitedly. Then I asked, "Are you sure?"

"Sure, Mike, I'm very proud of you and you always help out with dad. You deserve it. Besides, you put new tires on it when you got a flat." Uncle Jake had been lending me the truck to go to work for several weeks now, and as a display of gratitude I put new tires on the truck.

As I had done so many times in those years, I explained to Uncle Jake that I was the one who should be saying thank you because I got to spend that time with grandpa.

"Uncle Jake, you don't need to thank me for that because I'm thankful that you trusted me enough to take care of grandpa. I'm grateful for the time I spent with him."

I graduated from the Santa Fe Indian School about a month later and went to work for Bill Richardson in Washington D.C. as an intern, no doubt something my Uncle Jake set up. I remember the sweaty July morning he called and asked, "Would you be interested in going to Washington D.C. to be an intern?" I remember being really excited. Going to Washington to work in a political environment was one of the many things Uncle Jake did as a way of grooming me. It was a step towards being a person who would "be involved with service" as he explained. By "service" he didn't mean, "Do you want fries with that, sir?" He meant being a public servant.

"I see you being that person, Mike," he would often tell me.

About two months after my return from Washington, I found out that I was going to become a father. Thanksgiving rolled around, and this was turning out to be a day to remember. After eating Thanksgiving dinner with my girlfriend's family, which was the first time I had ever done such a thing, I was taking my brother back home to my parents. We were cruising along when he asked, "Can I drive?"

After only a moment of thought, I decided to let him drive. So here we go again cruising along; my thirteen-year-old brother Fermin and me. He was so small and skinny, but he is my little brother. I don't even think he could see over the steering wheel.

When it came time to turn off from the Nambé Pueblo road onto a dirt back road, I could see that he was not going to make the turn. So I reached over to pull the emergency brake and all at once we hit the left side of the concrete base of an iron cattle guard that separated the concrete road from the dirt road. After that it gets kind of foggy.

When I woke up, I was sitting almost in Fermin.'s lap. My left knee was throbbing and resting against the smashed stereo. I wonder if a boxer who has been knocked out feels like I felt. My vision was blurry, and I could see stars. As my vision came into focus, I noticed that the windshield was shattered and strands of hair were hanging between the squares. I don't remember getting out of the truck, as I was still very dazed from attacking the windshield with my face.

In a shaky voice and tears in his eyes, Fermin said, "I wrecked your truck." Not that I ever had, but I wonder if he thought I was going to beat on him for it. This is when I noticed the white shirt I was wearing was now red. There were cars driving by and Fermin was trying to get someone to help us, but no one would stop. Eventually, I gained enough equilibrium to start the truck and drive back to Lenora's house.

A couple of days later, Uncle Jake came to see me there. Those days are still a haze, but I remember him being upset about the truck and the news that I was to become a parent. He said that things can happen "… even when people have the best intentions." Before he left, I remember him saying with disappointment in his voice, "Well, what's done is done."

*

Two years after wrecking the truck, I was sitting across the table from Uncle Jake at his home explaining what I needed in order to expand the business I was now running. He was very encouraging, as this was my first business venture. Imagination or ambition must have really gotten the best of me. Who opens a business at age twenty-one? As usual, Uncle Jake showed support for what I was doing. He did so by helping me get a storefront and a small business loan. Unfortunately, three years later inexperience and youth drove Smoke Signal Communications into the dirt. I was then twenty-four years old. Uncle Jake and I didn't talk for several months. It was my fault. Avoiding him seemed easier than looking him in the eyes and saying I failed. For some reason, I thought he would hate me or something.

In the fall of 1998 my cousin Tsosie passed away. I hadn't seen Uncle Jake in almost a year. At the funeral, I saw him standing among the other people. There he was twitching, grunting and shaking hands as the crowd gathered around him. There was always a crowd around Uncle Jake, people loved him like he was some sort of celebrity. Only Uncle Jake was more like a people's celebrity.

I wasn't sure how to approach him, but I had a story to tell him. Oddly enough, Uncle Jake excused himself from the crowd and walked over to me.

"Hey, Mike. What's going on bro?" he asked.

"Not much," I responded nervously. "About the business, Uncle Jake," I started to say when he interrupted.

"Don't feel bad about the business, jito. You gave it a shot. Most people won't even do that. You should be proud of your experience and what you learned. Maybe it happened to you while you were young for a reason."

I couldn't believe what I was hearing. Where the hell was the speech about what a failure I turned out to be?

"How old are you now?" he asked.

"Twenty-five," I responded.

Then he started counting on his chubby fingers—twenty-six, twenty-seven, twenty-eight, twenty-nine, thirty, thirty-one, thirty--two. Why don't you go back to school and become a lawyer or something? You're going to be thirty-two in seven years, anyway. Why not be a lawyer?" he asked.

"Well, Uncle Jake, that's funny you should say that because I enrolled in school last week."

Where the conversation went after that escapes me, but one thing really stood out. He said, "I'm proud of you. I'm glad to hear that you are ready to stop sharpening the pencil. You know what I mean?"

I don't recall if I told him about the humid day in August that led me to this decision. That August morning I had just come from a friend's funeral. She was so young and had so much potential; she had died as a result of drunk driving. I smelled the odor of the burgers and French fries from a nearby Burger King. It was so humid that the air conditioner in my truck was useless and I was in a suit. Ironically, I was on my way to a client's house to collect their monthly life insurance premium when I decided that life insurance sales and customer service was a waste of my potential.

*

Not only was Uncle Jake encouraging, but he was funny too. One year he invited my cousins Philip and Gabriel, a family friend named Pamela, and my sister and me to go with him to Disneyland. On the way out of town we stopped at a department store. As Uncle Jake walked through the store he was followed by his entourage of teens. There was a silver haired lady with glasses looking through the items on a clothes rack. My Uncle Jake suddenly turned to her and said, “Hello, m’am. I’m a counselor at the mental institution in Las Vegas.” (Las Vegas is also the name of a town in New Mexico.) ”These kids are residents there. I take them out for the weekend so they can learn to socialize.” Talk about being put on the spot. The lady just got this blank look on her face that changed into something like, are you serious? I think she may have even considered running in the opposite direction. During the rest of the trip, everyone but me refused to go into any stores with him.

Uncle Jake was the kind of person who would drive all day and all night. On some trips I would fall asleep in one state and wake up in another. The funniest thing to me was Uncle Jakes' wake up call to everyone in the car. You know that moment when the only person awake in the car is the driver. On this particular night we had witnessed a drunk driver wreck his car, but after the excitement of the event went away, everyone fell asleep. So Uncle Jake rolled all the windows down and set the power lock so no one could roll them up. This was in December so as you can imagine it was quite cold. As everyone woke up he said in a playful voice, "Oh, did I wake you up?"

On one trip he turned onto a dirt road and woke me up.

"Mike," he said, "sorry to wake you, but can you do me a favor?"

"Sure, Uncle Jake. What do you need?" I asked.

"I'm really sleepy. Do you think you could drive for a little bit?"

"Yeah," I answered. "Where are we?"

"We're in Gallup," he said. "We're going to my friends' house so I can get a couple hours of shut eye. I'll show you where it's at. I just don't want to fall asleep at the wheel."

With that he hopped in the back seat and I put the car into drive.

"It's just up this road a little ways," he said.

As we drove along, I could see the homes along the dirt road in the early morning light. I began thinking, "This road looks like the one at home." Then I saw a tree that really looked familiar and thought to myself, "Okay, if the old gray cottonwood tree is on the other side of the hill, then we are home." Sure enough, as the car's hood ornament cleared the pinnacle of a hill, I could see the gray stump of what was once a huge cottonwood tree just below the site of the old pueblo.

"Are we home?" I asked in a tone that indicated the jig was up.

Uncle Jake started laughing and gave me a hearty slap on the shoulder. "Sorry, Mike, you were snoring so loud that I just couldn't help myself."

I tried the same thing with my kids one day, but they caught on much quicker than I did.

*

During the summer of 2004, I was working as a student advisor for a summer youth program called Upward Bound, at Fort Lewis College in Durango, Colorado. The dorm room was cool and dark. I could hear the sound of sprinklers outside, as if they were all marching to the same tune. Tic-tic-tic-tic-tic. It took a minute before I realized I was awake. Uncle Jake was on my mind. You know when you wake up from a dream that is so dramatic that your mind is still showing you the movie with your eyes open. The dream was so real.

The dream seemed like the scene from a soap opera, one of those scenes where a person is remembering a recent conversation and the edges of their view are all blurred out. Well, that's how some dreams are. They almost seem like you're in them but looking at them from a distance. Uncle Jake was lying in a bed with white sheets. He looked so peaceful and wasn't snoring. The fact that he wasn't snoring stood out because Uncle Jake had a snore that could blow curtains like in old cartoons. Then I heard a woman's voice say, "The governor had a heart attack." This must have been the moment I realized I was awake.

Sadness was all around me like the darkness of the room. I wasn't sure what caused the dream, but I decided to call my uncle Jake. The red numbers on the digital alarm clock read 3:10. Slowly, I got up from my bed and walked on the cold floor to the telephone hanging on the wall. My fingers found the familiar shape of the number pad and began punching Uncle Jake's number. Somehow I knew that Uncle Jake would be awake. Uncle Jake would stay awake for days at a time. People called him at all hours of the day and night. "Jake, can you get me a job?" or "Jake can you bail me out of jail?" they would sometimes say.

"Hello," answered the voice on the line.

"Uncle Jake. What's happening?" I inquired.

"Hey, Mike. What's going on bro?"

"Not much, Uncle Jake. I just had a dream about you and I wanted to call to let you know that I love you." I think this surprised him because no one called at three in the morning just to say I love you.

"Oh thanks, jito. I love you too. You know you're one of my favorite nephews." Then he asked, "So when do you graduate?"

"In December, Uncle Jake. It took me a semester longer than I thought it would."

"That's all right," he said "Hey, you did it. I'm real proud of you jito." Then he went on to say, "My schedule is real busy, and I travel a lot, but I can have you work with me."

"Well, I hope you don't mind, Uncle Jake, but I was thinking about going to work in the courts. That's if I don't stay in Colorado."

"Why would you do that? I hope you don't mind me asking," he said.

"Well, Uncle Jake, I'm having trouble deciding what to do when I graduate."

"That's normal, Mike. Lots of people feel that way when they reach that point in their lives."

"Well, Uncle Jake, I know the tribe has a policy where everyone starts off at a certain pay rate, and I know I didn't spend all this time in college to go home and work for six or seven dollars an hour."

"You won't because you'll have a degree."

"There's another thing, Uncle Jake. I don't know how I feel about going home to deal with tribal and family politics. My perception has been changed by the things I have learned. Last summer during my internship at Nambé, I couldn't believe the disregard and disrespect the other governors displayed at a governors' meeting. I don't know if I could be a part of that. Plus, I like it here."

Then he said the words I really wished he hadn't because they were exactly what I needed to hear but didn't want to face.

"You know, Mike, everywhere you go you're going to find that. At least here you have family, and the pueblo needs you. Besides, you're going to make a great leader, Mike. All those things you dislike are up to you to try to change."

We talked about this for a few more minutes before we moved on to talk about Grandpa Fermin, the truck, and life as a growing process.

As we talked, I said things like: "I used to think that maybe you should not have given me the truck but now I know that there was a lesson to gain from the whole thing."

Uncle Jake and I often talked about things like this and how life is a constant growing process.

"You'll find that you're going to grow your whole life," he said.

We talked for about forty-five minutes before he asked, "Mike, are you coming home for the Fourth of July?"

"I sure am. The kids want to light fireworks, so I really should be there."

"Do you have enough money to come home?"

"I do, Uncle Jake. My job pays for my meals, so I've been able to save some money."

"Mike, I hope you don't mind but I would like to send you some money anyway."

"You know you don't have to, Uncle Jake."

"I know, but I want to."

"I really appreciate that, Uncle Jake."

"Uh, Mike, I hate to do this, but I need to hang up now because I took my medication before you called and I almost dropped the phone just now."

"You tired Uncle Jake?"

"Yeah, and tomorrow I'm leaving for Mexico for a few days, but we'll talk more when you come home."

"Okay, Uncle Jake."

He said, "Call Marcia tomorrow to have her remind me to send you some money."

"All right, Uncle Jake. Thanks again. I love you, Uncle Jake."

"I love you too, jito. We'll talk more in a few days."

Two days later I was sitting in my apartment, as I had the mornings off, when the phone rang. The caller I.D. said Antonio M. Lopez, which meant that it was my family calling.

"Hello Carmella," I joked with my wife, Lenora. Carmella is her middle name.

"Mike?"

"Yeah," I poked.

"I have something to tell you. Are you sitting down?"

"Sure, what's up?" I said sarcastically

"Me and the kids were at . . . I don't recall whose birthday party it was . . . they came to tell your aunt Phoebe that the governor died."

My God. It was like a truck load of bricks had just been unloaded on me.

"Are you okay?" she asked.

I just sat silent and numb.

"Mike, are you okay?"

"No. No I don't think I am," I said. "Ah, I gotta go, Lenora."

Then she said, "Okay. Be careful."

Again I sat silent.

"I love you," she said.

I could tell she was trying to reach out to me but I just said "Bye," and hung up the phone. Then I stood up from the garage sale couch I was sitting on and began to pace and hold my head in disbelief.

My cousin Angie and her husband John live in Durango and I used to hang out with them a lot while I was there. John happened to be at my apartment playing chess when the call came.

"What's wrong?" he asked as I went and sat on the carpet behind another couch. My head hung low as I placed it between my knees with my hands still holding my head.

"What's wrong?" he asked again.

"Lenora told me that Uncle Jake just died."

"What?" he said. "You need to call Angie."

"John, I can't."

So he began dialing the number to his house. I could hear Angie answer the phone.

"Hello."

"Angie, Mike needs to talk to you," he said, and tried to hand me the phone.

"John," I said and shook my head as I tried to not let the words escape my mouth. If I said it out loud again, I would have to stop being numb and face it.

"Angie," he said, "Mike just got a call from Lenora and she said that the governor passed away."

"Ahhh," she screamed into the phone. "No, it can't be true."

But it was. John wanted me to go with him to be with Angie, but I couldn't move.

"I can't, John. Just please leave."

"I'm afraid to. I've never seen you like this and I'm worried about Angie."

"John," I said in a monotone, "just go take care of Angie."

"Are you going to be okay?"

"I don't know, John, but I need some space. Please," I pleaded.

I remember calling my parents' house to see if they had heard the same thing. I was grasping for a straw that would make this an ugly rumor instead of the truth.

"Dad, did you hear what they said about Uncle Jake?" I asked.

"I'm not going to believe it until I see his body," he declared. "George, Frank, and I are going to El Paso to get him."

I don't remember the rest of the conversation. As John finally left, the anger, sorrow, and shock mixed inside me like tomatoes in a blender. I just remember feeling the pressure build inside me. My fists shook and tears warmed my cheeks. I felt like I could just explode. It took me several hours to compose myself. It wasn't until I realized that the sun had gone down and I was sitting in the dark that I could get myself off the floor to make the four-hour trip home to Pojoaque Pueblo.

It was the middle of the night when I got home; everyone was asleep. The first thing I noticed was the black upright piano along the white wall of the living room. I sat down and just started playing a sad tune that I have never been able to play again. As my fingers found their way around the keys, I sat there and cried. The next day I went to his house, but I didn't stay more than three or four hours. I just couldn't be there. Seeing everyone in the state they were in was too much for me to handle. The next few days were the loneliest I had ever felt and I didn't want anybody around me. Not knowing how to reach out or knowing how to let anyone reach out to me, I sat alone and cried. At some point during all of this I went to my sister Denise's house to eat, but I couldn't. My brother-in-law Sonny whispered to everyone else, "Hey, watch Mike, because he is really hurting."

Whether or not I was supposed to hear that I don't know, but thinking about it now, all I did was sit on the couch, cry silently, and stare at the front page of the newspaper hanging off the arm of the couch across from me. The front page had Uncle Jake's picture on it. He was smiling on the day that photo was taken. During the next few months I found myself in the midst of an internal struggle. My last conversation with my uncle told me what I had to do, but I didn't want to come home. Durango seemed like a world away from Pojoaque. It was a world away from the desert below the Sangre de Cristo Mountains. It was a world away from the world of the curse, the blessing, and the responsibility that comes with being a pueblo person.

At my college graduation, I missed Uncle Jake tremendously. I know he was very proud of me and always talked to me about living up to my potential. I'm still not a lawyer, but I have a bachelor's degree in political science. Law school is still one of my interests, but in the meantime I have the joy of seeing Lenora taste the power that comes with education. She is almost finished with her associate's degree and has already decided to go on for her bachelor's. I have stopped perhaps short of my goal, but I know Uncle Jake would still be proud to see me supporting Lenora on her quest for knowledge.

While writing through these experiences, I finally realize why I took a job that has nothing to do with politics. I think that maybe I've been afraid of my uncle's memory. As much as I have tried to avoid it though, committee memberships and political inquiries seem to find their way to me. When I was having trouble deciding whether or not to come home, the drums were calling to me, but I didn't want to hear them. Who knows why, but people, no matter where they come from, will always have something calling them home like the magnetic north that calls the ducks to their summer ponds. No matter where a person is, or how hard they try to avoid it, or what kind of citizen they are in their communities, home is where they belong. Home in Pojoaque Pueblo, working to honor the drums of my ancestors is where I belong. Although he is gone, and cannot tell me so, I find myself trying to do things that would make my uncle Jake express his pride in me. It is an extraordinary thing to have someone influence you so much. I hope to live to be the man my Uncle Jake always told me I am.

ANNA MARIE SANCHEZ

Anna Maria Sanchez was born and raised in Santa Fe and recently relocated to the Pueblo of Pojoaque. She is daughter to Jeanette Vigil and John R. Sanchez, granddaughter to Minnie Gutierrez and Reynel Vigil, and great-granddaughter to the late Petra Montoya and Juan I. Gutierrez.

THE DANCE

Dawn was just a hint across the sky when I awoke that morning. The breeze coming in through the window smelled of lilacs and high summer, while a cacophony of sound from the highway going towards Los Alamos filled the room. As I climbed from the bed, careful not to wake my sleeping sister, nerves and excitement flowed through me in anticipation of what was to come. I remember looking out the window, high on the hill, watching the early morning travelers as I stood there waiting for my mother to come wake us. There was something beautiful about that morning, something that stirred in me a yearning to understand where I come from. Though I didn't realize it at the time, the feast day in Santa Clara was the first step I took towards learning about my Native American heritage. Even now, almost twenty years later, I remember that day with a clarity that only happens a few times in life. Like a stone thrown into still water, the ripples formed and echoed, multiplying across the events that are my life.

The morning of the feast day, my grandmother, my mother, and my aunts dressed my sister and me in the traditional outfits of a Pueblo dancer— the manta (the heavy woolen top dress), leg wrappings, skunk pelts, scarves, and belts had been handed down or loaned to us from various family members. Only our moccasins were brand new, my grandmother having bought them especially for the feast day. Cedar perfumed the air as the boxes were opened and the ladies set about dressing us. First they wrapped our legs in animal hides, then put the moccasins on our feet and tied the skunk pelts around our ankles, and finally placed the thick, heavy manta on top, and laid out colorful scarves to be taken with us. I had no idea what was going on, just that I was turned this way and that as each of the ladies completed her part in dressing us.

When all was done and the boxes were put away, my great-grandmother and my grandmother walked towards us, an old wooden jewelry box held between them. I remember my grandmother pulling me aside as she sifted through her jewelry. Piece by piece she decorated me with her own jewelry, until my neck was heavy with turquoise and coral, hands and fingers gleaming with silver. Before leaving the room, my grandmother and great-grandmother blessed each of us in turn. One by one, my aunts followed suit, until there was only my mother left. A look came into her eyes that I've only seen once or twice since my childhood, a kind of understanding of what we were going through, and a mother's pride. Sometimes there are no words needed between a mother and her children, a single look can speak volumes.

The sun was high in the east, the heat already upon us, and only getting stronger when we finished getting ready. Pictures were taken and last minute preparations were made before we left for the pueblo. I don't remember the car ride, but I do remember walking towards the Kiva, saying good-bye to my family, and climbing the ladder up and into the center. I was okay until my mother left to stand with her group of dancers, but then it all changed. Everything closed in until it seemed that all I could hear were the restless motion of the dancers, the sound of the rattles and bells, the murmuring of more than a hundred voices, and I think I would have lost it completely if my sister hadn't grabbed my hand. When she squeezed my hand, and looked at me, it all stopped. I was still aware of everything, but I knew that if I freaked out, she would be worse. So I held her hand and concentrated on the kids standing in front of me, thinking about all the practices we'd gone to during that week in preparation for the feast day. Attendants came up and, moving from one to another, prepared the dancers.

One by one,we collected our evergreen branches as we filed out of the Kiva. As I climbed up and into the sunlight, I looked out and was met by a sea of faces. Trying to pick out my family was near impossible, so I just concentrated on following the line of dancers down the steps and into the pueblo. At the sound of the first drumbeat, my heart jumped to the time, keeping the beat as my feet itched to dance. I was near the back of the line when the dance started and when my turn came, all thoughts of what people were thinking when they looked at me vanished. I lost myself in the beat of the drums, my feet finding the steps on their own. Never before in my life had I felt as I did then, with the drums booming in my ears, and the men's voices raised as one, chanting in a language as mysterious as it was beautiful. I didn't know what the words meant, only that at that moment, my soul felt alive and free.

Time didn't exist for me that day when the drums and the music carried me to a place I'd never been before. Sometimes memories of events long past can carry an air of unreality, or seem to be surreal, but I know that day I was taken to another place, one outside myself and shared only with a select few. Every August since then, I go down to Santa Clara to watch the dances, and I get to remember what it felt like to dance in the summer heat, to feel the drums beating against my feet and to hear the men raise their voices as one. Never again, since I was seven years old, have I participated in a dance other than to observe and watch the newest generation of dancers find their way into the Kiva, drums beating the air and thunder under their feet. It is a beautiful thing to be a part of something greater than oneself, and to be able to share it with others. This story is not new, but rather it is an addition to the long tapestry of stories weaved by our people, yet it is mine all the same. This was the first time I was fully exposed to the Native culture I was born into, an awakening to the second half of me that I didn't even realize existed. This is the beginning of my life's story, of two cultures merging within one person, and the discovery of what it means to live in harmony with both. Every person, young and old, has to make a choice as to how they want to live their life. My choice is to celebrate who I am and to respect where I came from. To forget our culture is to lose our identity and our way of life.

As the day drew to a close, the sun slid behind the blue Jemez peaks, streaks of light filling the sky with colors dazzling to behold. A final beat of the drums and ringing of bells as the dancers moved about wearily closed the feast on that hot August day. The slight breeze coming down off the mountains was a welcome relief as the sweat rolled off my face. My arms felt like lead and my legs like jelly, yet I'd never felt better than I did at that moment. As my mother collected us and we began to wind our way through the pueblo, I remember looking at the evergreen branch I had clutched throughout the day. It was broken and slick with sweat from my hands, but when I lifted it to my nose, the smell of the tree it came from was still strong, making my nose tingle and itch. I was about to throw it away when my mother stayed my hand. She led us towards the stream that flowed near the pueblo, murmured something, and knelt down by my sister and me, took our hands holding the broken branches, murmured something, and had us toss them into the water. She said that to return the branches used in the dancing ceremonies to the water from which they came was to thank them for the sacrifices made, and that it was a blessing, a prayer for the future.

MARY ANN KATHERINE FIERO
Yán Tsáwá Poekwí—Willow Blue Spring

Mary Ann Katherine Fierro, known to all as Kathy, was born and raised in the Pueblo of Pojoaque. Her parents are Gilbert Mascarenas and Phoebe M. Petty. Phoebe Petty is the daughter of the late Fermin Viarrial and Feliciana Tapia Viarrial. Kathy is married and has five children and eight grandchildren.

TRADITIONAL BREAD MAKING

I remember when I was eight years old and my grandma Feliciana, my mom Phoebe, Aunt Josie, and Aunt Dora were preparing the horno to be plastered before feast day. The horno is an outdoor oven used for baking. It is made of adobes, dirt, straw, water and looks like an Eskimo Igloo about six feet in height. The plastering is done with a trowel, and hands are used for smoothing the surface.

I remember when the plastering was done, a mud fight broke out between my grandma, mom, and aunts. Of course, we kids got in the fight too.

We were all standing around, laughing at the way we looked, packed in mud from head to toe when the insurance man showed up. His expression said, What the heck is going on? Do I stay or do I run?

He was about thirty-two years old, my mother's age, so I think my mother was so embarrassed that she felt like being swallowed up by the ground or disappearing. But they took care of business as usual, and laughed through it all.

The mud dried so hard on our bodies and faces that [after the insurance man left] we all had to be washed down with the water hose, which was worse because the water was very cold.

Then we had a water fight.

Then came the time for making the dough, which included flour, lard, yeast, salt, baking powder and warm water. Grandma always said that the children were not to stick their hands into the dough, but to watch and learn. After the dough was prepared and kneaded twice, loaves were formed and placed on pie plates, and covered with dish towels or clean sheets to rise one last time before being put into the horno for baking. When it was time to heat the horno for baking, Grandpa Fermin would chop the cedar wood.

When grandma wanted to check the horno for the temperature, she would throw in some pieces of dried cornhusks, and if they burned too fast, the horno was too hot. She had a bucket with water and a wooden stick mop used to mop the inside of the horno to cool it down and try the cornhusk thing again.

When the horno was at the right temperature and the loaves had risen, each of us carried the dough loaves out to the horno. The baking takes more or less forty-five minutes. So while the bread was baking we just hung around the horno, and you could smell the baked flour and yeast, and savor the wholesomeness …. Oh, you could almost taste it!

When the bread was done baking we would place it on the living room floor on top of a clean sheet. And, of course, our thoughts were YUMMY, now we can eat some with butter.

But grandma said, "Don't be eating the bread hot. It will get you *empachada* (sick/constipated)." The cure at the time was a very painful massage that my grandma gave.

While grandma and mom were out front tending to the baking, my sisters and I would sneak in through the back door and steal a hot fresh loaf of bread and take it out back and sit in an old abandoned car and eat it. Of course, we would get thirsty and drink water. So what happens—we get sick! Then comes the massage.

After grandma passed on, the tradition of baking bread and curing constipation was not continued. So when our annual feast came around, we usually bought the bread from nearby pueblos. One day my mom and my daughter, Beverly, decided to call the women in the family and talk about learning how to bake our own bread. We thought it was a great idea, so my mom and my daughter, Beverly, got in touch with a longtime friend of the family, Anacita, from the nearby pueblo of Santo Domingo. Anacita was very honored, as we were to have her teach us. In the past, Anacita would make bread for our Uncle Jake, the late governor.

Since then, all the women and girls in the family get together before feast day and prepare for baking bread, prune pies, and *bootsies* (thick biscochitos).

Keep the tradition alive!

LUCY ANN TAFOYA

Lucy Ann (Tapia) Tafoya is the daughter of Juan Ignacio and Crucita (Cata) Tapia, both deceased. She is the third oldest of seven children. In 1957 at age twenty-one, Lucy married Joseph Luis Trafoya from Santa Clara Pueblo. They had five children, one of whom passed away at age ten. They now have two girls and two boys, three grandsons and four granddaughters. Lucy mades black carved pottery with a corrugated background. She became famous for her pottery before she began silversmithing. Lucy passed away in 2012. This article is based on an interview.

Working

When I was small my dad used to have a big garden. He raised all sorts of vegetables—corn, tomatoes, chile, squash, turnips, red beets, pumpkins, radishes, onions, garlic, cucumbers, and watermelon.—plus cantaloupe, Indian melons, peas, pinto beans, green beans, yellow waxed beans, carrots, and cabbage. My brothers and I used to help him hoe and water the garden and pull weeds.

We had to go for our water in Nambé. I would go to Nambé on my horse Molly by myself to turn on the water. The water comes from the mountains, but there's a reservoir, and when it was our turn to get water we would channel the water into our ditch. We shared the ditch with other families, except we had certain days to water. The Spanish had certain days. We have water gates all the way down the system of ditches. A lot of people would have their water gates closed and I would have to open all of them so the water could go down to our place.

It is maybe three or four miles between Pojoaque and Nambé, something like that. If it was our water day and I turned the water on and later it was getting low, I would check and see that some of the Spanish people were closing the gates. They just wanted to be mean or something. And I would go back and open them up. Sometimes they would stand there and argue with me, and I would say, "I can't help it. It's our turn to use the water and your turn will gradually come."

Our garden had rows of chile and rows of assorted vegetables and we watered it row by row. The water flows off the main ditch into channels and into our garden, starting from the end of the last row at the end of our field, eventually coming up to the last row.

When we went to school in September, I used to bring some of my friends home from school. I would ask them, "Do you want a Halloween pumpkin?" and they would say, "Yeah," and I would bring them to our garden and I'd tell them, "We have to haul them out." And I had my friends all straight in a row, in a line, and we would hand pumpkins to one another until we got them to the house. I mean that whole yard was filled with pumpkins and watermelons. And before they'd leave I'd give them each a pumpkin for Halloween. My dad would say, "You're very smart."

I helped pick the apricots and cherries and I helped my mother make apricot, pineapple, cherry, and plum jam. (We had wild plums.) I helped my mother can all the time. I helped wash the jars and drop them in boiling water to sterilize them. And I used to help her dry fruit and vegetables.

I have cooked since I was eight years old. My mother had a housecleaning job at a doctor's home and at the homes of some people she knew. We had a wood cooking stove and she told me to have the boys chop wood and have kindling to start the fire. She would tell me to have them haul water out of a spring, which was half a mile away. They hauled two buckets at a time, but had to stop and rest once in a while.

After they brought the water, my mother would tell me to cook. As a little girl my mother taught me how to make tortillas, how to mix the dough. We make tortillas with flour, a little bit of salt, a little bit of baking powder and not too much Morrell lard. Morrell lard comes in a box. They've had that for ages. I would add a little warm water and mix the dough. She told me, "Don't put in too much water. If you put in too much it gets sticky and you can't roll it." And I had a little box that I stood on to reach the table to roll out the dough, and then I would be careful. I would grease the stove a little, wipe it and clean it.

I would put the tortilla on the hot wood stove. Then I would keep an eye on it so it wouldn't burn or cook on just one side, but flip it over and do the same thing—flip it around, change it around, till it was done, then lay it on a dry dish towel. I would make about twelve or thirteen tortillas at a time. That would take care of that dinner meal.

And in those days what we used to eat a lot were pinto beans, green *chile*, vegetables out of the garden, and sometimes, well, we had pigs. My dad would kill a pig; we would freeze the meat, and we would use that to make stew or whatever. We also grew corn, so we used to have corn-on-the-cob or fried corn or corn stew.

I washed the beans thoroughly, rinsed them two or three times. My mother always used a pressure cooker to cook them. My mother taught me that. She said it's the fastest way to cook. Would you believe I have four or five of those around the house for cooking, and then two or three big ones for canning. I don't let the beans soak, I just put them right into the pressure cooker and in forty-five minutes the beans are done.

What we did was we used to roast our *chili* in the oven and on top of the stove. But you have to do that all day, flipping them over. But now in the modern days we have these *chili* roasters. They have a grill on them. They have a little motor and it keeps turning and roasts the *chil*i as it turns. Now we do it that way, but before we used to cover it so they would steam and we could peel them.

On weekends, I would have the boys go haul water. We would get the water out of the ditch and put it in a big galvanized tub. We heated the water outdoors. We would build a fire under the tub in order to wash our clothes. We had a wringer-type washing machine and that was my job on weekends. And sometimes if our machine wasn't working then we would have to use a washboard, one of those old-time washboards. My mother would say, "Wash the socks." We had homemade soap; we didn't have detergent like we do now.

On weekends, my mother usually made me clean the house and wash clothes and the boys would have to chop wood, clean the yard and gather some wood chips to start a fire with. When I was busy on weekends doing laundry, the boys would have to go out to the garden to help their dad. He would not let us lay around or play around, he made us work constantly.

Like at lunchtime, we would be sitting at the table eating and he would tell one of my brothers, "When we're done, you go out and pull weeds and start hoeing around the *chile*." And then he would have another working in the cornfield and he would tell him, "If there's three or more stalks of corn in one bunch, leave two and pull the rest out." (You have better corn.) Then you have to put dirt around the corn stalk.

And then, in order to keep the corn from getting worms, he used to use Wesson oil or olive oil and open up the corn on the end and put three or four drops of oil on the tip of the corn so the worms would not get into it. And then that way you have nice perfect corn.

As I grew older, my responsibilities changed a lot. I went to school here in Pojoaque and I had a car accident. I was going to summer school at Santa Fe High because I was going to be a senior that fall. My brother, Richard, worked at Santa Domingo with the railroad and came home on weekends. He came home on the

Fourth of July and drove us to Nambé Falls for a picnic. I had to drive him back to his job that night, so my mother, my sister and I drove Richard to Santa Domingo. Driving back home we had a very bad head-on car accident at Rio Tesuque. There used to be a very high hill and there were a lot of cars coming from the north. We were the first ones coming up the hill when a car pulled up from the north and hit us head-on. There was no way for me to dodge the accident because the car was all the way to the right.

It was a very, very bad accident. I was pinned behind the steering wheel and they couldn't get me out. They took my mother and sister to St. Vincent's Hospital while they were trying to get me out, and I could hear somebody yelling and calling, "Somebody send out another flare." That's the last I remember. I was in a coma for a week. After that I was transferred to Albuquerque to the Indian hospital. I had a crushed femur and was torn up all over my face, my chest, my arms. I went through a lot. I was flat on my back for a full year. It took me a long time to learn to walk. My brother, Richard, used to come over and help me walk. Finally, I came out of the hospital and came home.

By that time, my classmates had all graduated from high school. I never graduated with the class. I took my GED test instead and passed it right away, so that's what I'm using now, my GED.

But I didn't use my GED that much because I started working on pottery and became famous with it. I worked on it from 1972 up till 1997. I worked and I did a lot of shows. I was traveling all over. I was in Kansas, I was in Oklahoma. I showed in Texas and Arizona, at the Santa Fe Indian Market and at the Eight Northern Pueblos Show. I did the Heard Museum [in Phoenix], I did the Pueblo Grande, but now I don't travel like that any more.

In 1997, I turned to jewelry, to silversmithing. I took a class for eight years in silversmithing and now I'm in a well-known jewelers' book that all the famous jewelers are in.

FRANCINE B. MAESTAS

Francine B. Maestas was born in Santa Fe and raised on the Pueblo of Pojoaque and has lived here most of her life. She has certificates of completion in jewelry, pottery, and stone sculpture from the Poeh Arts Program. She also has an Associates of Fine Arts Degree in Visual Arts and an Associates of Arts degree in Fine Art. She received a Bachelors of Arts degree in Studio Art and a Bachelors of Fine Arts Degree in sculpture, and has completed a year of graduate study at the University of New Mexico where she would like to receive her Masters degree in Studio and Fine Arts with an emphasis in sculpture. She is also the Founder, Director, and Instructor at the Family Cultural Learning Center on the Pueblo of Pojoaque.

MEMORIES AND ACTIVITIES

I can remember the gardens that my grandparents had when I was a child growing up on the Pueblo of Pojoaque. Lush green fields of corn, beans, squash, chili, and other vegetables and fruits covered the landscape and seemed endless.

I remember coming home from school and my grandparents would be out in the fields working, and if they were not out in the fields, they were tending to the animals, which included cows, horses, goats, sheep, chickens, and hens. My grandparents were always busy and worked so very hard, and raised nine children with their farming.

When the growing season was over I gathered corn to hang or freeze. I have memories of my family gathering yearly to roast green chili. Some were hung to dry and the rest were left for freezing, which seemed like an endless chore. The chili that was allowed to turn red was split and dried, then ground into powder, and the seed was saved for the following year.

When my grandparents became too old to care for their animals and plant their gardens, these memories faded away. The next memory I have of my family gardening was that done by my uncle, who was the youngest of the boys. In his yard he had fields of various vegetables that reminded me of what my grandparents had grown years before.

My main reason for starting the Family Cultural Learning Center in May 2005 was to bring back Traditional Arts and Crafts. Although I did not come from a family of artists, I felt that raising livestock and sustainable gardening were arts in themselves.

The focus of the Family Cultural Learning Center is intergenerational teaching and learning. Classes in red, black, and micaceous pottery, stone carving, red willow basket making, drum making have already taken place with great success.

In the fall 2005 I was honored to meet a couple from Tierra Azul Farm in La Mesia, New Mexico. The couple gave me $150.00 to start a garden project. I had never really gardened before, but had childhood memories that encouraged me to start preparing the soil for planting. With the money that was given to the Family Cultural Learning Center, we were able to plant a cover crop of winter wheat, which was a great success. The focus of the garden project was to emphasize the use of dry farming techniques, which include waffle and terrace gardening techniques which our ancestors used for generations. The main reason for using these techniques is to conserve water, and to retard evaporation of water being used for watering. Historically the waffle garden was above ground and mud was used to make the grid pattern. Rock was used for both the waffle and terrace gardens, which gather the heat from the sun and extend the growing season. Both methods have been practiced and documented historically.

During the winter months, I went online and was able to get seeds donated from various organizations, and in early spring was able to get soil and compost donated as well. The terrace and waffle gardens at the Family Cultural Learning Center each measured 1200 square feet.

During the summer, the Pueblo of Pojoaque Boys and Girls Club attended an eight-week garden program for both tribal and non-tribal children. The Pueblo of Pojoaque Early Childhood Development Center also took part by allowing me to plant a garden of beans, corn, and squash with the three-to-five-year-old children.

Overall, the Family Cultural Learning Center has been a great success and a wonderful experience for me, and I feel that it can only grow and encourage more tribal members to take part in ongoing classes and activities.

MARIA PHOEBE PETTY

Maria Phoebe Petty, known as Phoebe, was born May 9, 1936, in Pojoaque Pueblo to Fermin Viarrial and Feliciana Tapia Viarrial. Phoebe has three daughters, Linda, Kathy, and Genevieve Mascarenas. She also has fourteen grandchildren, and many great grandchildren. As a young woman, Phoebe obtained her degree as a head start teacher and served many children in the Pojoaque Valley district. She obtained many other certificates and recognitions while serving the children and elders in her community. During her younger years, Phoebe enjoyed preparing traditional home-cooked meals, gardening, dancing, and most of all, spending time with her family and friends. This article was based on an interview.

RECLAIMING TRADITION

I am thinking about my parents, my siblings and myself and what we have endured in our lives.

I am both Spanish and Indian. My dad was Spanish and spoke nothing but Spanish. My mom was from the tribe, Pojoaque Pueblo. My parents, Fermin and Feliciana Tapia Viarrial, along with my grandfather, José Antonio Tapia, reestablished our Pueblo. They wanted to come back to the pueblo because it was abandoned and because my grandpa read in the paper that the land was going to be given away. I was born in '36 and they came in '34.

They came here in horse drawn wagons. My mother was pregnant with my brother, Ben, when they came from Colorado. Ben was ruptured from my mom bouncing in the horse wagon. Ben was born here, and they had to take him by horse wagon to a hospital in Santa Fe. One of the neighbors probably helped them.

I think there were about three or four families that came after dad and mom moved back to the pueblo. It was a very small pueblo. There were only about four or five houses to the pueblo then.

I was born in 1936 at home, along with my twin sister, Dora. We were born ten minutes apart. We do not look alike, but we do have a great deal of characteristics in common. My sister and I weighed two pounds each at birth. In those days there were no incubators, so we had to be placed in the wood stove oven at home to keep warm. My complexion is dark like my mother's, and my sister's is light like my father's. My older brother, Ben, says that's because one of us was conceived at night and the other during the day. I think I was left in the oven longer and my sister was not left in long enough.

Food

My father had two horses, Goldie and Chestnut. My brother, Jimmy, and I loved to harness and saddle our horses to prepare them for work. We would work all day hauling wood and picking fruit with mom.

The best memory of all was when I would return from school and smell my mother's homemade tortillas—mmm!—that would fill the entire house. I loved to pick up the dried apples from the orchard and eat them with the tortillas. But there were times when we had not much to eat, so my mother would cook us apricots and that would be our lunch or dinner.

We canned the green chile, the spinach, and the verdolagas (purslane). We canned or dried the corn to make chicos (dried sweet corn kernels). And they would make ristras (strings) with the chiles. They would pickle pears and dry apples for pies, and make jellies. Once in a while, when there would be cherries, they would make jelly from them, and from the apricots too. They used to can pork and beef. Or dry the beef to make jerky.

For the hog, they would boil water in a barrel until it got hot, and they would shoot the pig in the forehead and then they would lay him on a table with a slab on it and put those gunny sacks over him and pour the hot water over the gunny sacks and let it set there a little while to soften the hair and skin, to scrape it off. Then they would cut the pig skin into strips to make pork rinds, and they would use the head for tamales, whatever. They used to scare us with the pig head when we were small.

At one time, my dad was going to pour water over the pig and the water from the dipper went into his rubber boots and it was so hot we had to get other help. He had to go to the hospital and was burned so badly that he lost his job at Los Alamos.

I remember one time my dad and others were going to shoot this cow, and while they were separating the cows from the calves, this calf came after him. He fell down but picked up a rock and hit the calf on the head between the eyes and it fell over dead. So they had to butcher that calf instead of the cow.

Learning Tradition

When I was about eleven or twelve, my aunt, Petra Gutierrez, from Santa Clara would take me to Santa Clara with her for the summer. They were teaching me Tewa, but I forgot it growing up. I knew a little bit, but not much. They used to talk Tewa a lot there. They would sit at the table at supper and talk Tewa ,and I would ask my aunt, "What did they say?" Or she would say, "Pass the salt" or "Pass the bread," in Tewa. They would explain words to me so I wouldn't feel left out. They were kind to me and treated me good, like I was part of the family.

I raised my daughters to get involved in the culture, in the dances. My oldest daughter, Linda, was Indian Princess at her high school. My youngest daughter, they used to dress her as a boy to take the place of a boy in the dances. I only danced once for the Pueblo, the corn dance. I just didn't try to participate, and now I wish I had. I still try to teach my grandkids and great-grandkids to get involved in the dances. The little ones start early, at two-and-a-half and three years old. What I'm proud of is that my children and great grandchild are so involved in the dancing, the Kiva, getting educated, and helping others.

We have other people from other tribes to teach our children the Tewa language because we were raised here as non-speaking people. We've had drummers come in to teach them dance. That's good. I hope it continues and that someday our children will grow to know more about what's going on around them, that they can pick up where our ancestors left off—continuing their traditions: learning to plant gardens again, learning their language, their dancing, everything.

SANDRA ROMERO

I am a tribal member of the Pueblo of Pojoaque and have resided on the pueblo most of my life. I have three children and am a grandmother and great-grandmother. I speak my native language Tewa, as well as English and Spanish. I am a jeweler and enjoy traveling and getting together with family.

TEWA SPEAKER

Here I am, five years old, with Tewa as my only source of communication; I spoke no English whatsoever. All communication was done in Tewa, even though my parents both spoke English. When I was adopted, my Santa Clara grandmother told my parents, "Teach Sandra to speak Tewa." I don't know if that was because that was her only way of communicating.

So guess what, here I am, taken to the Pojoaque Valley Public School System to start my education. What an eye-opening experience for me. Today, I can still picture the classroom as it was then. The walls were a yucky light green color, with the ABC's, the numbers one through ten, and different shapes to show the eight basic colors. The brown desks were all lined up, the smell of polish on the floors and desks wasn't pleasant.

From the start, my young life in school was a nightmare. It all began when my parents didn't mention to the teacher that I did not speak English. Even the teacher, Mrs. Madrid, was a sight to look at—tall with black, shoulder-length curly hair and black-lined eyes, and the brightest red lipstick. Kind of like someone who was ready for Halloween. I'm sure there were a lot of us who thought the same of that teacher. A lot of the children were terrified of being left in a new place when they realized that their parents were leaving. That included me. Parents were trying to reassure their children—some were being held, hugged, kissed, and softly spoken to. But in the end, we all stayed.

But wait! Who do I see if not my cousin Charlie Tapia, almost right next to me? Charlie was my lifeline at the time, even if it was just for a few days. Charlie was able to explain some of the daily routine to me. It didn't take long for Mrs. Madrid to put an end to that. She had Charlie moved to another classroom, in an attempt to encourage me to learn English.

The children were cruel, just downright mean. I was taunted, teased, and had my long beautiful black braided hair pulled apart. I'd get home and have to explain that to my mother. The teacher was determined that I learn, so she would put me out in the middle of the playground. It became a monkey see, monkey do during the recess time—in the morning, after lunch, and afternoon. It was me who was doing the act, imitating them, trying to fit in with the rest. The play area was provided with a number of items to play on. There were the swings, teeter-totter, merry-go-round, slides, monkey bars and basketball court.

Sometimes, during recess or lunch, I saw some of my relatives, but again the language barrier arose. They either spoke English or Spanish. Boy, life was difficult for this little Indian girl.

As I look back, I wonder if learning English was a good or bad thing. Why? Life was even more difficult due to all the prejudice in school. Derogatory words or statements were used against us, such as: "Those damn Indians," and "They're stupid, poor, and dumb." We seemed not to be recognized when we accomplished anything. It was passed off. "Ignored" would be a better word. Life was a great struggle in the so-called English world.

Today I'm proud of the way I was raised, speaking my Tewa language, because of the beauty it has. Our language is our life and will continue to be spoken. I am making an attempt to teach my children and grandchildren the Tewa language, so that it may be carried on for generations to come. I am a proud Tewa speaker.

SANDRA ROMERO

GREEN CHILE

I remember life on the pueblo as a place full of activities.

*

My parents were farmers who grew food to survive. They loved the land since it provided for them. They planted maize, chili, cucumbers, squash, tomatoes, radishes, and beans. Sometimes there was an abundance of garden vegetables, and relatives and neighbors got to enjoy them too. And at times, we even made a few dollars.

The planting season started in March and ended toward the first week of November. I was taught at a very young age to help in the fields, some of which I did not enjoy. I remember following my mother or father in the rows where all these veggies were being planted, and covering up the seeds with a small amount of dirt. Hoeing or weeding the garden was a chore I did not look forward to. Sometimes, I purposely chopped a few plants. Then another row was given to me to do. At times, I'd start out doing the task at hand, but be side-tracked and start chasing butterflies, bugs or grasshoppers. I liked to just sit in a row and daydream.

A saying I heard from my parents was, "No work, no food." I was stubborn at times, not wanting to work in the garden. So, sometimes they would go in for lunch and leave me alone in the garden. But then I would see the apricot tree or the apple tree and go munch on the fruit and I'd be all right. But the nights could be a little rough, if you get the message.

Sometimes, it got very hot and uncomfortable. We would go take a break. So it was either early morning or late evenings when we would return to the fields.

Irrigation was part of what I liked, because I would go splashing in the ditch. The person in charge of letting the water go, the *mayordomo*, would either call or come by the house to let my father know when it was his turn. Or, at times a neighbor would be the messenger. My father got the water at a lot of different times, in the morning or in the evening. We got our irrigation water from Nambé, and sometimes a fish or two would swim down and end up in the garden. They would be flopping and jumping because there was not enough water for them to swim in. So we would catch and eat them. There was no need for a fishing pole then.

As the fruits of the field began to ripen, we started sampling the first vegetable that was ready—usually the radishes, fresh and crispy, washed in the ditch or water faucet outside. Umm, so delicious with a little salt. Boy, I can almost taste them. Sweet peas usually followed, which were really tasty also. Every vegetable had its day.

My mother would take time out to make a fresh pot of beans, homemade tortillas, freshly roasted green chile with a little fresh garlic and salt, or zucchini with sweet corn. Oh, what a treat that was! Nothing but fresh, wholesome garden food. No store bought tortillas in those days for us.

When the time for harvesting came, it turned into a family affair with help from relatives or friends. It was time to pick green chile. We'd roast it and either froze or dried it. To dry them, we'd peel the chiles, leaving on the stems to be able to tie ten or so on a string and hang them out to dry. Or, we'd partly roast them and split them open and lay them flat to dry outside. Later we'd fry them with grease and eat them plain. We'd pick the sweet corn and cook it and tie it up and let it dry and turn it into chicos. We could cook the chicos up with beans. Beans were also picked in their dry shells, put in a basket or placed on a stretch of canvas. The beans were either shook in the basket or else the canvas was folded in half and you used your hands or a broom and gently hit the canvas to release the beans from their shells. We would place the dried chicos and beans in empty flour sacks to store for the winter.

Going out and finally picking the red chile to make ristras was even more exciting. We filled gunnysacks with red chiles, which we would take to the pantry where some finished ripening. We piled up gunny sacks of red chile against the wall, leaving room for my parents to put their little stools to sit on. Making the ristras (strings of chile) was usually done after supper. Then we would go into the pantry, get comfortable and start the job. I didn't know how to make ristras, but I contributed by placing the piles of chiles in front of my parents. They made it enjoyable by sharing their lives with me. It was a time for storytelling, and time for relaxing; we laughed and teased on those occasions. Sometimes I'd fall asleep and get awakened late at night to go to bed. Just to think of all that red chili brings back good memories of my childhood and how life used to be.

Almost every morning after breakfast, my father would go out and take out the finished ristras and hang them on the warehouse. People would come by and compliment my father on how beautiful the ristras looked, especially hanging up against the gray colored warehouse. They were usually about ten feet long, but were doubled to shorten them so they'd be easier to handle and hang. It was picturesque, and I'm sure it gave my parents a sense of pride, just knowing that it all was worth the hard work.

Those days were so special, and I now appreciate what it was like to be brought up in such a culture. Now I can visualize and appreciate the art of farming, or growing, and living off of what was given to us through nature.

VILLAGES TOWNS AND CITIES

SANTA FE

To someone who had grown up in the East, Santa Fe, which calls itself "The City Different," was exotic. Santa Fe and Taos both had exerted a pull on Eastern artists and writers from the early twentieth century on. The lure came not only from the vast land with its mesas and mountains, or the raw colors of its earth, rocks and trees, but its Native American and Hispanic cultures. The industrialized East Coast with its dark cities and factories incessantly pouring smoke into the skies, with the sounds of automobiles and elevated trains, all these told the intuitive artist that Western civilization had hit a dead end. Thus, when the first Eastern artists ventured to Taos and sent back reports, they told of a land that was rich with possibilities for art. This was a time when artists, writers and intellectuals wanted America renewed by a quiltwork of regional cultures, and here was a land unfettered by the machine, whose traditional cultures remained uncontaminated by modernity.

In time, a colony of Taos artists developed and named themselves The Taos Society of Artists. Taos also attracted American socialite Mabel Doidge, who knew Gertrude Stein, D. H. Lawrence and other European arts' luminaries. Dodge persuaded Lawrence to come and visit, and the visit changed him. "I think," he wrote, "New Mexico was the greatest experience I ever had from the outside world. It certainly changed me forever."

Santa Fe's art colony developed a bit later, perhaps because so many prominent artists had already arrived in Taos. Canyon Road, which began a short walk from the Plaza, ran into the mountain foothills, was where most of the artists chose to have their homes and studios. It remained the center of the bohemian colony until Santa Fe began attracting a steady flow of wealthy newcomers, which raised real estate prices. As the older artists and residents of Canyon Road died, younger artists could not afford the new rents, and began moving elsewhere, some even out of town. Now the studio-galleries of the old artists are galleries selling high-priced commercial art. Claude's, a bar that once burst with life on weekends, filled with artists and writers and a mix of cultures, is long gone, symptomatic of Santa Fe's loss of its original character. As one friend put it, "Santa Fe has lost its poetry." The stories in this section describe Santa Fe at a time before the transition.

ED LARSON

Ed Larson lives in Santa Fe, New Mexico and now in his nineties continues to create in his home studio after many years of having his own gallery and studio on Canyon Road. Ed is known for his talent in a wide range of subject matter and style in his paintings that range from Cowboy Folk Art to Abstract Expressionism. He also carves and constructs animals from wood. He is gaining recognition for his Story Quilt designs as these quilts are shown in various museums across the country. You can see his work at edlarsonart.com

JESUS SAID BUY FOLK ART

The first time I came to Santa Fe was 1949. I didn't know where Canyon Road was. The next time I came forty years had passed and everything was different. I had money. Not important money, but a lot more than I had in 1949 and I had this vague idea that Canyon Road was the place to be.

But in 1986 I was still living and exhibiting my folk art, paintings, wind toys, big fish, (fish that looked like giant pike plugs) and twenty-some picture quilts in Chicago. The gallery was in an area of Chicago called Noho. It was called the Zolla Lieberman Gallery. Zolla Lieberman was located in a long wooden five-story warehouse covering an entire block. It was the center of the Chicago Gallery World. I was doing okay.

One night the block-long wooden warehouse began to smolder. By nine the next morning the entire block was a roaring inferno. A friend called me. I was in a loft two miles from the gallery. I ran all the way to the fire.

I arrived at 9:30 thinking I could rescue my work. I couldn't. There was a cordon of police around the building. Where the Zolla Lieberman Gallery had been, fire roared from every window. All I could do was watch as this fine old wooden building burned to the ground. It took several weeks to cool. It looked like World War Two.

All my work for the past several years disappeared overnight. I thought this work was like, “me.” I thought I was all gone. Everything was destroyed. I had some rethinking to do.

Unlike most of the artists who exhibited there, I was lucky. My gallery had insurance. I came away from the insurance settlement with just under fifty grand. My buddy L. D. Burke was already in Santa Fe. He told me, “Come to Santa Fe, it will change your life.” That sounded good to me.

I already had representation in Santa Fe. It seemed like a good time to make a change. I moved to Santa Fe. This was 1989.

I went to what I thought was a first class real estate firm on Paseo de Peralta to see what I could afford to buy.

The firm I picked was surrounded by a prim picket fence. Everyone was busy. I was welcomed by one of the many agents.

I told her I was looking for a “fixer upper.” My Agent wanted specifics. “What price range would I be able to handle?”

I hiked my stake as far as it would go and claimed I could afford something just over $100,000. There was a long pause. My agent slowly closed the book of offerings. The next words I heard were, “I don't believe this is the town for you.” I was on my own.

I started driving around Santa Fe looking. It took awhile, but I found a property that would be a fantastic find today. In fact, it would be incredible.

There was a lot to do but there was room for my studio, and I began to paint. I also got busy making folksy furniture, carving birds, making wind toys and that is how I met Santa Fe Dave.

Santa Fe Dave had just opened a furniture store on Cerrillos Road in an abandoned service station. Dave and the people leasing the station claimed 42,000 cars passed by every day. Santa Fe Dave needed products he could sell. I placed some of my painted furniture with him. We did alright. Dave came over to my studio and when he saw my wind toys and off-the-wall art I became a part of his operation.

I became a contributing supplier of items to Outlaw Furniture, AKA, It Is Not On The Plaza—meaning we were out of the high rent district and could therefore beat down town Plaza prices. I was part of the Santa Fe scene.

It wasn't too long after this that I asked Santa Fe Dave, “What are you doing tonight?” Dave answered by saying, “I'm going to a meeting.”

“What kind of meeting?”

There was a pause.

Finally Dave said, “An AA meeting.”

I could not have been more surprised. “How come you are going to an AA meeting? You aren't an alcoholic.”

Dave, who is a big guy and maybe fifteen years younger than I am, is an easy guy to talk to. In fact, he talks all the time. He was very slow to answer.

"Because," he said, "when I drink I have blackouts."

To me this was a great relief and I told him that. I didn't want my friend to be an alcoholic. "Oh," I said, "Hell, that's nothing Dave, everyone has blackouts."

Dave said with a smile, "Maybe you should go to the meeting with me."

So I did. May 12, 1989. I haven't had a drink since. It wasn't that easy but I will try to flesh out the details as we go along.

Besides AA, Santa Fe Dave and I had a lot in common. We became very good friends. Outlaw Furniture became my hangout. On snowy days we sat around a wood stove and told stories. If people came that was okay. If they didn't, we invented things. We thought of new things to do. At one time we were going to do a musical on Billy the Kid. We got as far as the casting process. When the subject of how we would pay the actors came up, the project began to fade.

Dave talked me into making a perpetual motion machine. The result *looked* like a perpetual motion machine but we never tried it out. Our explanation to customers was that we had not perfected a proper brake and therefore were afraid we might never be able to get the machine to stop.

We actually sold this with a caveat that we were not responsible for our machine if the customer attempted to release the forces we had harnessed. We were not to be held liable.

We bought and erected a windmill. It creaked and so we filled up the oil well with oil. I never knew there was an oil pan that kept the mechanical part of the windmill lubricated. The wind blew that oil from the well all over our frontage till it was hard to walk without falling down. We found out the oil pan should have had a cover on it to keep the oil contained.

We created a hand-operated bull ride. Customers could ride our mechanical bull at their own risk. That sold right away.

Buster the skull man came by. He brought his skulls, so we sold skulls. Cow skulls. Goat skulls. Antelope skulls. But Santa Fe Dave had his principles, and he drew the line with Buster. We offered no human skulls.

Most of the people there were like me. We were all in the program and new to AA.

It made for interesting days and nights. Each of us worked the twelve steps in our own way. Sometimes that was funny. Sometimes it was hard. Some of us went back out.

We sold old boots, painted jackets, rugs, and furniture that cowboys didn't want anymore. We sold saddles and tack. We, well mostly Dave, did this. He sold an honest-to-God outhouse to a guy from Chicago. Shipping costs had not been properly estimated and I believe we lost money on this deal.

We produced a Billy the Kid bean bag game. I made it with directions from Santa Fe Dave. Billy never looked so good. He stood out front everyday till someone spirited him away.

Then there was this dangerous unknown kind of Rat we had caught and caged. Dave and I showed this very dangerous caged animal to only a few select clients. They had to be customers who had a heart strong enough to take a real shock.

This animal was caged in a box about the size of large boom box. It measured 30 inches by 12 inches by 12 inches. A sturdy screen covered one-half the top of the box. The other half of the box top was hinged and covered where this animal could den up. He usually hid there all the time.

The viewer would be told, "There is a kind of rat-like animal in there. We don't know what it is, but it looks very snaky. The damn thing stays in its cage and it is hard to get it to come out." All the while we would tap on the box to get the thing to come out of its den.

Then Dave or I would pick up the cage and shake it vigorously. I would suggest that the viewer get a little closer and maybe he or she could see it through the hole which it used to go into its den.

When the viewer was positioned just right, we would release the spring-loaded lid. The lid would snap open and out would fly a tanned squirrel's tail.

Some people ran all the way out of the shop.

Jack Palance looked into that trap and when it exploded Jack hardly moved. He didn't think it was a bit funny though, so it was hard to laugh while he was in the shop.

Pat Boone jumped.

Dennis Weaver didn't jump quite as high as Pat Boone did.

Everyday we moved all our furniture out of the garage and every evening we moved it back in. We added such Santa Fe Dave favorites as frying pan ashtrays, horseshoe clothes hangers, horseshoe lamps and cowboy signage like: "Wipe the shit off your boots before entering the kitchen." This was our Mother's Day special.

And to stay up with the rent money, Dave kept searching for new investors. Meanwhile, we kept taking in more program folks and forgetting the city gross receipts tax.

Stuff like this happened too often: Dave loaned one of our program people fifty dollars from the lease money. He promised to pay us back on Monday. And, of course on Monday he was a no show.

Well, stuff happens. Maybe the guy had a slip, i.e. maybe he had gone back out and started drinking again. We did have this rule that if you were using or drunk you were not to come to work. But we could not raise this guy on the phone, and when calls to his digs were not answered and two weeks went by, we had to figure it was time for those of us who were partners to pony up to pay the guy's receipt tax.. And then, finally he calls us.

"I am sorry I didn't pay you guys."

"Where are you?"

"I can't say that."

"Why not?"

"I can't."

"What's the matter? What happened to your promise to come in on Monday?"

"Well you know, I was coming in . . . . . . I just can't come in . . . ."

"Are you still there?"

"Yes. . . . . I robbed a bank."

"Oh. Well, now can you send us the money?"

"Not right now."

Later our guy tried to hold up an Armored Car in New England. He used a toy gun and it didn't turn out well. The last we heard, he would not be traveling our way for several years.

We drank a lot of coffee and we heard a lot of tales sitting around our wood stove. One of our guys lost his house because he owed back taxes. Then he lost his two front teeth due to a little too much of the grape.

He came back. We got a lawyer in the program to get his house back. I bought him two new teeth. He was looking really good. We felt great pride in this. We didn't give up on anybody. He went out again. This time he lost the teeth I bought him and shortly after that the house was gone too.

One day a customer came in and asked the price of a cane chair. Dave told him it was twenty-five dollars. The guy wanted a deal. He asked Dave, "Would you take twenty dollars?"

Maybe Dave was thinking about the fifty dollars, or the bank robber, but whatever he was thinking about, Dave lost it. Dave said, "You dirty blankety blank. . . . . You no good blankety blank. . . . . No good. . . . . blankety blank...." Dave could be very understanding, but he could also be very intimidating when he got started.

He chased the guy all the way to his car. The guy rolled up his windows and spun his wheels to get away from Dave. Gravel sprayed everywhere as he fishtailed out and somehow squeezed into the traffic going up Cerrillos Road. We were all stunned. Dave turned around and started walking back to the wood stove. I had followed him out of the store.

"Dave," I said, " I don't believe that guy is coming back here anymore."

We had a guy from the program who had been a speechwriter for Richard Nixon. He was a great guy. He was an educated man. He could be very funny. We all liked him. His problem was binge drinking. He consumed as much as three quarts of vodka in so many days. One day he went out, did his thing all in one day. It was too much. In less than a week he was dead.

This can happen to anyone. It is all one day at a time. (As I write this both Dave and I are still in the program, the twelfth step is all about helping others, one day at a time.)

In keeping with the twelfth step, part of Dave's thing was to take us all on outings on Sundays. He would load us in his van and off we would go to odd places Santa Fe Dave thought we should see. It might be an abandoned shale mine. Or maybe Ojo Caliente, where we would take the hot baths. Some of us needed that more than a visit to a shale mine.

Then we started getting very successful. People slowed down to see our latest offering. It just got better and better. Then it got too good. It all happened when Santa Fe Dave met this wealthy investor.

He was a producer with several successful hits. He wanted us. Well, not exactly us, he wanted the store. It was just too good to be. He saw our store as the nucleus of something ready to go nationwide. We had a gold mine. He saw in our store something special that we didn't know how to expand, and he wanted it to take off.

Did we have a gold mine? The store was really Dave’s, but I thought of it as mine now. I had stock in the store. If we had a gold mine, was I rich? Our investor was from California and he moved quickly.

He would take control. We would expand. We would become the source for cowboy furniture nationwide. Everyone would buy horseshoe towel racks. This nationwide thing had us going. Things happened so fast I don't know what happened. We started out seeking outlets in the East. Six weeks later we had nine new outlets. The next week we learned we were broke.

During the post mortem you could see what had happened. We did have something special, but it was not another Walmart. It was Santa Fe Dave and the way he took care of his drunks. We worked together and we loved the place. It was that Chicago fire all over again; only there was no insurance settlement this time.

A friend, “Whitey,” took me in up on Canyon Road. He had a space up where the glass blower had been. Everybody referred to this place as “the glory hole”. Whitey left after a bit for a career as a character actor in Hollywood, and I took over Whitey's space on the Road.

I was also showing at the Horwitch Gallery. Elaine died and that morphed into the Lewallen Gallery. Now I was showing at the Lewallen Gallery. Arlene died. The gallery world is not without change. Then I heard that George Millar was leaving the Stables, and he would leave his studio to me…if I wanted it.

George was a buddy. He was like everyone in Santa Fe, undergoing a mid-life crisis. He was going back to Canada. I could move in and just take over payments. No lease. No nothing. All I had to do was do it. George said if he came back in a year I would have to agree to leave. A year passed and he didn't return.

Okay. I would do it. The Stable's, as this compound was called, was owned by Juan Vigil. Juan was a wonderful man. His family consisted of twelve children. They had all grown up on Canyon Road. I knew one of his sons, David. He had given me a piece of signage that I had converted into a picture of the Airport west of Joplin on old Hwy 66. I'm from Joplin, Missouri. I painted all the bi-planes I remembered seeing out there at that old airport on that old signboard. It sold and I made my first rent. Thanks, David.

As George moved out, I moved in. The next month the only difference was I paid the rent, not George. I felt like I had arrived. I was on Canyon Road, where I am now, on the street called "The Art and Soul of Santa Fe." But being on Canyon Road is only one part of the equation. You have to pay the rent.

Canyon Road is not particularly selective, but it is quirky. First thing that happened was almost my swan song. I put up a big wooden sign. The sign read, "Ed Larson's Studio. Cowboy paintings, Wind toys, Big Fish and Nudes." George Vigil, one of Juan's sons, came over and told me that wasn't acceptable. Mr. Vigil said nudes were something he did not want to be associated with. He did not want me showing nudes in his stables.

I took the hint. I painted out nudes and changed it to poems. If you come by, I now offer poems free for the taking.

Now I have been in place on Canyon Road almost ten years. Twelve if you count the time that I spent with Whitey.

You can recognize my place next to the Tea House at 821 Canyon Road. There is a big green fish over the door. Under that fish is a sign that reads: JESUS SAID, BUY FOLK ART

Some people want to know where in the Bible it says that. I think you can find that in Ephesians.

FRANCINE FRIEDMAN

Francine Friedman is a psychotherapist by profession and a writer by passion. Originally from New York City, she has lived in SantaFe for thirty-six years and has weathered many changes to the city that pass for progress. She is also a jewelry historian because she needed to work with things beautiful and silent.

SANTA FE IN THE SEVENTIES

Nineteen seventies Santa Fe certainly had its share of characters.

The Camera Man was an elderly gent who lived in my neighborhood on Don Gaspar Ave. He was, at best guess, in his seventies. Summer and winter, he wore a drab overcoat and a hat with earflaps that were always down. He also wore two cameras around his neck, the old-fashioned accordion-pleated type. Every afternoon he would walk to the camera store opposite La Fonda Hotel and ask, "Are my pictures ready?" and every afternoon he was politely told, "No sir, you'll have to come back tomorrow." Needless to say, there was never any film in either camera.

Rubber Lady was an "artiste." She was dressed head to toe in what looked like a black wet-suit and had two spare tires around her waist. Her face was also covered in something that looked like Latex. You would see her either draped around a lamp post or standing on the Plaza frozen in an artful pose. No one ever found out who she was but the story goes that the police gave her a ticket for something like “disturbing the peace,” and she was never seen again.

Pablito was short with a round sun-weathered face that made him look like a dried apple. He was Super-Christian. He would walk around the Plaza with a Bible in his hand and stop anyone he could, quote some scripture and sing a few hymns. This took about half an hour and it was nearly impossible to get away. More often than not, if he saw a woman walking alone he would stop her and tell her: "You are a whore." After being his victim one time too many, I told him to watch his mouth, and he never came near me again.

Winnie Beasley was a hero and a character. Watching her tool around town in her vintage motorcycle, complete with sidecar, was a vision. She also wore an aviator's cap complete with goggles. Winnie was a pilot and carried mail during WW II. It was clear that she was reluctant to give up that exciting part of her life. Winnie had a stroke sometime in the Eighties and one of her sons took care of her and the beautiful horse ranch they had in Tesuque, a small village five miles north of Santa Fe.

Horace Aiken was Winnie's opposite. When I knew him, Horace was in his eighties and had an apartment in La Fonda Hotel. Rumor had it that he was a remittance man, that is someone whom the family paid to stay away. Mr. Aiken was always impeccably dressed for his daily constitutional in a homburg and navy pin-striped suit, red bow tie and white shirt with frayed cuffs and collar. He carried a silver-topped walking stick.

A bit later on, Skirt Man came on the scene. He was a Vietnam vet who walked the Santa Fe streets in an army jacket, combat boots, knapsack and skirt. His choice of skirts was fairly ordinary except for the white satin wedding gown, which he seemed to favor. The local newspaper did a small story on him in which he maintained skirts were much more comfortable than pants. Skirt Man was a vehement protester against nuclear weapons and would go up to Los Alamos, home of the atom bomb, to voice his opinions. After a few years, he just disappeared.

It was important to stand down-wind if you ever encountered Stinky Sam. Sam came from an affluent Pittsburgh family and was an antique dealer before succumbing to schizophrenia. He was also a remittance man. He lived in a storage unit—his girlfriend lived in an adjoining one—and conducted the business of buying and selling jewelry as he went from one store to the next. Sam, regardless of his non-existent hygiene, was one of the most honest people I've ever met. At that time I had a small booth in an antique mall. I always let him take a piece of jewelry from me if I felt he could make a few bucks, and he always came back a few days later either bringing the piece back, or with money to pay for it. At last sighting, Sam was taken back to Pittsburgh because his illness became more active.

We don't have characters in Santa Fe now. The city has grown and we have become more uptight so that street performers like Rubber Lady would not be tolerated. The seven-foot transvestite who frequented the old Safeway downtown, silently guarding the oranges, would be quickly and quietly dispatched to somewhere else. We have lost a lot of what made us The City Different and we have sadly become The City Same.

TOM HAMILL

A New Englander by birth and a New Mexican by adoption, artist Tom Hamill arrived in Santa Fe in the mid-1960s. With a bold style that fused realism with abstraction, Hamill's large oils depict the Maine mountains and the New England coast. He was a graduate of Bowdoin College who later studied at the Art Students League in New York and at the Skowhegan School of Art in Maine. Tom died in 2018.

FINN O'HARA VERSUS CLAUDE

An Incident at Claude's Bar

Claude James owned a bar on Canyon Road, a meeting place for a cross section of Santa Fe. Everybody came to it. It was a "mixed bag of assorted cookies." Claude was an incredible woman—gifted, raised in Paris and New York, migrated to Santa Fe—with a charismatic and unique personality.

Finn O'Hara was one of the "assorted cookies." He was one of those talented failures, an alcoholic who wasted his talents. But he had charm and was liked, but had a bitter and acid tongue. Claude didn't like him and vice-versa.

Then came a Saturday night, bar packed to the rafters, all the "cookies" plus Hal West and me, and then it happened! Finn was drunk and so was Claude. She was holding forth with tales of Parisian life. Then Finn moved in, not wanting to be upstaged. He insulted her. His back was to the wall and Claude, who had an arm like my thigh, swung at him. He ducked and her fist hit the wall with a loud THWACK!

The bar became silent as a tomb.

Finn said, "Is that your best shot, Claude?"

Finn was ushered out quickly and didn't appear for some time. Next day, Claude with a bandaged right hand was her usual self. That was her gift. Nothing fazed this remarkable woman, my dear friend.

TOM HAMILL

A DAY A SOFA WAS SAWED IN TWO

I lived on Canyon Road for twenty-five years.Willa Palou was my landlady, a wonderful, generous lady. We were close friends. During the Seventies, the hippie invasion occurred. Willa had two rental houses, besides the one she lived in. I lived in one. The remaining one was rented to a couple of St. John's students.

All went well until Willa noticed that this unit was visited endlessly by young people, hippies, at various hours. I noticed it too, and got suspicious. One day she heard a hand-sawing noise coming from this house. She thought it strange and called me. I hadn't heard it because my house was in back. The door being unlocked, we entered.

The fumes of drugs were overpowering. But what was shocking was the sofa. It has been sawed in two. The couple were giggling and sitting on the parts, with the saw and sawdust in-between, proud of what they had done.

"Why did you do it?" I asked.

"We wanted to make a love seat."

It was a life draining experience for us both. Poor Willa, who had not been well, had to be supported. We called the police, who had been staking out the house, to come at once and arrest the couple who had been dealing and using. They paid for the sofa and vanished to jail, never to attempt to saw another sofa. Hopefully.

TOM HAMILL

TOMMY MACIONE

Tommy Macione had been born in Sicily and lived there until he came to New York City about the 1930s. He studied art at the Art

Students League and then moved to Santa Fe. He had about twenty-three dogs and two were always limping. He never had any money and sold his paintings occasionally. Years later the city supported him after taking away his dogs, for hygienic reasons.

One day I saw him in Tito's Market, trailed by two dogs only. He spotted me and said joyfully, "I sold a painting." I congratulated him and looked into his cart. I saw one large T-Bone steak and four cans of Alpo dog food.

I said, "You're going to have a big steak dinner tonight!"

Then he said, very seriously, "No, that steak is for my dogs. The Alpo is for me. It is quite good."

I was surprised but I knew he was serious. That evening he and his dogs had a delicious meal.

PRISCILLA HOBACK

Priscilla Hoback lives in Galesteo, New Mexico where she has a ceramic studio, six Arabian horses, and a large garden. She is a regional artist inspired by archetypal images, native clays, and village life.

JOEY & ELVIS

I had ten neatly folded twenty-dollar bills stuffed deep in the pocket of my jean jacket. This money had been carefully saved to buy a horse of my own.

There were large cattle ranches north of Las Vegas on the open grasslands, good horse country. Every spring ranchers sold a few of the three-year-old colts.

I remember that Sunday afternoon so clearly, stepping carefully around clumps of dead yellow grass, a chilly spring wind made walking difficult. The sky was a brilliant blue, and I had to squint my eyes against the glare. It was one of those vivid New Mexico days.

We walked downwind toward the small herd of horses. A sturdy buckskin colt caught my eyes. Born on this ranch, he had been bred to be a cow pony; his history and blood showed in the color of his buckskin coat and tiger striped legs. His eyes were bright with intelligence.

This was my first venture in “horse trading”. I handed over one-hundred-fifty dollars. We shook hands, and I had my horse and the money to buy a used saddle.

One of the cowboys got a rope on him. We pushed him, stiff legged and shaking into the old trailer and drove back to Santa Fe. On the ride home I named him Joey. Probably because I always loved the folk song, “Little Joe the Wrangler.”

We were headed to a new stable on lower Alameda Street, next to the old WW2 internment camp.

Twenty miles away, you could see the twinkling lights of Los Alamos. Every day, Jack Blevans drove a big rig up and down the dangerous switch-back road carrying building materials, but on weekends he and friends roped calves and helped build the sheriff’s posse stables.

This stable was the center of my universe for the next few years. I thought of it as my home, my school, my job and the most wonderful place imaginable.

This posse rode as a mounted troupe, dressed alike in elaborate turquoise shirts, black and white chaps with initials branded deep into the leather. Many collected beautiful silver studded saddles, bridles and the horses to wear them.

I remember the architect, Mr. Kruger, bought a beautiful, spirited palomino horse in California. This horse, Goldie, was parade and high school trained. He pranced and bowed and was so fancy, and I was so smitten. Goldie opened a new world for me, one of show horses and trick training.

I grew up around cowboys and cow ponies. I had worked several summers at the Bishops Lodge Dude Ranch, saddling horses and helping with trail rides. Now I was around show horses, grooming and exercising them during the week to make the money that supported Joey and my pickup truck.

The wrangler who ran the barn was an old cowboy named Jim Bryant, recently released from the state prison on Cordova Road where he served time for robbing the Santa Rosa bank. Before he turned to crime, he had worked on a cattle ranch in Texas, where he trained young horses. He had the wry gentlemanly manner that comes naturally to western men. He knew a lot about life, survival, men, and being on one's own. He took me under his wing. I was a sponge and probably learned some things he never meant to teach.

But he did want to pass on everything he knew about horses. He showed me how to move slowly and speak softly around spooky horses, and to stay calm and always pay attention. He would coach me while leaning on the fence. "Feel his mouth." "Feel his feet." "You are so owl headed." Or "Quit running with your tail up." He thought of horse training as a one, two or three cigarette problem. This meant: "Slow down for as long as necessary. Relax and wait."

Joey quickly responded to saddling, riding, shoeing and vigorous grooming. No more shaggy tangled hair or cockle burs on his shinny black tiger striped legs. I polished his coat till it shined like copper.

The posse members were very kind to me. They rewarded my hard work with encouragement, support, and occasionally presents. One of my most prized gifts was a leather hand-tooled cup that attached to my right stirrup and securely held the flag pole. It is a proud thing to carry a flag horseback in front of the band.

There were many local rodeos in small towns that were called affectionately “pumpkin rollings.” They were all pretty much the same. A parade through the center of town, and a Saturday night cowboy dance with the dance hall decorated with twisted crepe paper streamers. Pickup trucks with kids and dogs and blankets backed up to outdoor arenas. Lots of local young men showing their skill, proving their courage and earning their manhood.

Rodeos began with the grand entry, the presentation of flags and the playing of the “Star Spangled Banner.” Posse members and contestants alike rode this serpentine parade. Often daddies carry their young children in front of the saddle, and handsome cowboys rode double with their sweethearts.

Then begin the main events of bronc riding, steer wrestling, calf roping, and bull riding. Mid afternoon, when they reloaded the bucking shoots with fresh stock, there was a crowd pleasing competition for the ladies. Ranchers' daughters and rodeo queens compete in a barrel race.

I trained Joey to run and turn. Barrel racing suited him: he was quick, handy and sure footed. Competing in front of the crowds was something new, scary and tough on the nerves, but one just “cowboyed” up. Slowly, I rode better, ran faster and this thrill grew in my blood.

Joey was “cowpony fast”, but not “thoroughbred fast.” Often our winning times were made because he could turn on a dime and give you five cents change. When racing the stopwatch you need to hurry every chance you get. I carried a quirt and would swat him on the straightaway but he ignored it most of the time. Being confident or perhaps a little lazy and much too smart for his own good, he preferred tricks for treats. He performed many of the very ones I first admired when performed by the palomino, Goldie.

Horses were welcome in Santa Fe then, and Joey would jump into the bed of my pickup, just like a big dog. We would go up San Francisco street, then around the plaza. There was a horse watering trough provided by the city next to the library. One time on a dare, a double dog dare, a friend and I rode into the Hotel La Fonda lobby, stepping gingerly up steps and across polished saltio tiles and then on into the bar. We were graciously asked to leave.

I remember being at Bert's Burger Bowl one afternoon with Joey in the pickup. I can clearly see my friends wearing pearl studded shirts, black rolled cowboy hats and sporting a few pimples on their lean faces. Peter La Farge put dimes in the jukebox and called me over to listen to a brand new song he was excited about—"Heartbreak Hotel."

I thought I would never have a bad day.

SUE WEST

Sue West grew up on a ranch outside of Santa Fe. In college she studied creative writing and began teaching ballet in Wyoming in 1979 while raising her three children. She has been artistic director for two dance companies, and has received three NEA grants. Voice of America *named her an outstanding artist of Montana, for her ballet,* The Dry Spell, *which won numerous awards. She is founder and producer of Synergy Videos, an exercise video on-line. She lives near Las Vegas, New Mexico.*

BEFORE SANTA FE BARS

The home on the ranch where I spent my childhood was adobe, made of mud bricks by Mexicans a hundred years before my youth. Imperfectly shaped to the closeness of the brown sod, and with each room built without forethought to go up and down with the shape of the land. The front porch that held the imperfect, thick walls was supported by white pillars of carved wood, chipped by years of dry winds and blowing New Mexico rains. I adored this home. It had a soul that made each of the children raised under its roof reach out for color and drama in their lives. I was born there in December 1946, the youngest of a family of six, freckled faced, near sighted and slightly redheaded.

"Chaquaco" was our name for this home where I spent my first twenty years. The memories of this time were seldom slow and quiet but exciting and hectic, for the West family had a certain zest for living, a capacity to make each occasion special, stretching it even beyond its due importance.

There is not one childhood memory more clear in my heart than the memories of country dances held in the large living room of Chaquaco. I can hear the music and laughter, the whooping and chatter. It wasn't just the dances themselves that I loved but the planning for weeks, and the thrill of the first headlights coming down the hill to reflect off the top of the windmill, followed by the headlights of a long line of cars coming to our dances.

My Irish mother fussed thoroughly about these dances, spending days waxing the brick floors on her knees with her head wrapped in a red bandana, washing windows and baking pies. My daddy on the other hand was easy going, putting off till the last minute the evening milking, and cleaning his boots with his pocket-knife in the kitchen as the first guests would arrive, smiling with easy charm while mother cleaned up the mess. The dances were the center stage of daddy's life, the fiddle player his director and each fat or skinny, pretty or homely woman his adoring fan.

The neighbors would come from miles away, the wife with starched petticoat and special cake; and the man, freshly shaven, smelling like the whiskey bottle tucked under his arm. The children came too, very much a part of these nights, running loud and boisterous in and out of the Virginia Reel, playing hide and seek through the rambling dark adobe rooms. We giggled, dancing with timid boys—step one two, one two. Weren't we good at it too? For days before we practiced dancing around the brick floor, often the palm of our own hand on the imaginary cheek of our boyfriend. We would eventually fall asleep on a pile of coats to be awakened at dawn when the party ended and the morning milking needed doing.

Perhaps it is the fact that those days and times are gone forever that make those nights so important to cherish. My children are making their own memories now, but those type of country people with their complete openness, coming from so far away as families to dance, drink, and visit, no longer seem to exist.

I have a sketch of a country dance hanging in my new home and this sketch is titled "Before Santa Fe Bars." The children in this picture are laughing, weaving in and out of dancing couples, the women poke their heads out of the kitchen, gossiping, a fat lady dances with a tall man and a baby sits on a daddy's shoulder while he taps his foot to the music. This picture is a part of my childhood, my past. Those people came to Chaquaco with rustling skirts and Stetson hats. The faces now become clear in my mind as I see each one. I can even feel daddy lifting me to his shoulder to dance high above the floor, twirling fast to the quick beat of the fiddle.

ANDRES ROMERO

THE HAMBURGER CONSPIRACY

As I was growing up, my best friends were two boys who lived next door. Of the two, I was closest to the younger. This was probably because he was the one very near to my age. He was about three weeks older than me. He was born on February 19th and I was born on March 8th.

The older brother was eighteen months older than both my friend and I. In those days, experience-wise, that was equivalent to a five-to-seven-year span in age difference today. To his younger brother and me, he was in another world.

I remember quite vividly that for most of my childhood, preteen and early teenage years, their mother would always have a birthday party for the younger brother on the Friday following his birthday. His birthday fell right in the middle of the Lenten season. All the little boys in the neighborhood would be invited to his birthday party, and we all knew that everybody would be served hamburgers. There were always ten to fourteen boys at the birthday party. Everyone would have hamburgers. That is everybody, except me. Being a Catholic, and out of respect for my devout and religious parents, his mother would fix me a fried egg sandwich. Everybody would be chomping away on his mouth-watering, juicy hamburger with (or without) cheese, tomatoes, lettuce, onions, and pickles. Some would be generously lavished with mustard, catsup, or maybe even mayonnaise. Boy, how I would crave a hamburger. The sight of a hamburger with all the trimmings would cause me to salivate.

I did not know it then, but I began practicing a very rudimentary form of visualization. I would fall into a kind of a trance and dream of biting into a warm meat patty with cheese. As it slowly melted in my mouth, my palate would simultaneously taste the semi-tart mixture of mustard and catsup. Awakened to reality, I had to force myself to eat a plain old egg sandwich.

God, there is only so much one can do with a fried egg sandwich, and besides, what else can one put on it, except salt and pepper? For a sandwich, an egg can only be fried three ways; sunny-side up, medium or thoroughly cooked.

After my friend's birthday parties I would come home and go to bed disappointed, frustrated and mistrustful of the justice in the universe, and then dream of hamburgers tumbling over a fence.

My earliest ambition at this very young age was to someday own a hamburger establishment. This was eons before the advent of hamburger franchise chains.

Weeks before the birthday party I would try to think of ways of solving my birthday party dilemma. One time, I even thought of fibbing to my friend's mother by telling her that I had a special dispensation from the Vatican to eat meat on Fridays.

It was only my strong altar boy background and my exemplary Cub Scout training that prevented me from doing so. It's not that I didn't try other approaches, because for weeks before the party, I would tax my imagination by trying to come up with a plausible explanation as to why I should be allowed to partake in this hamburger feast that, by now, I considered a special delicacy. Try as I might, I could never really figure out how to circumvent this seemingly insurmountable obstacle that lay between me and a delicious hamburger. One time, the boy sitting next to me at one of the birthday parties, seeing my anguish, offered me a bite out of his hamburger. Boy, was I ever tempted! For a second there, all the religious instruction and Cub Scout training came close to flying out the window. I almost succumbed to temptation.

Suspecting that the devil was behind this, I quickly weighed the consequences of this temporal pleasure as opposed to eternal damnation in the fires of hell in the company of Lucifer and his gang. So I resisted. I didn't take a bite. Besides, I told myself, I have this severe aversion to heat and, temperature-wise, that hell place didn't sound too inviting.

Another time I really thought that I would solve this dilemma by becoming a Protestant—a Presbyterian or Episcopalian or even a Baptist—for a week. I thought that perhaps I could get a week's leave of absence from Catholicism and thereby not have to abide by the canons of the Church.

One birthday gave way to another and the years passed, and before I knew it we were out of grade school, out of junior high and out of high school. Years later, sometime after my stint in the military, and while in college, I read in some newspaper that the Vatican had changed the rules governing the eating of meat on Fridays. Imagine how shocked and disappointed I was when I read that any Catholic could now eat meat, including hamburgers, on any Friday during the year, except on Good Friday during Holy Week.

Now, every time I have a hamburger, I remember my friend's birthday parties and all the hamburgers that I couldn't have and all the fried eggs sandwiches I had to force myself to eat.

To this day I still crave and thoroughly enjoy a good old fashioned hamburger with all the trimmings. Someday, when I approach the autumn of my life, I know that I will pray that reincarnation doesn't exist, because if it does, I would really hate it if I came back to this earth as a chicken or an egg. Or is it an egg or a chicken? Oh, well . . .

BEVERLY McCRARY

Beverly McCrary was an English teacher who lived in Santa Fe for most of her life. Her passion was designing clothing based on Middle Eastern garb and embellishing the dresses with charms, beads, sequins, buttons and mirrors. Her writing is based on childhood experiences growing up in Santa Fe. Beverly died in 2002.

MY CHILDHOOD SCARE

In 1949, on a warm spring day at Wood Gormley School in Santa Fe, I was a pre-first grader in Mrs. Grace Yontz's class. On that particular day I was to go to my dancing class after school. When the afternoon dismissal bell rang, I gathered my lunch pail, my dancing clothes and shoes, and Margo Gerber and I walked the block and a half to the studio on East Manhattan Street where Mrs. Dorothy Parks taught tap and ballet to little girls. It was a big room, empty save for dance bars against the walls, a line of chairs and a record player on a small table.

All the girls changed clothes and put on their tap shoes. Ten little bird-legged girls clacked our way along the wooden floor to a space at the dance bar. I, being the very tiniest child, had to reach way up to wrap my little fingers partially around it. Mrs. Parks showed us the steps and started the music. Tap, tap, tap, tap, slide. Turn left, swing your arms. Repeat. Slowly spin around. Begin again. After dancing this for fifteen minutes or so, we stopped to rest and change our shoes for ballet.

Mrs. Parks left the room and went out back to use the outhouse. Our dance building had no indoor plumbing, so during the break before changing my shoes, I went out too.

I skipped slowly down the alley looking at the rocks and weeds, turned at the rear of the building and walked up to the outhouse. When my teacher came out, I went in and hooked the door. It was a small, dark place. I waited for my eyes to adjust, then stood on my tippy toes and sat on the wooden seat to go to the bathroom. It seemed so black in there that I did not want to stay long. When I was ready to leave I unhooked the door and pushed. Nothing happened! I pushed harder. Again, nothing. I stood there scared, not knowing what to do. My tap shoes clicked against the floorboards. I looked up to the ceiling in case any spiders might be coming down to land on me. The place smelled. I shoved the door harder and harder. Still locked! And then the tears. Rolling down my little face, dripping onto the front of my purple tutu. Small gasps as I began to sob. I could see the dirt outside through the cracks in the wall boards, could see the sky, the weeds, but I was shut in. Stuck! Alone! I didn't know what to do. Then through a small crack at the edge of the door I saw that the outside hook was latched. On no!! Oh no!! Sob!! My little body was shaking as I cried even harder.

It could not have been too long that I was in there, but it seemed forever. Later when the door did open, there stood Mrs. Parks, who had absentmindedly hooked the outside of the door when she left. When she opened that wooden door, she took my hand and gently pulled me into the sunlight. She hugged me, told me that everything would be all right and took me back to the dance room. I was still quite upset but knew I was safe.

I do not recall ever going into that outhouse again. Fortunately, there are very few outhouses still in use in Santa Fe, but even now I rarely use an outhouse and if I must, I always make certain to put a rock in the door to keep it part way open.

ANDRES ROMERO

ORALE! JOHN WAYNE

(*Note*: *"orale" means "okay," "alright," "come on."*)

I had a lifelong friend whose idol was the late cowboy actor, John Wayne. When we first met, he told me his nickname was "Duke." Out of curiosity, I asked him who gave him the nickname, or how he came to get it. "I gave it to myself," he told me, "because John Wayne has always been my hero."

Even when he was dating the girl that later on became his wife, it was widely understood that if there was a movie on television featuring John Wayne, all other activity would be automatically canceled, or postponed. He was truly a devout fan. Later on, when he married his long time sweetheart, they had a son he named Sean Wayne.

One Tuesday evening in the early part of May, I became somewhat bored staying home and decided to go out and treat myself to a drink. I decided to go to this restaurant-nightclub named "The Zambra," where a good friend of mine tended bar. As I entered the nightclub, I noticed that it was rather empty. As I approached the bar, my bartender friend greeted me with, "Too bad our friend 'Duke' is not here. His hero, John Wayne, and his friends are sitting at that big table having dinner." It turned out that John Wayne was in town filming, *The Cowboys*. As I sat down at the bar, I asked my bartender friend to send a round of tequila to the table where John Wayne and his co-workers were sitting. I was the only one sitting at the bar. After about fifteen minutes or so, John Wayne came up to the bar and asked the bartender, "Who is this gentleman named Romero?" Being the only one at the bar, the bartender pointed to me. John Wayne came over to me and said, "I want to thank you for the round of tequila. I would like to reciprocate. Is there a specific reason you chose to buy us a round of Tequila?" I explained that his number one fan in northern New Mexico was a good friend of mine, and I had bought and sent over the tequila in his honor. Before I knew it, John Wayne and I had consumed three rounds of tequila. Not being a drinker, I became very light headed rather fast. I remember stating that I had a problem, to which John Wane countered “What kind of problem do you have?”

"I don’t know what to call you. Do I call you Mr. Wayne, John or Duke?"

I will never forget his answer. “Son, I don’t care what you call me, just as long as you smile.”

Next thing I knew, I was inviting him to a Cinco de Mayo Party that would take place the following Friday evening at this place that I patronized, called the Estrada Room.

“Our film office is located at the Desert Inn. Stop by and leave the address to the place, and I will see if I can make it,” he said.

The next day I dropped off the address at the Desert Inn. Friday finally got here and I went to the Estrada Room right after work, thinking John Wayne was so busy he would not show up. After about an hour, I decided to leave and to go pick up my date. As I left the premises, I ran into John Wayne and his body guard as they were coming up the ramp.

“Hey, Romero, is this place? Take me in and introduce me to the proprietor.”

My friend "Duke"and his wife had gotten here early and were sitting in a booth. As luck would have it, he was facing the wall and did not see me and John Wayne and his bodyguard come up to his booth. I tapped my friend on the shoulder and said, “Duke, there is someone here that I want you to meet. Duke, I want you to meet John Wayne.”

My friend was speechless and could not believe his eyes as John Wayne said, "Nice meeting you, Duke" and shook his hand.

GERRY WOLFF

Born in San Francisco, Gerry Wolff studied landscape architecture and environmental planning at the University of California, Berkeley and at Stanford University. Gerry relocated from San Francisco to Santa Fe several years ago and is now exploring her new environment and its inhabitants.

ADAN

(*Note: This story was written after workshop participants had read aloud "The Good Anna" by Gertrude Stein and were asked to write a story imitating her style.*)

Work. He knew what work was. More than anybody I know of, he knew what work was. He, Adan, was from Mexico—the middle of nowhere, Mexico. A small town with an Indian name, somewhere between Guadalajara and Zacatecas, but a bit closer to Zacatecas, where saddles were made and cattle were roped. Adan rode horses and roped cattle. He even won a local rodeo contest roping cattle and tying their feet—the fastest.

Work. Adan—Adam—was the first son. Adan was a needed worker. His father, Juan, took Adan from their home ranch and deposited him at the family's other land holding, to take care of the animals—horses, cattle, pigs, goats—to feed them, milk them, guard them—and to grow squash, melons, beans, corn, peanuts, chiles, tomatoes. Adan was alone at this holding—all week. Adan cooked for himself—tortillas, vegetables, meat that he had slaughtered—and he was only seven years old!

"I wasn't afraid."

Adan got only a few hours each Sunday with his mother, Altagracia, who took him to church, then cooked the Sunday meal at the main house and ranch, until his father, Juan, returned Adan to his solitary station and responsibility to start yet another week of work. He was alone. And Adan was only seven years old. It was his station for another seven years until the second boy arrived to assist in the work. Any thought of attending school was only a fleeting thought. No chance. Work had to be done, relieved only by his mother's Sunday meal—his time of learning values—and a Sunday visit to church.

School. There was a school nearby—maybe two miles away—an easy walk—but not within reach. There was neither time nor money—where time is money—to permit Adan to go to school. Not even for one day did Adan go to school. Therefore, Adan did not learn to read or write. What he could read or write he taught himself by being observant. Adan taught himself English, not correct English, but workable English. Adan was intelligent. He saw all and said little. He was smart and a bit psychic. He could read people and their motivations quickly and accurately. But more important, he had integrity. Adan was honest. He learned this from his mother, Altagracia.

Rest. Rest is the payoff. Rest is the reward for a lifetime of hard work—farming in Mexico and garden installation and maintenance in the United States for over forty years. Although rest is not yet at hand, rest is within sight: Adan "retires" at New Year's from work with big, demanding, pressure-driven landscape firms. But after fifty-five years of hard work, Adan will not stop working. He cannot. He needs the income. And work is part of his soul, his honor. Adan will continue to work but at a slower pace, at his choice of time, and for people he chooses—in their gardens. And, maybe, he will even have a chance to rest in his white,

Mexican string hammock for which he has been saving symbolically for just such time—his time of rest; or actually, his time of slower-paced work.

PATRICIA D'ANDREA

Pat D'Andrea grew up in New Mexico and has lived in Santa Fe since the 1970s.

TAMALES

Santa Fe is the "City Different." That means that the whole city is supposed to look like it's made of adobe, whether it is or not. There are neighborhoods here which are more than a hundred years old and not made of adobe. One of these is a small neighborhood one block south of the capitol that was built when the railroad almost got to town in the 1860s. It's one short street called East Santa Fe Avenue. Most of the houses are brick bungalow style with pitched roofs, porches and small fenced yards. There are big elm trees along both sides of this street and the sidewalks have all buckled because the tree roots have pushed them up at the seams. Little skateboard ramps—up and down. It was hard to walk on those sidewalks in 1973 when I lived there.

That year Sofía, the Escamilla's daughter from next door, had moved back to town from Mexico City with her husband and their three boys. He was a professional wrestler, a real one, not a showy TV wrestler who wears silver capes. There wasn't any work for him in Santa Fe. So they decided to cook for a living. Sofía was a wonderful cook. I guess she said, "Why not?"

One Christmas, Sofía, Antonio and their boys decided to make tamales for the Christmas trade. The boys were little, rambunctious, and not useful in the kitchen. That left Antonio, also not useful, Sofia's parents (too old), and, finally, Sofía.

She had started by making *biscochitos*, which were very popular with the neighbors. Tamales were more difficult, complicated and demanding, but Sofía was determined. Would I help? she asked. Sure, I said. Little did I know.

Sofía got together a team—Olivama (short, stout, and quiet) came from up north in Peñasco. Julia and Rosalinda, dyed-blonde sisters from Delicias in Chihuahua sang a lot and worked so fast no one else could keep up. The big work began on December 23, a Tuesday, but before that Sofía had boiled the chicken and pork, shredded the meats and mixed them with Chimayo red chile powder, garlic, oil, comino, salt and pepper.

Olivama mixed the *masa* (dough) with the broth, chile and comino and kept the big table supplied with huge bowls of the dough. She was also responsible for soaking the *hojas* (corn husks) in the sink until they were soft, then spreading them on a towel at the big table.

Julia and Rosalinda smoothed the masa on the corn husks with spatulas, then laid them on the table next to me. I put a tablespoon of meat on each. Sofia folded and wrapped the tamales, stacked them in the big steamers on the stove, and set them tocook. When the tamales were cooked and then cooled, Olivama wrapped them in waxed paper, Sofía put them in plastic bags, one dozen in each, and then into the big refrigerator.

The dark kitchen seemed brighter in the heat from the stove, full of the smell of good red chile, garlic, comino and anise. The little boys ran in and out, Julia and Rosalinda sang, Olivama worked quietly, Sofía was everywhere, full of energy, her dark hair standing out like it was electrified. When we stopped for *empanadas* (a pastry) and coffee, Sofía told us, "We've got to make eighty dozen by tomorrow." By seven we'd made twenty dozen. Long night ahead.

Not being a cook myself, I'd offered to do this work in exchange for a "lifetime supply" of tamales, biscochitos, and empanadas. Also, I had the idea that being a neighbor meant helping out, something I'd already learned from our small street.

About eleven thirty Antonio came in with a bottle of José Cuervo Especial and a bottle of Rom Pope.

"Remember," he said, "José Cuervo does not do time."

That started Julia and Rosalinda on a round of jokes and toasts."*Viva Méjico!*" "*Viva tamale!*" and so on. The tequila was sharp, the Rom Pope was smooth and sweet.

Pretty soon I had a little bit more and we sang a version of "La Cucaracha." By this time, even Olivama was singing. We toasted each other again.

After a while, Sofía said, "Time to go home," and I remember her guiding me to the door and me stumbling down the steps, through the gate and into my own back yard, breathing in the cold air and the smell of red chile on my hands.

Sometime the next morning (it seemed like it was really early but maybe not), I heard the front door bell. It was Sofía.

She looked at me closely and said, "Could you do a little more?"

"Sure," I said.

By then they were on dozen number sixty-three and they were all tired, so I took over one job after another while each one rested. And I ate a lot of tamales, the ones that weren't perfect. By that afternoon when we finished, I had probably eaten two dozen tamales.

After all the tamales were delivered that Christmas Eve, the kitchen seemed too quiet. We all had bowls of *posole, Noche Buena* beer and laughed about the two dozen tamales I'd eaten.

Then we hugged each other and went out into the snow to go home.

LIZ JEFFERSON

Transplant Liz Jefferson has lived in northern New Mexico for more than half a century. Her integration into New Mexico culture happened through other transplants. "Brinck" is the story of one such influential encounter.

BRINCK

John Brinckerhoff Jackson looked me in the eye with a direct approach that managed to be both gracious and honest. Dressed in felt cowboy hat and leather boots, blue jeans braced with a leather belt latched with a silver buckle and a turquoise stone, we were almost eye to eye.

"Hello, and how are you?" he asked.

Landscape Magazine was advertising for a part-time person to assist with circulation. A Canyon Road address. Editor and publisher, John Brinckerhoff Jackson. A magazine business housed in a two-room, adobe-looking building, certainly not a corporate establishment. I was face to face with *the* John Brinckerhoff Jackson. Brinck was a professor at Harvard and UC Berkeley. Fluent in languages, he spoke seven, as I recall.

A brief interview covered the basic skills needed. Business manager Sylvia Loomis was in the room and part of the interview. Even then, Sylvia was gray haired and had the demeanor of a purse-lipped maiden lady. She was far from that. Sylvia was a Quaker. Socially and philosophically she was a liberal, walking around in grandmotherly-like gathered cotton skirts and flat shoes.

I soon realized that her soft-spoken manner disguised a will of steel.

My own flat Midwestern voice, tailored suit and hose covered a pedestrian attitude that did not blend with the general atmosphere. We stood there, all aware my outlook was different from theirs. Would our personalities blend at work? Brinck's New Jersey accent, Sylvia's soft spoken demeanor, and my own unadorned pragmatic expressions were to form an unlikely trio.

"The job is part time," Brinck informed me, "six hours a week. Magazine circulation is about three thousand and you would be responsible for the mailing."

Sylvia asked: "Can you prepare the mailing list and update the subscriber information?"

Armed with my resume, work skills, and experience, I answered, "Oh, yes."

Brinck decided I would be added to the staff.

"Sylvia is business manager and your position is circulation manager."

Editor, business manager and circulation manager, all work was part time and all had titles. Operation of the business affairs was assigned to Sylvia and to me.

Brinck was concerned that *Landscape Magazine* project a professional appearance. Its covers were a blend of interesting photography with glossy exterior and creative type styles to project sophisticated literature. The polished veneer provided a bold introduction and insight into the content.

La Cienega was a small community near Santa Fe. Local residents were mostly Spanish. A small and active community, local fiestas and celebrations were routine. J. B. became a patron to La Cienega, sponsoring events and projects for resident families. His decision to build a swimming pool became a time consuming project. Dealing with business details caused him to pace in and out, back and forth, muttering to himself and talking to us. The land, dimensions of the pool, dealings with the local advisors and contractors were interruptions and intrusions on his academic pursuits and interests.

Interested in people from all cultures and walks of life, Jackson took every opportunity to talk with everyone around him. A visit over Danish in his kitchen was interrupted by a young local woman knocking on his back door. Immediately he began assessing some papers she showed him. He counseled her on classes. His manner was that of financier and professor. Quietly observing them, I had an image of him sitting on the steps at UC Berkeley in jeans, hat and boots, with an intense face, a student by his side, gently guiding her thought in good directions.

Inquiries about my life were interspersed with our office conversations. A busy year 1959. My marriage was ending. My sister was getting married in my Santa Fe home. I needed legal advice concerning my divorce. Without being asked, Brink provided that. Next he asked about the wedding—where, when, and those involved.

My mother arrived early for the wedding. Immediately Brinck invited the bride and groom, mother and me, to his ranch for dinner. A gracious host and excellent cook, Brink did it all. Totally organized, the dinner was on the stove, and the scent of old fashioned cooking filled the house. Included with the hors d'oeuvres was an invitation to view his private pond. It was Jackson's routine to skinny dip in the pond each morning, which was recessed in an area of green meadow, surrounded by trees. The groom accepted the invitation. Quiet and inviting, the water's temperature was refrigerator level. The groom came back to the dinner party looking pale blue, wondering if four days to his wedding night were enough to recover.

Brinck received the wedding invitation and asked, “Liz, I’d like to come to the wedding. Do you mind if I ride my motorcycle?”

“Arrive on whatever," I responded. "Just come."

He explained further: "On Sundays I ride my cycle to northern New Mexico to chart points of interest and inspect roads."

I still have a vision of him standing on the entryway of my adobe-looking home in Casa Alegra. Eyes wide, observing this mostly Los Alamos working class group, motorcycle parked among the cars. Attending the church ceremony, then the reception, it was a world of people and conversation with which he had little familiarity. The abundance and quality of the gifts, the humor and easy conversation intrigued and amazed him.

Our working relationship changed as my life changed. As I divorced, remarried and had a child, we lost contact for a number of years. In my dotage, I decided to go to college. The best advice around would come from Brink Jackson. I telephoned him.

"Of course," he said “come on Thursday at 10:00 a.m.”

We met and he welcomed me as if he had seen me yesterday. Of course, we talked in the kitchen. An antique looking stove stood by the wall. Reaching for the tea kettle, for a pan of muffins, for cups for coffee, he asked questions. Mulling over my responses, he provided insight and direction.

We made sporadic contact over the years as I visited New Mexico family and friends. At times he revealed a little of his background, and finally that he was ill. In 1993 he received the Pen Award for a book of essays. I last saw him about 1995. Evidently ill but still mobile and alert, we talked intensely during the brief time we had. I learned of his passing via a clipping of his obituary. John Brinckerhoff Jackson is buried in the cemetery at La Cienega, the community he loved and lived in with gusto.

Always a life in transition, originally he was John Brinckerhoff Jackson, known as Brinck. Then he became J. B. Jackson. His last request of me was to call him John.

LIZ JEFFERSON

MERRY-GO-ROUND HOUSE, OR CHASING ONE'S TALES

Opening one eye as the alarm rings, I jump out of bed and start to throw on my clothes. Pulling up my panty hose and tucking in my blouse, I run out of the house, across Don Gaspar, into the Bataan Memorial Building, just in time to report to a new job.

Heels clattering on the floor, my shoulder bag slipping off and the drooping purse clutched in one hand, I step into a hallway and enter the new Technical Services Office.

"Hello, I'm Liz Jefferson," I say to the man behind the desk.

We shake hands.

"I'm Tom Reed," he says.

The room is sterile. A chair, a bare desk, an empty file cabinet. Later, the calm atmosphere turns out to be deceiving.

I open my desk drawers and notice a confusion of papers. I tell Reed, "A file system needs to be established, from scratch."

Reed nods in confirmation. "`I'll take you to meet the chief, and then the district officers."

I follow him silently down the corridor. I notice looks of apprehension on faces peering out the doors from their desks. Living in Española, the cultural gap between Anglos and Hispanics is familiar. This organization of local Hispanics with an Anglo boss had raised apprehension.

As newly appointed Chief of the Bureau of Revenue, Martin Johns was both respected and feared. He was recently appointed by the governor. He is a respected attorney, short with intense eyes behind round glasses; his posture and body language shouts confidence and authority.

His task is to shape up the tax collection system. Up to the present, tax records and submissions have been manually handled. Johns intends to computerize receipts and records to plug the holes—missing records—that patronage has created and that results in tax evasion.

The chief's office is spacious with a reception room staffed by a slim-lipped older woman.

Mary greets us: "Welcome to the Bureau,"

One side of the room has a door to the chief, on the opposite side an entrance to the deputy chief. A tiny room to his right is reserved for the deputy's secretary.

"Pink memo pads are the exclusive use of Mr. Johns," Mary informs me. "All departments and division heads will use green forms."

She tells me that the Bureau has seven divisions, and that information and requests are to be routed to Johns, and through her to the deputy chief, then through his secretary to division heads. Around and around the merry-go-round of halls in the Bataan building travels the bureaucracy.

Division chiefs mentally, if not physically, tiptoed in and out of Johns' office. The Bataan building's square corners are a pathway for chasing one's fears, dreams and anticipations. Santa Fe headquarters begins to be regarded as a "command post." Departments down the hall and around the corners receive the reports of the seven division offices. Their mandate is to carry out tax laws and collections and to distribute information. But accurate reporting has not been the practice.

Patronage was. "Bill, my sister needs a job. Her husband is ill, her kids have to take a bus to school, rent is due and there's no food in the house." That kind of story got a typist a job and an auditor a desk.

Johns announces that tax auditors will have training sessions in Santa Fe. He reinstates tests that are already in place but not given, and establishes qualification standards. Fear is rampant. The staff responds by smiling, by saying, "Yes sir, of course," but are resentful. Johns also announces that he will visit district offices regularly.

He has desks removed and replaced with tables. Desk drawers full of unfilled, unreported paper are pulled out and dumped on the floor. Green memos from the staff fly to the Chief of Tech Services. Pink slips from the chief are returned with comments or instructions.

Attorneys are now used to drive the chief and business is conducted every mile on the road. Johns brings stacks of scratch sheets for notes. When he returns from one of his trips he calls Reed into his office. Reed returns, holding out his hand to me he asks, "What's this?" Wide-eyed, mouth open, a little in shock, he held over a hundred tidbits of work assignments to take care of.

The staff responds with constant passive resistance.

"Oh, did you want that today?"

"I cannot find that file."

"Matilda promised me I would have your answer later today."

Each of these is logged and sent to the chief, and from him it goes to the deputy commissioner. Nothing is ignored or lost.

One day I leave my room and return to find more papers. I look for a document, it is no longer where I put it. "What is this?" I wonder as I read a paper I did not remember seeing before. Another day I return to my office to see Jean in front of my desk, standing in her white go-go boots and stylish short skirt, black hair framing her intent face. She holds a large fistful of papers in one hand, and with the other is inserting a smaller set into papers already on my desk.

"What are you doing?"

"Uh, oh, I was just…" she mutters and spins around, into the hall, white boots clattering on the floor, shoulders erect.

I am relieved to know that I am not losing my mind, that memos and correspondence are being lifted from, and inserted into, the work on my desk. The paper game by Jean continued to my last day.

Words, words, and more words. So much information. I cram it all on one page, but Johns tells me, "Content should be placed like a piece of art in a frame. Don't jam the message—use white space."

With all the hustle and scuffling, everything moves along. We become more professional and business-like in appearance. Auditors are trained. The wheels spin efficiently in an ethical yet compassionate operation.

Sylvia was head of Word Processing. When she left her job to follow husband and family to a new location, a car accident took her husband before arriving at their new life. Word reached the Bureau immediately. Her resigned supervisory position is put on hold, waiting for her. She returned to Santa Fe.

Many friendships develop with women struggling to support homes and children, as I am. The male supervisors, entrenched long before Martin Johns, or myself, are another matter.

Personnel routinely posts announcements of state jobs. An opening in another newly established office, the Governor's Policy Board for Law Enforcement, lets me exit the Bureau on a high note. Though perhaps slightly falsetto.

I am blessed with a replacement, Victoria, with two weeks to train her. She has passed her qualifying skills exam, and we rework six-month old files. As we check files, making new categories, we open what had been an empty drawer.

"Those papers were not there earlier," she exclaims. Jean has continued her paper sabotage to my last day.

Friday afternoon I do the amenities, says adios to Reed, Mary, Johns and others. My purse on my shoulder, slipping only slightly as the door slams behind me, I cross the street.

"Hi," my daughter greets me.

SUSAN CLOUGH

Susan Clough, a native Californian, considers herself a citizen of the world. A long, hot stint in Libya followed by a long, cold stint in Alaska preceded her 1990 move to Santa Fe where she found the weather just right. She is an incorrigible hiker, lover of wine, food and languages.

BORDER CONTROL

In 1990, following decade-long stints in Libya and Alaska, I put down firm stakes in Santa Fe, New Mexico. A wasteland merely in terms of annual rainfall, it oozes culture and the greatest of outdoors. I tilt toward the latter. Putting one foot in front of the other, poking on trail and off, I'm a trail gypsy in this magically eroded land. Molly Bloom, my old golden retriever, is my default hiking buddy. Sometimes she and I hook up with other trail gypsies. We stay high when it's hot and low when it's cool. As the trail years added up, we shelved the hiking guides and pick up local topo maps. We leave the security of beaten-down trails. Time to be off the map.

High drama on a hike is rare, but happens. One January Wednesday in 2000, five gray-haired, gung-ho women and two dogs gather west of town, set to hike the arroyos till we hit the big 'ole Rio Grande. Spirits high, we tough through deep arroyo sand. Rag-tag fences cut through this desolate, prickly space. Looks like poor grazing land. I hear it's BLM land and fence jumping's okay, as is slithering under rusty tatters of barbed wire while crossing arroyos.

I hear shouts.

"Stay where you are!"

A man jumps from behind a juniper tree. He's no friendly hiker. We freeze at the sight of him. He wears a camouflage shirt, combat boots and is packing heat.

He yells some more: "You are trespassing on Tesuque Tribal land."

Stony silence in our ranks. Will he shoot us? He's wearing some sort of badge. Has he been following us? The dogs must sense fear and stick close. He takes out his radio and calls for support. Against us??? What are we in for? There's a hill not too far to the north and someone's up top. Oh, my god, a sentinel. The word "ambush" rushes in. I think about being scalped or, more likely, raped. That gun keeps me and the others rooted in the sand. Two scary thirty-year-old Libyan memories rush in.

1967 in downtown Tripoli I'm being attacked by a boy with a big fat stick. Behind him thirty others glare with hate-filled faces, rocks in hand. I run like hell as the volley of hefty stones glance off me. Enemy American! Jew lover!

Another ambush. Lonely Libyan beach. Early 1970s. A military Land Rover and a Saladin tank churn up the sand and stop six feet from our umbrella. The Land Rover is stuffed with soldiers. Uzi carrying Libyan soldiers hang all over the tank. "Emshee!"—"Get the hell out of here!"—someone shouts. After tossing off more menacing Arabic, they head back down the beach. We wonder why they are on our case. We grab towels and beach umbrellas and make a beeline to our cars. 0nly to find out that our friend's hefty station wagon is stuck in the sand. Push or pull, we can't budge the beast. What next? The tank and the Land Rover come back. The teenage Uzi bearing Libyan soldiers hop from war cars and mingle menacingly. They hook a cable from their Land Rover to our stuck car's bumper. The car's bumper falls to the sand. Losing face can make us dead meat or certified CIA. Five silent soldiers push the car. Crisis resolved. We scoot. Whew! Ghaddafi has taken the beach for a training camp.

Back in the Santa Fe arroyo, four hefty trucks fighting through the sand are heading our way, rooftop lights flashing. All the Tesuque Indians piling out of the trucks are dressed identically to our accuser. With guns at hips, these Tesuque reinforcements seem embarrassed at what landed in their net and merely paw at the sandy arroyo with their big black boots. Number One accuser demands our names and addresses, searches our packs. What can he say to dog treats, dog leashes and celery with peanut butter? What he says is that we must appear asap at Tesuque Pueblo headquarters.

"Now. And bring your drivers licenses."

In stunned silence we slog through the arroyo back to our cars, relieved that we are alive but sad and mad about the sting. We all drive out to Tesuque Pueblo.

Our accuser snaps up our licenses, slaps a traffic citation pad onto the bare wooden table and silently and meticulously fills out five criminal trespass citations. No such luck as a slap on the wrist. This is extortion, plain as day. One week from today we are to appear for our trial. Minimum fine per person $500. Maximum fine $5,000.

Trial morning, one week later, my phone rings. In a terse voice the Arresting Indian informs me that there will be no trial today.

"You have two choices. You can settle out of court with me—and maybe one of my bosses—without the judge. You will each pay what we decide—$500 to $5000, or you can set a new trial date, pay the same fine plus court costs. Our trucks take a lot of gases. You have to decide right now. Bring cash or a money order. No checks or credit cards."

I spend the week before we settle out of court talking over this nasty business with lawyer friends, the FBI, Representative Tom Udall and Governor Johnson. Their gut reactions vary but bottom line boils down to, "Pay up and move on. We can't touch them 'cause they're a sovereign nation."

A week later we show up at the pueblo. We are to negotiate an out-of-court settlement. The venue is a seedy back lot trailer, a single light bulb dangling over the formica table, bringing to mind vintage KGB. We face three Tesuque Ranger Police, including our Accuser. A lawyer friend has coached me how to behave. "Remain quiet, let them lay out their game plan. No strident American voices. Speak in a monotone. Don't look them in the eye. Be humble." We do as advised and are each fined $500.

"Not fair" we say. "We are here to negotiate." They stand up. One says, "Stay where you are." They file out of the long, narrow trailer room. Three minutes later they file back in, one at a time, expressions inscrutable, sit down, and the Accuser announces in an officious tone: "We have decided to fine you $250 each. Pay now at the tribal office."

It boiled down to being in the wrong arroyo that Wednesday morning.

GAYLE POLLIT

Gaye Gravely Pollitt describes herself as a "late bloomer." She learned to water ski in her twenties, fly planes in her thirties, ride Harleys in her fifties, and got involved in politics in her sixties. She also loves to "cowgirl up," travel anywhere she has never been and, most of all, spend endless hours with her husband, Harry, and giggle daily at their Portuguese Water Dog, Raven.

THE INDIAN WAY

I grew up in Phoenix. My family moved there when I was five. Phoenix may be in the heart of "Indian Country," but not once in all that time did I ever even bump shoulders with a Native American.

Oh, for sure, I saw them depicted at the Heard Museum during a class trip. And every time I passed the corner of Central Avenue and Indian School Road, I wondered what went on in that ominous looking place on that huge sprawl of land. I knew I loved their turquoise jewelry, but it was always sold by non-Native people at shops in Olde Towne Scottsdale. I also knew that the painted wooden Indian sitting in front of the same store was disrespectful, like a mascot. I figured out enough from my Catholic school history lessons (even though the accounts were written from the perspective of the colonizing conquerors) to know that all American Indigenous people suffered grave, irreparable injustices.

But the Indians were not real people to me. Not breathing beings. Not grins, greetings and laughter. Not the playful and good-humored people that Santa Fe has given me. Not until I came to Santa Fe did these First People of our land become real to me, become accessible, enriching to my daily life.

Let me tell you my story.

It is September 2003. In front of the Palace of the Governors. Under the portal, facing the famous Plaza. There's serious commerce being conducted and serious fun being had. Sixty-some Native Americans sit on the walkway, blankets spread in front of them, the blankets festooned mostly with jewelry, all of which they've designed and made. Tourists and Santa Feans alike walk along admiring the work, leaning down for a closer look. I eavesdrop.

"You're welcome to pick it up," comes a deep-voiced invitation from the tombs of a barrel-chested Native. He has followed his customer's gaze and prodded a handsome belt buckle slyly in her direction. My eyes meet his and he winks at me. We share his conspiracy!

"I made each of these pieces myself," explains an elder a few spaces down. Her deeply tanned, life-etched face captures my heart; I never notice her work.

"All stones are genuine," assures a younger Native man with black braided hair entwined in red cloth.

"How much is this?" a timid woman shopper inquires. I can tell she's in love with the delicate baby's bracelet studded with tiny turquoise stones that she's holding gently.

"What's your best price if I buy three?" asks a gruff Easterner a few more spaces down the line.

"Let's see," says the Native American. "Forty dollars times three is…"

A pause. The Easterner leans forward, expecting his discount.

"…one-hundred twenty dollars," he finishes with a completely straight face.

I'm not the only one listening in on this conversation. And there's a light laughter in the crowd as the Eastern shopper straightens up stiffly, looking miffed.

"It's not cheaper by the dozen, brother," the Native artist gently explains. "Each one is all handmade."

The man hurries off without a purchase. And those of us who have heard the exchange get an even better appreciation not only of the quality of the work we see, but of the wry sense of humor and love for banter we've witnessed. I'm coming to suspect it's a widely shared Native American trait.

I stop at one woman's spot. Earrings. Pendants. Bolo ties. Necklaces. All silver and most set with two or three stones in dramatic color combinations. Simple, elegant designs that speak to me. I look up now for the first time to see the artist. I guess she's maybe in her late fifties. She has very smooth skin; her black hair pulled back. She is bundled in a heavy jacket against the cool September day. But it's her smile I really notice—how it lights up her whole face, especially her eyes. She has been watching me and silently greets me with that huge, big smile.

"Hi," I say. "Your work is lovely."

"I design it with my daughter. But she doesn't like to sell, so I do."

I've picked up a pair of earrings.

"You can try those on."

"What kind of stone is this one?" I ask. It's deep purple, my most loved color.

"Charoite. It's one of my favorites. Pretty color, isn't it?" A pause. "Where you from?"

"Ohio," I answer. "Just here for a few days. My husband, Harry, is a wood sculptor and we're here for a meeting of collectors of wood art."

We chat like old friends. I buy two pairs of earrings with an elegant combination of stones and three silver bookmarks with a single turquoise stone perched on the end. She thanks me. I thank her. And we say good-bye.

"You'll be back, I think," she replies with a knowing smile. Her name is Mary. Our entire exchange took less than fifteen minutes. I thoroughly enjoyed it.

It's now August 2004. Harry and I have returned to Santa Fe. We've talked of little else the last eleven months. We've returned, we think, for a two-week vacation. We rented a tiny casita with a kitchen six or seven blocks from the Plaza. We want to pretend we live here. Go to the grocery store. Cook. Take long walks in town. See if we like Santa Fe enough to come back to live. The plan, we think, to move to in three or four years.

We arrived Sunday afternoon, August first. It's now Friday, the sixth. Yesterday we made an offer on a house. This morning we signed the contract. So much for our "plan" to return in three or four years! We will cut our vacation short to return to Ohio. We've a house to sell and I have a career-long job to resign. But that's tomorrow morning.

This afternoon we're seeing Santa Fe in a completely different light. It's our town. The sky and mountains are ours. The low adobe buildings are ours. The adobe homes behind earth-tone adobe walls punctuated with brightly colored trim and gates are ours. The narrow streets in the downtown historic district are ours, even those many streets that, to our amazement, remain dirt!The "coyote fences," the pinions and junipers—all are ours.

And, the Plaza is ours. The fabled Santa Fe Trail terminated on this spot and it marks the town's heart-center. It's a gathering place—a square-block of people pushing strollers, playing with dogs, relaxing on the grass and benches, or cutting across to visit the shops, restaurants, bank, or the 5 & 10 cent store that border it.

There's also a tin-roofed gazebo for community events. We love the Plaza and return to it.

We're looking for Mary, not sure we will recognize her. It has, after all, been almost a year since we met. I see a woman I believe is Mary. At the same moment she looks up from working with a customer. Her quick smile shows immediate recognition; then she returns to her sale. (Harry told me later that he, too, felt certain that Mary recognized us immediately, but that she was going to wait for us to approach her, to see if we recognized her.)

We stop at her space. She finishes her transaction and greets us.

“Hello. You're back. I knew you would be.”

I'm stunned. Mary deals with thousands of customers every year. Not only do our white, Anglo faces look familiar to her, she remembers that Harry is an artist! How impressive!

“Mary, guess what?” I blurt. “We just bought a home today. We're moving to Santa Fe.”

She grins. “Congratulations! You must come to my home for dinner after you move in.”

“Wow! Mary, that would be great. Yes, we would love to. Thank you. We'll come find you again when we get back.”

Harry and I are dumbstruck and deeply honored to have been invited to her home. Mary barely knows us! But somehow we feel a sense of connection. I am particularly surprised and delighted. (Remember my description of growing up in Phoenix?) Later, when we tell friends who had lived in Santa Fe for many years, they express surprise and they admit that they're rather jealous. They have never been invited to a Native American's home.

Thus began an unexpected and precious friendship. You know how sometimes when strangers first meet and feel a kinship, they say, “We must get together,” and never do. I admit I thought Mary' invitation was just such an exchange. Happily, it was not.

We saw her three months later, in November, after we moved—lock, stock and studio—to Santa Fe. We saw her under the portal on the Plaza and at ceremonial dances. Again, she invited us to her home and we set a date, December 26, for lunch and feast day dances.

The day is here now. Harry drives to San Felipe Pueblo where Mary lives. I navigate the forty minute trip south of Santa Fe. Exit 252 on I-25. Turn right, away from Hollywood Casino, and pass through an area of newer, somewhat identical-looking homes lining the road and some official Pueblo offices. The land is December-brown, semi-rolling. After a small creek crossing, take the first right, we look for a house under a tall tree as our landmark—and hesitate. We're unsure. But only for a nanosecond, because a young woman, who instantly knows we're visitors (unfamiliar red truck, white couple) points to a home matching the description of the one Mary has given us of her home. Later, we realize the helpful young woman was Mary's' daughter.

Harry and I are a little nervous. We are unsure of etiquette or protocol. The front door is ajar. We knock anyway. Mary greets us warmly, her two youngest grandchildren crowd around us, both trying to see who can get closest. And we are family. Our needless uncertainty melts.

As we enter we are astonished to see we are Mary's only guests! She has cooked a feast sufficient to feed a cast of thousands, but we and her family are the sole object of her feast-day cooking. She has invited us into her home to meet her daughter and jewelry partner, Ann; her five grandchildren; and Daniel, her friend from Cochiti. We sit around a large table in the kitchen, getting acquainted as we eat. The youngest grandchild, Joyce, snuggles close to show me her toys.

I devour the venison stew, so tender and delicious I wonder what I can forego in order to have seconds. But, to be polite, I taste her *posole* (hominy). Now I'm really in trouble. I cannot pass over the hot and yummy *posole* either. Approving groaning noises coming from Harry's direction assure me he also loves this meal. Mary and Ann had baked bread early this morning in their outside *horno* , a round beehive-shaped mud oven. We sop up the stew and posole broths with this unleavened, slightly sweet bread. Perfect! Harry says the bread reminds him of funnel cake, minus the powdered sugar that we always treat ourselves to at rodeos.

There's more food, too—pork ribs, a pasta salad, gelatin salads, desserts and ice tea. We both eat to bursting and, just like my Italian grandmother, Mary keeps saying, “Eat, eat. You eat like a bird.” This universality of life does not escape me. I smile even bigger.

Conversations flow easily. And after the meal, we are invited to relax in the living room. When we first arrived at Mary's, I was so occupied with the greetings that I had no chance to take in her home. The living room is graced with displays of Mary's pottery and jewelry collections. (On a visit months later to Danie’s daughter-in-law's home at Cochiti, we will enjoy an equally extensive collection of Native American art.)

Mary laughs, telling us how the large framed addition to her eighty-foot mobile home now makes it possible for her youngest grandson, Shawn, to do wheelies and race-track-laps around her living room on her granddaughter's bike. Shawn, age nine or ten, immediately obliges with a dizzying demonstration. The teenage middle-grandson, Robert, watches TV with a friend and pays little attention as Shawn repeatedly wheels in front of him.

Occasionally Mary speaks in her native Keres to her youngest grandchildren. They seem frustrated and even annoyed at her, but she ignores them and persists. She offers them ice cream in Keres that somehow they understand. She feels adamant; they should learn their native language as part of strengthening their heritage.

As we leave, Mary tells us that the next time we come, we must just knock on the door, say, "Hello," and come in. When we express some hesitancy about that, she says it is their custom. We happily agree—first, because we will be delighted to visit again and secondly, because we feel privileged to be learning her customs.

Since that first visit, we have been Mary and David's guests three other times, at their home and at Daniel's daughter-in-law's home. We invited them to our house to celebrate the opening of Harry's studio, but David's duties at Cochiti prevented it. We're long overdue for inviting them again. And, now almost three years later, we're still learning their customs. Mary recently admonished me that I had still not learned "the Indian way" when we failed to attend a feast day at her home because I thought we needed an invitation for the day. She chided us: "You knew the date! You are always invited. I do not have to call you ahead of time for each feast."

I regularly look for Mary on the Plaza so we can catch up on each other's lives. The reason I need to search for her is that on mornings when there are more Native artists who have traveled to Santa Fe to sell their work than there are spaces under the portal, their day gets determined by a lottery at 8 a.m. Mary and the others never know if and when they will "win" a space, or which space will be theirs. If they draw a blank (literally), some of the artists will share a space, but most drive home, sometimes great distances, and return another day to try their luck. It seems difficult to work under those chancey circumstances, but the Natives themselves share in determining and regulating the program which includes a regular pre-approval process in which every artist's work must pass rigid, high quality standards in order to even participate in the portal program lottery.

We cherish a number of pieces Mary and Ann have created. I especially treasure a beautiful turquoise and jet pendant Mary gave me for my birthday. Harry loves to sport his handsome silver bolo tie with a grand single turquoise stone which together Mary and I designed for him. And, at the moment, I eagerly await a pair of earrings that I asked Mary to design for me to wear under my motorcycle helmet. The stones will be turquoise, charoite and jet to match my Harley's black, turquoise and purple paint scheme! We wear each of their pieces with great warmth and pride—and true and valued friendship.

TONY PADILLA

Tony Padilla's first language was Spanish. He did not begin to learn English until first grade.Tony has a master's degree in English and is a retired English teacher who spends his ays reading, biking, skiing, fishing and playing pool. He is also an excellent native New Mexican cook.

GROWING UP IN SANTA FE

All of my mornings are taken up either by a bike ride or a workout at one of the municipal gyms in town. On one particular morning I decided I'd do my workout at the Chavez center way out on Rodeo Road. I left the house and eased on to St. Francis Drive, which would lead me to Rodeo Road and the gym. By mistake I took the inside lane on St. Francis Drive and all I could see around me was a mixture of aggressive driving and speeding. Many motorists were swerving from lane to lane, only to be held up at a red light down the road. Whatever happened to Santa Fe? I wondered.

I remember the sheer joy of growing up in Santa Fe. It was the land of mañana where if things didn't get done today there was always an abundant supply of tomorrow.

I grew up in a neighborhood that loosely resembled a family compound. Everyone was related and I spent my days playing sports and romping around in the hills nearby with all of my cousins. Daytime was synonymous with perpetual motion, and I grew up thinking that this was the order of the universe.

Evenings, on the other hand, were entirely different. When the summer sun finally called it a day, so did we. It was time to settle down and listen to the quiet and to stories told by my great-grandfather. He was the patriarch of the compound and with that came limitless awe and respect. He was a regal, kind, and soft-spoken man who was first and foremost a true gentleman. He lived with a grace of Spanish decorum that no longer exists. I never saw him casually dressed. He always wore a suit. His storytelling most often would leave me breathless. I remember him sitting on that porch propped on a chair wearing a suit as he told his stories.

Everyone in the compound grew up speaking Spanish, and the compound was the center of my universe until it was time to start school. I still remember that first day of school, and particularly the smell of chalk and sharpened pencils. I remember sitting at a desk with a small book featuring a blond boy and a curly-headed blond girl. I have never been so terrified as I was that day. That feeling hit the top of the Richter scale when the teacher began speaking and I had no clue what he was saying. It was totally foreign, and I knew I was in deep trouble. I came very close to wetting my pants. The day was long and it remains a blur. I walked out of the school building that first day and my shirt and pants were wet with a sweat caused by fear and stress that remains vivid sixty years later.

Next morning, I told my grandmother I did not want to go back, but she dragged me to school anyway. My grandmother was a grand, smart lady and she quickly realized that mistakes had been made. She began to rectify these mistakes by keeping me up till very late at night, pounding English words and phrases into my thick skull. Her English crash course began to show positive effects. By Christmas I was speed reading the book about those strange blond kids with a dog named Spot. Learning came at a fast clip, and I was awed that there was a huge world outside of the compound and the quiet, majestic town surrounding it.

We lived two blocks from the plaza. Greeks owned many of the restaurants around the plaza and on any given day you could see many of the old timers sitting on plaza benches and speaking in their native tongue. It was an easy time living in Santa Fe in those days, and there was a peaceful coexistence among all of its inhabitants that, looking back now, made it seem utopian.

I often wonder how so many of these small groups found their way to a place that was virtually unknown and secluded from the rest of the country. Were they the disenfranchised?

School continued at an easy pace and by now I would go to and from school on my own. There was no traffic on the streets, and I remember walking along the Santa Fe River most of the way home. When I hit the compound, my first stop would be at my great-grandmother's house. My chore was to gather and split kindling for her wood stove. This I did on a daily basis. I would then go into the kitchen and sit at the table where my great-grandmother would set a steaming bowl of red chili. No milk and cookies, just a bowl of red chili and a tortilla and some butter with the lady of the house. I then went home and had red chili and beans and tortilla for supper. I loved it.

Growing up in Santa Fe was not all fun and games. My entire family and the community at large was deeply rooted and involved in the Catholic religion. By second grade, I was an altar boy, along with the rest of my cousins. In fact, it was an older cousin who trained all aspiring altar boys. He taught us the moves and helped us to learn the entire litany of the mass prayers and responses. I still remember the tears in my grandmother's eyes when she saw me in my altar boy garb. She so wanted me to be a priest, and I so didn't want it.

Anyway, the priesthood thing died my freshman year in high school. I discovered girls, and I found that being with a girl was better than going to a Cantinflas movie at the Aller theater or eating homemade ice cream at the Santa Fe Creamery.

Santa Fe, in those days, may not have been much for providing ballparks and tennis courts for the young, but there were teenage dances everywhere. I learned quickly that I was a natural on the dance floor. At those dances, girls anxiously waited for me to ask them for a dance. Most guys couldn't dance, and those that did, danced poorly. And so I had a monopoly going.

High school here in Santa Fe was a period of constant laughter and joyous times mixed with lots of serious academia. I attended a Catholic all boys school taught by the Christian Brothers. It was a no-nonsense school where corporal punishment was a daily occurrence. I remember sitting in an algebra class and the brother went a bit too fast explaining a formula and he lost me. I asked a question, he looked at me, stepped next to my desk, hit the top of my head with his knuckles, and asked, "Are you stupid?" Everyone laughed, including me.

As a junior, I didn't study for a civics test, so I put my name on the paper and placed it in the basket of the teacher's desk. The result of that foolish act was that I scrubbed toilets and washed windows for three consecutive Saturdays. Arrive late to class? You bend over, grab your ankles, and your hamstrings get whacked with a board. One whack for every minute that you were late. You let go of the ankles? The process starts over again. Ah, St. Michael's and Santa Fe. Those were the good ole days.

And so, Santa Fe remained pretty much the same during my high school years. The laughter, the joy, the camaraderie of those days in this mystical, magical town will always pulse in my veins.

I joined the Army three days after high school graduation. I traveled all over the states and much of Europe. I went where the Army took me, and I'm thankful for that. I left Santa Fe to see what was out there. It expanded my horizons and it took me away from that compound that had been the center of my universe, but it also gave me an undying appreciation for the deep roots that are embedded like concrete in this city.

After three and a half years of military life, I came home. From 1959 through the Sixties Santa Fe pretty much remained as it had always been. The pace was slow. Everyone knew everyone. There still remained that laughter and joy that I experienced in my high school days and everything seemed as it has always been. A person could buy a three-bedroom house for under $9,000 with more property than you could manage. City league basketball and softball gamers were in vogue with beer parties after the games. Things were still good in the Sixties, but those of us who were born and raised here could already begin to sense a change in the air. No one admitted it, but the uneasiness that no one could identify was there. It was not till about the mid to late Seventies that the change hit like a brick to the forehead.

The compound? The center of my universe? The house where I was born is still standing, although it has been upgraded and redone. A cousin tells me that where my great-grandparents lived now stands a condo sort of thing that is selling for $500,000. One cousin still lives in the compound, but I haven't seen her for a couple of years, and I suppose I oughta visit. I would like to know if any of her neighbors have asked her if she eats regular food like roast beef.

I recall going to a party years ago when Bill Richardson had just dropped into town and was running for his first Congressional seat. My wife worked with Barbara (Bill's wife) at the time, and that's how we ended up at the party. So, here I am drinking wine and eating some exotic cheese and holding up a corner or a huge living room, as if putting my back up against it I could keep the wall from collapsing. This woman, wearing too much turquoise and wearing a "Santa Fe outfit" spots me, identifies me as a native, and saunters straight towards me. I realize then that I didn't do such a good job of making myself blend into the wall. Anyway, she walks over, makes with the chit-chat and then she drops a bombshell of a question: "Do your people eat regular food like roast beef?" Has Santa Fe changed? You bet it has.

It doesn't end there. The son of a friend of mine is an electrical contractor. He was working on some electrical stuff in a new housing development south of the city. He was listening in on a conversation between two women. One lady from New Jersey, who has been in the neighborhood for a year or so, is talking to a recent arrival. Recent arrival asks Jersey, "So how do you like the area?" Jersey responds, "I like the city and I like the neighborhood, but there are just too many Puerto Ricans here." I heard that little anecdote, and I laughed so hard my abdominals hurt. That was beautiful. It's better than the roast beef story.

Has Santa Fe changed? You bet it has. For that matter, I have also. I eat roast beef every now and then with my Puerto Rican cousins and friends.

POJOAQUE, NEW MEXICO

MARGARERT RICE-JETTE

Margaret Rice-Jette was a painter inspired by the enchanted landscapes and skyscapes of northern New Mexico amid the rich diversity of Native American, Hispanic and Anglo cultures. Originally from Baltimore, she lived in Santa Fe County for over thirty years. She earned an MFA in painting and was an artist-in-residence at Mercy University in Macon, Georgia, taught locally in private schools, and held workshops for teens and adults. Margaret died in 2018. Her three sons reside in Santa Fe.

ONE SNOWY EVENING ON THE EL RANCHO ROAD

The cold was quickly growing more intense as my sons piled their skis in the back of the car and jumped in, excitedly chattering about their day on the slopes. We pulled out of the school grounds and onto the El Rancho dirt road. The first snowflakes were already falling. The flakes weren't melting but sticking to the dirt.

We had driven a short way toward home when I noticed a small figure walking along the side of the road. His shoulders were hunched against the cold wind. Snow was settling on his hair and clothes. Wearing jeans and only a thin jeans jacket, from the back he appeared to be a young teenage boy. I slowed down and stopped beside the boy.

"Want a ride?" I asked.

Turning his head, he grinned at me, then leaped into the passenger seat. Not a teenaged boy but a small thin man in his middle forties, I guessed. He began a fast paced story. Nonstop, he talked about wanting to visit his cousin at San Ildefonso Pueblo, which was five miles down the road. He said he had walked from

Nambé Pueblo, where he lived, and wanted to get to his cousin's house by dinner time.

The car reeked of the odor of alcohol, and when I looked in the rearview mirror, my sons were looking at me incredulously. Some of the whiskey must have spilled on his clothing. He suddenly began to sing.

"Ah, yeh, yeh, yeh, ... AH, yeh, yeh, yeh," he chanted in time to an imaginary drumbeat. This man was certainly in the euphoric stage of inebriation.

"Come with me – we go dancing!"

Muffled snorts erupted from the back seat. Meanwhile snow was thickening, whirling as the man's chant grew louder.

"AHH, yeh, yeh, yeh," he shouted, palms slapping knees with every beat.

Suddenly I recalled the story my mother-in-law had told me about going out one very cold morning to find an Indian from the pueblo curled up in the dry irrigation ditch on her property, an empty whiskey bottle still in his hand. He had evidently come from the El Rancho Bar the night before, gone to sleep, and had frozen to death in the sub-zero cold.

With this warning in mind, I was going to head straight for the pueblo.

Now I could barely see more than a few feet in front of me. The small area swept by windshield wipers was the only part of the car not covered by snow. I rolled down the window to try and see farther. There was the turn-off to our home—barely recognizable. We drove past at a snail's pace. Two miles farther at a crawl and a form loomed at my left—the El Rancho Bar—no lights—closed by this storm. I knew we were more than halfway there. It was now dark.

Inside the car, time telescoped—suspended in silence but for the chanting. The rising wind moaned—the chanting rose and fell with the wind. Outside, snow blew in horizontal fury . . . white out.

Suddenly the pueblo was there in front of us. We slowly crawled the wide arc of the plaza. It was empty. No light shone from surrounding adobe homes.

"Where is the house?" I interrupted the chanting.

"Ohhh, I think he lives THAT way." His left hand swept towards me, nearly clipped the top of my head. We drove "that way." No lights from any house lining the plaza. I gripped the wheel tighter in silent desperation. More silence from the back seat.

"Or maybe THAT way." His right fist hit the window next to him. He was now very drunk.

We circled the plaza for the third time. Way off to the right I thought I saw a faint light. A house? Beyond that first cluster of homes? Hopefully, with someone home. I headed for the light and pulled up beside a tiny adobe.

"I get out here," the man grinned.

"It's your cousin's house?" (Bite your tongue, I told myself. At this point any safe house would do.)

"Hey, yeh, yeh, yeh—Might be", he said. He stopped his singing and drumming for a moment to look out.

"Must be." He opened the door after a few tries, stumbled out of the car and nearly fell.

Collecting himself in stages, he staggered to the door of the only house with a beacon. He banged at the door with both fists.

The door opened and there was talking back and forth. He started to go inside, reeled back outside, waved to me, went back in and the door closed behind him.

MARGARET RICE JETTE

STRANGE ENCOUNTER ALONG EL RANCHO ROAD

It was a Disney technicolor day in early spring—trees leafing out, bees from my neighbor's hives buzzing, tiny white and yellow butterflies fluttering, puffy clouds drifting in the brilliant turquoise sky. The sun was warm on my arm as I drove with all windows open, down the El Rancho road. I was about to put on a tape to suit my mood when by the side of the road I noticed an incredible struggle going on.

An old woman straight out of the pages of a folk tale was attempting to drag a foot-thick tree limb as long as half the width of the dirt road. She paid no attention to me or the car as I slowly came to a stop. She was trying to drag this tree-sized limb across the road to the other side. Under five feet tall, she had a bent humped back and thin legs so bowed she wobbled on the outer edges of her feet. She supported herself leaning on a stout stick used as a cane in one hand while trying to drag the heavy limb with the other. I had stopped the car far back from her, and she hadn't noticed me or the car rattling over the washboard ruts in the road. She was obviously very old, and she might be deaf, and I didn't want to startle her, or kick up dust from the road.

A dark red shawl was tied around her head and across her shoulders. She wore a black dress and an apron that had been white, both now dusty from the road and her struggles. She had very thin arms and legs, but a thick body and shoulders. She somewhat resembled a spider struggling with a much larger creature in her web. Her face was furrowed and red from her efforts.

I turned off the engine, got out of the car and walked towards her. She looked to be in her nineties and in danger of a heart attack.

I could hear her labored breathing. Speaking a greeting in badly accented Spanish, I approached her.

"Buenas dias Señora. "Como esta usted?"

She finally looked up and saw me. She directed a rushing stream of angry Spanish at me when I tried to indicate that I'd help her with the giant limb. The only word I was able to recognize in this tirade was spat at me—"Gringa!" while she pointed her cane horizontally at me. Then she began shaking her cane up and down so close I thought she might strike me! She glared at me, still spitting out angry words.

I was so astonished and shaken that I walked back to the car and just sat there, watching her snail's pace across the road. Every few steps she turned her head toward me, glaring fiercely. I couldn't go anywhere. She and the great branch were blocking the road, and I wasn't about to go near her again.

"Poco loco en la cabeza", the Spanish phrase for "a little crazy in the head" came to mind.

I wondered who she was, why she was so angry—amazed by the force of her anger and of her stubborn spirit as she continued to drag the limb to the other side of the road. The more I watched her, the less I could shake off the eerie feeling of unreality—the feeling that I had slipped from the present back in time when myth and reality blended.

I told myself she must be someone's great-grandmother, not a *bruja* (witch) who jumped out of the chamisa waving a stick as a wand to cast a spell.

MARGARET RICE-JETTE

THE SMALL THEFT

It was a drought year in all of New Mexico. In Pojoaque that summer the fields were so dry that walking through them raised clouds of yellow dust. Hordes of grasshoppers rose in front of me as I hauled pails of water to corn already stunted.

One morning Pablita came over with serious advice on the practical way to steal water from the Acequia Baranca.

"You only open the gate a little. Prop it with a stick, a small one, you understand, so it looks natural. If you do it right, it won't be noticed. Besides, your garden needs to survive. A bad year."

Since there are famous El Rancho stories of people being shot for just such a small invasion of water rights, I listened but was not tempted.

A few weeks later I witnessed Pablita's monumental anger. She had been caught at it. She, Pablita, wife of the *majordomo* (ditch boss)! The indignity of the fine was one thing, but the laughter of her neighbors and all her many relations who enjoyed a good joke was hard to take. All day her face burned from keeping her own tongue in check. Adolpho's added teasing, no matter how sweetly sly, stung more than mortal woman should be expected to endure.

She had delayed facing her husband by inviting me over for coffee.

Adolpho spoke to me, but the content was for Pablita. "You see, Margarita, it doesn't pay to steal. Look, we will have a good rain soon. God provides."

Pablita slammed out of the house. The screen door jumped on its hinges.

"The good God provides," she said. "Yes, if I help!" She threw a lethal look back at Adolpho through the screen and then turned to me. "Margarita, don't listen. This is the first time I've been caught in many years, not so bad, you see!"

Adolpho came slowly out of the house and looked innocently up at the sky as if he could see high clouds piled up over the mountains. Wisps there each afternoon only to drift away from the valley.

"It will rain tonight."

"Adolpho, you grow old. Now your bones tell the weather. If it rains, it will rain in the mountains, not here."

The air crackled around Pablita. She carried her personal storm out to the garden to hoe away her frustration.

That night wind carried the storm clouds into the valley. It began to rain. It rained all the next day.

On the following day when I woke up and found it was still raining, I put on old clothes and a slicker, took a shovel, and went to my garden before breakfast. Across the fields I saw my neighbors marching like a silent army to their gardens, shovel weapons over their shoulders. My collies were having a good time getting in my way as I dug little trenches to drain the deluge from new plants.

Across the lower alfalfa fields I saw Adolpho helpïng Pablita save her tomato plants. He bent to speak to her. Maybe he whispered, "God will provide."

MARGARET RICE-JETTE

CULTURAL EXCHANGE

Pablita is excited about redoing her casita in wall-to-wall plastic.

"Those new trailers—they're beautiful! So easy to keep up. I looked at Eloy's and decided to do over this old house modern."

She has invited me over to share her enthusiasm for progressive change. I look. Try to think of something to say. She bubbles with details of her plans to paint the *vigas* (beams) to match the wash n' wear wallpaper she has chosen, with a resplendent pattern of roses and vines, vines and roses.

I think of the cool whiteness of plastered walls, the functional simplicity of hand-adzed beams, and try not to shudder. I look out her window at real flowers; the ones she wants on her walls have not yet leaped into her garden. I have run from plastic world; she has just entered it, an innocent. When I turn, her eyes search my face.

"Don't you like color?"

"Umm, it's just that . . ."

"You should paint yours. You'll see. Someday cover up those old beams, so hard to dust."

How can I tell her what I really feel? How do I dare throw cold water on that blaze of creativity? I am a coward. I smile and praise the color and shine of Congoleum.

How could anyone ignore that expectant face beaming: "Won't it be beautiful?"

ALBUQUERQUE

ROBERT EVANS

Evans is a retired civil engineer. After living and working in many of the United States, Libya, Abu Dhabi, Lebanon, Iran, England, Mexico, Japan and China, he has returned to his native New Mexico. He has neither need nor wish to leave.

THE HOUSE ON WEST MESA

The wholesale development of Albuquerque's West Mesa hadn't started yet in 1957, and the residents were a scattered assortment of old land grant families, rednecks, misfits and drifters.

I was working construction then, and had a miserable little apartment just off South Coors Road. I lived pretty much from paycheck to paycheck, and, except for covering basic expenses, I invested in houses and lots—houses of ill repute and lots of whiskey. My favorite watering holes were the Chesterfield Club on West Central and the Peacock Club on the corner of West Central and Coors. When I could afford it, I went out to the Paradise Valley Dude Ranch, in Tijeras Canyon. Prince Bobby Jack and his band played at the Peacock, and Dick Bills played at Paradise Valley. Someone told me that a young Glen Campbell played with Dick Bills, but I guess that was after I was going there.

I often ran into a particular couple of women at those places, Ana and Stella, usually together. I had known them casually for about a year before I started dating Ana, a small, dark, vivacious girl. She was a nurse, but considering her wild life and wild habits, I wondered how she had stuck with the studies necessary to become an R.N. Stella was a secretary, about forty, so we considered her almost an old person; most of our acquaintances were in their twenties and thirties.

Ana and Stella had a house about four blocks from the Peacock, had lived together for several years, and had dated and/or had an affair with about every man I knew. They were great fun to be around; an additional attraction was that they seemed to have an unlimited supply of alcohol, marijuana and heroin.

Neither of the two, to my knowledge, had ever been arrested, which surprised me when I first met them. But after I knew them for a while, I learned that several of their closest friends and ex-boyfriends were members of the Albuquerque and State Police Departments. It was not unusual to see uniformed cops in their house drinking and using.

Considering the easy availability of drugs around all of us then, I suppose that I'm lucky that I liked alcohol so much. Even though I tried about everything, I liked to be drunk rather than high on dope. As much trouble as I got into in those years due to drinking, it's hard to think that bourbon saved me from even more grief.

After a couple of months of dating Ana, I moved in with her. At that time, Ana and Stella lived in the house, and another woman, Ruth, was there often enough to be thought of as a resident. I liked all three very much, perhaps because all three were equally morally corrupt, that being part of their attraction. Their vocabularies were colorful at any time, and their use of profanity was, to say the least, imaginative and at times embarrassing, even to me. They were all heavy drinkers, regular drug users, and slept with any number of regular and sometime partners. Ana and Stella stuck with men, but with Ruth, gender didn't matter.

Money never seemed to be an issue, either. Ana worked as a nurse, and sold drugs that she stole from her doctor and from the hospital. Stella worked as a secretary, but regularly got money from her family, probably to insure that she stayed away from home. Ruth had recently gotten a big insurance settlement due to her husband's death.

To close these brief biographies: Ana contracted syphilis, went insane and died at the asylum in Las Vegas at the age of forty-two. Stella was shot during a drug deal that went sour down on South Broadway in Albuquerque about two years after I was no longer living at their house. Ruth married a used car salesman who went on to become one of the State's largest Ford dealers; she is now a regular at local charity events and political gatherings.

Not too long after I moved in with Ana, Maurice showed up at the house. How he found me, I never got from him, but there he was, dirty and beat up, with fresh blood soaking the left side of his torn clothes. He told us that he had been shot.

The fact that he was bloody I could believe, as I could see blood, but whatever else Maurice told me I doubted, as my history with him had proved that if a lie was available, truth wouldn't be heard.

I had met Maurice down in Socorro a couple of years earlier. I had been out of the Air Force a little over a year, had no real responsibilities, didn't want to get a job, nor did I want to work very hard. I had an interest in geology and some basic rock-hounding knowledge, so I supported my basic needs by collecting semi-precious gems and mineral samples from around south-central New Mexico. When my old Plymouth station wagon was loaded down, I'd go to El Paso, Albuquerque or Santa Fe to sell to rock shops and curio stores. The proceeds went to keep me fed and in gas and beer; that seemed at the time to be enough.

I couldn't understand at first what Maurice was doing in Socorro, as he presented himself as a worldly, sophisticated, Eastern-educated man, and as an Air Force officer and pilot who was medically discharged due to a wound suffered when he was shot down over Korea. He had the necessary Air Force uniform and the insignia, badges, medals and paraphernalia necessary to back up his story.

As I had been in the Air Force, certain parts of his story didn't ring totally true, but at first I put that down to my not knowing much about being a pilot. Then I met another of his "friends" and learned that he had never been in the military at all, was certainly not a pilot, and that the scars on his back and butt were from a police shotgun blast he received during an arrest and capture when a store robbery went bad. Maurice was just out of the penitentiary and was in Socorro trying to con and scam people, which was his basic lifestyle, and he thought small-town people would be more gullible.

At first I was taken in by all his bullshit. About six-feet tall, well-built, with dark, wavy hair, Maurice was a good-looking man. He was well spoken, intelligent, knowledgeable on many subjects and just generally a charmer. But his b.s. soon got old, and it became evident that many of his stories were just that: stories. He tried too hard to be what he wasn't. In spite of whatever attributes he had, he relied on making up stories about himself, always with the goal of eliciting sympathy from the listener. He didn't seem to have trust in being who and what he really was. But then, maybe his real self was less attractive than his fake persona, if that was possible.

About the same time that I learned that his "Air Force" story was false, and learned that he was originally from Cincinnati, he started talking about the "mob" people he knew there, and how easy it would be to go into one of their card games and rob them. He proposed that we do just that.

I may have been living a disorganized and unfocused life, but I wanted no part of an armed robbery. Certainly robbing from supposed "mob" people didn't sound like a promising venture, nor one that offered a long and healthy life. I told Maurice, "No thanks" and added, "I'll see you around." I moved my rock hunting activities south to Truth or Consequences, New Mexico.

Maurice had been nothing but a faint and distasteful memory when he showed up, dirty and bleeding, at the house on West Mesa. Had I been there alone, I may well have given him twenty dollars and told him to go to an emergency room. But Ana was there, as well as others, and the nurse in Ana took over. She got him in and on the couch and was examining him before I could say much. She cleaned blood off his side and wiped out his wound.

"You say you've been shot? This looks like a cut," she said.

"No! I'm shot! I'm afraid I'm going to die! Somebody mugged me at the airport!"

The Albuquerque airport was clear across town, so that in itself didn't sound right.

But Ana didn't know Maurice, so she couldn't know that whatever he said was suspect.

"Well, let me probe a little," she said, "to see if I can feel a bullet. This may hurt a little."

Maurice's grunt and grimace of pain didn't hurt me at all.

"I don't feel anything in there," Ana said. "But you ought to be x-rayed. Let's get you down to the hospital."

"No, no! I can't go to a hospital! For starters, I don't have any money. I was mugged, remember? And they might be looking for me."

"Who might be looking for you?" I asked.

"Oh, well. These guys, you know? Actually, I wasn't really mugged, not the way you might think. Actually, these two guys and I went into the Angus Lumber Company, and, you know, there was this money there—well, it actually was in a safe, but, anyway, we took it."

Maurice had used the word "actually" three times in telling us that he and two others had just robbed someone, so maybe it was true.

"You cracked a safe and stole some cash, and now you say you have no money?"

"Yeah, well, we were coming over here to go to the Chesterfield Club to get a beer, but these two guys decided to take all the money, so they stopped by the river and threw me out of the car and beat me up and shot me and took all the money."

"Who were they?" I asked.

"Hell, I don't know. Just two guys I met at a bar downtown, and we got to talking and decided to get some money, and Angus Lumber was right there, so we went there."

"Maurice," I said, "those two won't be looking for you. They probably don't want to ever see you again."

Ana jumped in. "No matter. Let's just go down to my doctor's office. I can x-ray you there and get some antibiotic, and then we can decide what to do."

And that's what we did. Ana and I got Maurice, groaning and acting like he was on death's door, into the old station wagon and went down to her doctor's office on North 4th Street. She cranked up the x-ray machine and took his picture. As Ana had surmised, there was no bullet.

"Well, okay then," Maurice said. "Yeah, that was it. They stabbed me. I remember now, they stabbed me. Am I going to live?"

"Not only are you going to live," Ana said, "but I'm surprised you bled so much. That cut's not long, it's not deep, and it's not even close to anything vital. What did they stab you with, nail clippers?"

"I'm going to be okay, then? Wow! I thought I had really hurt myself." Maurice smiled and looked around. "Are there any really good pills here? You have any good codeine or morphine?" He put on a look of agony and groaned. "Oh, hell! Oh, God! The pain is killing me! Give me something, quick!"

Ana looked at him in disgust. "Knock it off. I've seen hang nails worse than this. I'll give you some morphine, just to shut you up. And if I ever hear of this office being broken into, I personally will find you and give you a real reason to bleed."

"Wait a minute," I said. "Maurice, you just said something about you were afraid you had really hurt yourself. What did you mean? How did you hurt yourself?"

"Oh, did I say I hurt myself? Well, maybe I did, a little. Those two guys dumped me down at the bridge, like I said, but they just kicked me out of the car and they had all the money, and I stumbled and fell down, and I got dirty and tore my shirt, and they drove off. So there I was, dirty, broke and still about half drunk, and no one would stop when I tried to flag them down, and, anyway, what could I do?"

He was wearing this hang-dog, poor-me look on his face. Ana and I looked at him, waiting for we weren't sure what.

"So you see," Maurice went on, "I didn't know what to do, but I still had my wallet, and somebody had given me your address and I had that, so I thought maybe you could help me."

He looked back and forth to me and Ana, expecting, I guess, for us to say we would take him in, or maybe adopt him.

"And?" I prompted.

"Well, I remember when you left Socorro, you didn't seem too happy with me, so I really wasn't sure you'd be happy to see me now, and maybe you wouldn't help me, so I figured you couldn't refuse to help me if I was hurt, so… there you are."

"So what the hell are you telling us? That you stabbed *yourself*?"

"Yeah, well, just cut myself a little, you know. There were all these broken beer bottles there by the bridge, and I used one on those. When I started bleeding, I thought I'd done too much. Hurt like hell, too. And I almost wasn't able to walk to your house. I'm sure glad you were at home."

Ana had a look of total disgust and dislike on her face. "Jesus H. Christ, Bobby! Is this piece of shit a friend of yours? This pathetic dumb-ass? I'm not wasting any more time on him! Get him out of here!"

My feelings about Maurice were the same as Ana's, as I wanted no more to do with him, either. I asked Ana to give me twenty of her strongest codeine pills, extra gauze and some tape.

I turned to Maurice. "I'm going to give you these and twenty dollars, and we're going to drop you off at the Greyhound Bus Station. Don't ever again call me, try to see me, or let me see you. Can you understand me?"

"Yeah, sure, man, sure! You'll give me the pills? Sure, I understand!"

Ana's and my relationship never had any hope of becoming permanent, but that evening marked the beginning of the end of whatever we did have going. She and Stella and Ruth would at times not be around when I got home from work, and they might or might not come in that night. There was one particular guy, one of the cops, around more than before, and I knew I was being replaced in Ana's sweet affections.

One Friday afternoon when I got back from work, three green plastic garbage bags were on the front lawn. As I got out of my car, Stella came out of the house.

"There's all your stuff. Ana doesn't want you here any more."

To say that my pride was hurt would be a big understatement., But I also felt a huge sense of relief. What I felt most, however, was surprise that my entire material life could fit in three green plastic garbage bags.

TAOS

INTRODUCTION

I never caught the meaning of the title of Zane Grey's novel, *Riders of the Purple Sage* until I first came to Taos. As you head north into town on the main highway, the sage-covered plains stretch westward for miles. Often, when I have driven this road, depending on the light, the sage takes on a purple hue. Sage, of course, is pale gray-green, but there is something about the quality of light in the Taos valley that works this magic, making the landscape unlike any other I have seen in New Mexico. This plain, the color, and the light create an appropriate entrance to this small city, which has just as good a claim as Santa Fe to the title "The City Different."

This city different is composed of cultural layers created over hundreds of years, one upon another: Pueblo Indians, Spanish conquistadors and colonists, French Canadian and American fur trappers, East Coast and European artists, hippies, New Age spiritualists.

The contributors to this section offer a few of the layers that existed in Taos not so long ago. Orlando Garcia and Bonnie Martinez both had glimpses of the bohemian community of eighty-some years ago that included Mabel Dodge Lujan, Freida Lawrence, Lady Brett, and Georgia O'Keeffe. The years they spent in Taos were, for many of us, the creative and artistic heyday of the city. For these artists and their writer friends, and for earlier artists like Blumenschein and Phillips who arrived in the late nineteenth century, Taos was exotic. Here were two cultures, Native American and Hispanic, that they had never experienced, and a landscape and architecture unlike any other they had seen.

In his book, *Mabel's Santa Fe and Taos*, Elmo Baca wrote: "What survives in the paintings, writings, photographs, letters, and other mementos of the bohemian legends of New Mexico is a profound joy and wonderment in the face of the miraculous."

Perhaps some of that feeling of wonderment (partially drug-fueled) inspired the hippies of the 1960s to establish five communes—Lama Foundation, the Family, the Hog Farm, Morningstar and New Buffalo—all within twenty-one miles of Taos. The hippie life, after all, was one of neo-primitivism: tipis, communal sharing, transcendence through drugs. Bonnie Larson's story is placed in this section. While Bonnie and her friend, Tom, did not live in a commune, they shared the primitive living conditions of the communards. They were friends with members of the Hog Farm, who visited them, and they were not far from Taos.

Years later, New Age spiritual seekers began finding their way to this city, or, as they might say, were drawn to the city by a spiritual force. That spiritual force, says contributor Jean Westland, resides in Taos mountain. And that mountain brings us to the Taos Indians, for whom it is sacred.

Not too many years ago you would see Taos Indians, wearing their traditional white cloth blankets draped over their heads and shoulders, lounging in Taos Plaza, but no longer. This is but one sign of change in the city that now has a major commercial strip along the south side of town and developments reaching several miles from the plaza into the country.

ORLANDO GARCIA

Orlando Garcia was born and raised in Taos. He was a World War II veteran who served with General MacArthur in New Guinea, the Philippines and Japan. He returned to Tokyo to teach school for one year in 1961, and later traveled to Rabat, Morocco for another year. He attended the University of Madrid in Spain for four summers, then the University of Quito in Ecuador. Orlando taught school in Taos for twenty-eight years. He died in 2024 at age ninety-seven.

FOUR TALES

Mabel, Lorenzo, and the Bohemian Crowd

Mabel Dodge Lujan's circle of friends were writers and artists. Mabel used to go to the best cafés in New York where the bohemians used to hang out.

Mabel also used to go to Italy quite often. That's where she met D.H.Lawrence. They used to call him Lorenzo here. She met him at a town near Lake Como. She had money. Lorenzo was there for his health. He had T.B.

Lorenzo came from the coal mining area of England where there are a lot of steel mills, and a lot of the people there suffer from lung ailments on account of the smoke. The doctors would advise people with money to go to Italy or North Africa where it was sunny and dry and that's how Lorenzo met Mabel Dodge. They say Lorenzo was told to move out of the hotels in Italy because the maids found blood all over his pillows and bed where he coughed all night. They told him he couldn't stay there any longer because he had TB.

Since Mabel had been to New Mexico, where the air is healthy and the climate is sunny and dry, she told Lorenzo that New Mexico would be the place for him. Many TB patients moved here. We were swamped with them. Some claimed they were artists or writers. Lawrence was the husband of Freida. Lawrence and Frieda came to Taos with Mabel and stayed at her place. Mabel had a tight circle of friends here in Taos, writers and artists—O'Keeffe, Strand, Steiglitz, and artist friends from Santa Fe. I know this because I had friends who worked for Mabel Dodge.

Tony Lujan was a Taos Indian, tall, heavy set. He was Mabel's driver and gardener. He drove her convertible, a very expensive car. She started making love to him, then later married him. During my youth a lot of friends died of appendicitis. We didn't have a hospital in Taos. In 1936 Mabel donated a huge house to Taos County for a hospital. There is a bronze plaque that reads: "Donated and dedicated to the Spanish Americans of Taos County by Mabel Dodge Lujan 1936."

The Band at La Fonda

From the Fifties to the Sixties I used to play drums with a trio at La Fonda Hotel. We played at La Fonda on Saturdays and on special days like fiestas. The piano player, Frank Montoya, was good at playing jazz music, and this was the only jazz music in town. We played all the Tommy Dorsey, Woody Herman, Glenn Miller, and Arty Shaw music. We had people following us who had been in the army when this music came out, it was their music.

The band had a great bird's eye-view of what was going on. Our followers had a great time, especially after having a few drinks or coming to the dance half drunk from parties. They came late. I remember Frieda Lawrence, Lady Brett, and Frieda's boyfriend, Angelo, a known Italian gigolo. They used to say she picked him up in Italy and that he left his wife and children. Angelo would come to the bandstand and request slow romantic music. He was very generous with the tipping, so we happily complied. Angelo had a favorite dancing friend, well known in Taos. While dancing with her, Angelo would constantly lick her ears. She didn't seem to mind. Frieda would sit and talk and drink with Lady Brett and her circle of friends while this dance went on. Frieda didn't notice, or pretended she didn't see anything.

Freida must have been in her sixties then. She was fat and ugly. She looked like a bale of cotton. Lady Brett was about the same age. I remember Lady Brett. You would talk with her and she was worse than I am— hard of hearing. She always carried an ear trumpet. She was pretty when she was young and gay, but not anymore.

Nat Flores and the Two Witches

A friend of mine, the guitar player in our band, was a gardener for Rebecca James, who lived right across the street from him. Her father had been business manager for Buffalo Bill's Wild West Show. She was born in England.

Nat would complain about the long-haired music that Becky James and Georgia O'keeffe blasted from their record player for hours while he was out in the yard cutting grass and cutting flowers. Nat, a jazz musician, couldn't stand the weird music these two women listened to.

Nat said both wore long black dresses and seemed to be in a trance drinking some kind of tea, which he thought was a peyote brew. He thought they were high on something the way they would yell and talk while the music was going on. Nat would sometimes say, "Those two witches are weird, they yell and holler while listening to that music."

When Rebecca died, she left Nat two O'keeffe paintings, one of a strange lily flower and another of pelvic bones.

Nat Flores and the Would-be Bank Robbers

Note: The backstory to this account is found in a wonderful little essay, The Great Taos Bank Robbery, *written by New Mexico mystery writer Tony Hillerman. One of the two would-be robbers was dressed in women's clothes, wore a wig, and carried a pistol under his purse. He and his partner stood in the teller line until looks from others so unnerved them that they fled.*

On November 12, 1957, the Taos bank was supposedly robbed. Two young men from Colorado came to Nat Flores' house after they tried to rob the bank, which was only one block away from the house. Nat Flores, the guitar player with our trio, knew one of the boys' fathers, Pablo Jaramillo, a good jazz sax player. The two bandits came to Flores' house to hide. Flores didn't know what they had done. When he found out what they had done, he tried to convince them to turn themselves in to the authorities, but to no avail.

Nat was doing janitorial work at the Pond Clinic run by Dr. Ashley Pond and Dr. Al Rosen. Dr. Rosen belonged to the sheriff's posse. While Rosen was communicating by phone or walkie-talkie with the sheriff's posse, Nat kept on mopping and scrubbing floors but listening to the reports and conversations going on. He went home and reported to the young boys what he had heard, where the hunt for them was concentrated.

One night, around one o'clock in the morning, I was awakened by a phone call. Nat wanted to talk to me, and asked me to come to his house. I thought he wanted to drink because he liked to drink. I told him I had to go to work the next day and I couldn't go. Days after that phone call and after the boys were captured, he told me that the phone call was to ask a favor of me, to take the boys to Costilla, New Mexico, right on the Colorado/New Mexico state line and get them off his ass.

He told me that he tried by every available means to get them out of his house. Since Nat's father had been a Methodist minister, he used every means—prayer and the Bible—to get them to turn themselves in. After he told me that he had wanted me to take them out of his house to Costilla, I told him, "You could have put my ass in the pen for helping fugitives to escape. What a hell of a friend you are."

BONNIE MARTINEZ

Bonnie Martinez was born and lived in Taos for many years. When she lived in Canon, four miles east of downtown Taos, she saw many celebrated artists. When her daughter moved to Santa Fe in 1987 to attend college, Bonnie followed in 1988. She has lived in

Santa Fe ever since. She reads a great deal, especially New Mexico history and folklore.

A TAOS TALE

I grew up in a very exciting neighborhood. There were artists and more artists. One artist that comes to mind is Georgia O'keeffe. The children in our neighborhood, as I remember, thought Ms. O'keeffe looked spooky. She never smiled, did not say much, and always dressed in black, so we called her the Lady in Black.

We thought she was a witch, perhaps because of the black dress. We saw black and we thought witches. Why? Who knows.

We tried very hard to avoid Ms. O'keeffe because we did have nightmares many times after seeing her. Ms. O'keeffe, for whatever reason, scared us. I don't think she stayed for too long in our neighborhood. But which of us from our neighborhood would have thought we were rubbing elbows with an artist who would become renowned. I mean renowned!

I went to work at the pharmacy on the Taos plaza. I was going to be fourteen years old the coming September, but I told the owners I was older, just to get work. It was the start of summer. I worked as a soda jerk, and I loved it. I stayed at that job until I finished high school. Besides the school kids, we had people come in from all over the globe. Movie stars and artists. Mabel Dodge Lujan came in a lot. So did Frieda Lawrence, who is buried by her home in Taos. Frieda, as I remember, had this loud, loud laugh. She was kind of tall and very round, with wild hair, and her belly would shake when she laughed. I was told she had been married to D.H. Lawrence. She would come in and have ice cream sodas and laugh and laugh. Her husband at that time—he had red hair —didn't come in. He stayed out in the car. He was a sculptor who came from New York.

Mabel wrote books, *Winter In Taos* among others. Other people wrote books about Mabel and Tony, her husband, and their life in Taos, their travels, etc. *Winter In Taos* is about her experiences discovering Taos and her life there; and about the love of her life, Tony. *Winter in Taos* also tells about the many small villages she visited, and of course Taos Pueblo, which she loved. She was a benefactor to many special Indian people there. Her other book is *Edge of Taos Desert*, mostly about her life with her former husband, and with Tony. Mabel died when she was eighty-three years old and Tony died shortly afterwards from a fall. His eyesight had gotten real bad and Mabel's son had put him in a quarter of the house that he was not familiar with. According to people who worked there, he did not fall far. It was a weird house, really.

BONNIE LARSON

Bonnie Larson came to New Mexico in 1970 with a Spanish degree from UCLA and a Montessori Teachers Credential. While her three daughters were children, she founded two cooperative alternative schools. Through her association with indigenous Huichol people of Central Mexico she produced a book of their art and myth and also co-authored a bilingual children's book based on a Huichol myth. She lives in Santa Fe, New Mexico with her artist husband, Ed Larson.

THE RIO GRANDE FLOOD OF 1979

It felt like an invasion. The helicopter was making tight circles over our heads. The wind it was whipping up was blowing my long hair into my eyes, but I could still see it was raising a huge cloud of dirt over our attempt to make a home out of a crumbling adobe, a couple of school busses and a tipi there on the remote side of the Rio Grande. An emergency vehicle with its blasting siren and flashing lights was arriving to the high ground on the other side of the river.

The river was in full flood. Huge logs and other debris were tumbling down in front of us like derailed freight cars. A voice from above, like God speaking, broadcast the news. “Two men, four women and three children stranded. One woman is pregnant.” The pregnant woman was me.

Then a voice yelling from the other side of the river into a megaphone asked, “Are you all right?” We could not be heard over the roar of the river, so we answered with affirmative body language like thumbs up and happy little dances. Despite our show of well-being, an incredibly strong young man jumped up and grabbed the cable upon which our now useless cable chair had ridden. He started across the river by flinging himself forward and re-grasping the cable with both hands, again and again. We stood watching in amazement. Certainly no one human could do this. We thought he would be afloat among the logs and debris at any moment. Miraculously, he made it to our side and dropped down in front of us. He asked us a few questions. Yes, we had food. No, the cable chair would not work with the river so high. Yes, I was very pregnant. No, the baby was not due for a few days.

Then, as if he were part Rambo and part Spiderman, he returned across the river the way he had arrived. The helicopter disappeared over the hill. There we stood, a bit more disheveled than usual, but the same as before: stranded on the remote side of the Rio Grande, watching the largest flood since 1942.

I came to northern New Mexico New Years Day, 1970, from a "back to the land" community situated in the beautiful, damp redwood forest of northern California. I probably would still be in that lush setting by the Russian River today had it not been for an unhappy marriage. When my husband informed me he wanted us to swing with another couple and that he had already been in the swing of things, so to speak, I left. Swinging was definitely not for me. I found this out after one awful, awkward encounter with Wacko, my best friend's husband.

I arranged a ride to L.A., but beyond that I had no plans and no destination. I was twenty-seven years old and I was sure that a better fortune awaited me somewhere. By chance, I encountered a friend of a friend in a health food restaurant in L A. The bearded, rosy-faced young man asked, "So what's up? Where are you headed?".

I could only respond with a teary, "I don't know."

Seeing that I was adrift, he offered to give me a ride to New Mexico where he lived. I knew nothing about New Mexico, but it sounded rural and I knew I needed the peace and quiet of nature to help me sort out what I would do. So without much thought I hopped into his oldVW bug and began an adventure that would shape the rest of my life.

I arrived in Santa Fe in the dead of winter with only a small, hastily packed overnight suitcase. My main outfit was a silky, blue miniskirt I had made myself and an embroidered voile Norwegian blouse. My clothes caught a lot of attention and, dressed that way, was almost like being naked against the weather. On the first drive north out of Santa Fe toward Española, I thought I had arrived on the moon. I had never before experienced such vastness of cold, barren open space. The scene was made ever more stark by the full moon illuminating strange rock formations and the shadows they cast on the snow-covered land. The mountains and mesas in the distance did not suggest sanctuary. No, this was an exposure to the elements I had not anticipated. Here nothing could be concealed. Soon I would not be able to hide even from myself the fact that I was pregnant, and I had run away from everything and everyone I knew.

The "friend of a friend" was Tom Watson, a gently eccentric refugee from Beverly Hills who had come to northern New Mexico via Denver in the mid Sixties. When I met him he was fresh from his experience of being part of the Hog Farm Commune's "Please Force" that was responsible for creating peace and safety at Woodstock. I felt protected and challenged by his strong intellect, ever-probing mind and idealistic point of view.

During a short stay with friends in Tesuque Village, a couple of the principal organizers of Woodstock arrived. Lo and behold, Wacko was with them. He did not even know that I had left my husband. Imagine his shock when I greeted him at the door in Tom's kimono. It seemed the movers and shakers of pop festivals and communes all had connections to northern New Mexico.

My first good look around the state was from a small plane with these guys as they searched for land which might be suitable to liberate from private ownership and make available for a communal settlement. Their mission was "to free the land for the people." The place was to be called Earth People's Park and was to be purchased by one dollar donations from everyone who had been at Woodstock. They selected an area near Taos, but were wisely turned away by the locals.

Shortly thereafter, Tom took me to see his home on the remote side of the Rio Grande. We pulled ourselves to the other side of the river, hand over hand, as we sat on a crude cable chair suspended over the river. There on the hillside was perched a hundred-year-old one-room adobe. It was little more than a ruin. Tom's few possessions were strewn about. The place had been vandalized. I attributed the disorder to the vandal's invasion. How was I to know that Tom had been living there in intermittent depression and quite out of touch with the "real" world except as it could be understood through physics and philosophy?

Now, nine years later, here on the isolated side of the flooding Rio Grande, I was pregnant with my third child. For weeks before our would-be rescuers arrived, we had been dealing with the flood. The more the water rose, the less weight we could put on the cable chair, which was really just a board hung from two wheels that rode atop a steel cable. Usually three grown people could sit and ride on the cable chair, les groceries, laundry and children. As the river rose, we had to lessen the weight on the cable chair to one man and one woman, then to two women, then to a woman and a child, then to one woman, then only to my brave nine-year-old daughter, then to no one. We were very careful not to overload the cable chair because, if the chair were to dip into the water, it could be pulled back by the current and then release its occupants as if launched from a slingshot.

Every spring and summer a few people would camp out with us to glean some insights from Tom on poured pumice construction methods, passive solar greenhouses, composting toilets, heat pipes and the like. Sometimes they stayed just to share in our whimsical lifestyle on the bank of the Rio Grande.

Work, play and philosophy seemed to meld into each other. We were living a back-to-the-basics lifestyle which was at the same time primitive and, for us at least, avant-garde. We gardened on terraces held in place by stone walls that we built. We experimented with various organic growing methods, and each year managed a beautiful garden of vegetables punctuated by

Jerusalem artichoke sunflowers and large sunset-colored marigolds.

Our most valued crop was the native blue corn. Every year, like our pueblo neighbors, we lived the corn cycle. We planted the best seed from the past year, irrigated, harvested, shucked, soaked, and ground kernels to purple-blue masa that we pressed out into our own handmade tortillas. They were delicious right off the wood cook stove.

My summer kitchen was built into a school bus parked beside the sandy arroyo. It had most of the conveniences of a modern kitchen. Even a juicer and the essential waffle iron. We were known, and often dropped in on, for our waffles made with flours we ground in the Corona hand mill and eggs we gathered from our Banty and Guinea hens.

Meals were served on a picnic table under huge old cottonwood trees that watched over our family and offered perspective to our serious and silly after-dinner discussions. Tom and I marveled as our growing daughters bounced up and down on the big trampoline these trees shaded and sheltered.

When the weather turned cold, our fair-weather guests departed and the water froze in the school bus kitchen. Life then centered around the wood stove in the old adobe house. With almost constant stoking it warmed our home, dried our mittens, heated our bath water, baked our bread and cooked our meals.

The summer of the big flood, my younger, funny and wise sister, Susan, joined us to help me. She was pregnant with her first child, but not showing. She hoped I would be her home birth role model. With her was her eleven-year-old stepson, Aaron, who just wanted to enjoy his summer vacation by the river.

Simon, an adventuring young Englishman from the high society of London, was also staying with us in the hope of making a fortune by growing marijuana on some flat spots up on the BLM land behind our property. For two summers he hauled water on his back to the plants and set elaborate trip wires warning systems around the plants, but the local Hispanic boys managed to harvest the crop both years.

Last, but not least, were two midwives from a lesbian commune in the South. Oma, the older and more fascinating midwife, I had picked up as a hitchhiker the previous fall. She had returned, as promised, to help me have a home birth. I say "fascinating" because when I first met her she was sporting a Mohawk and was full of tales of her life as a stiletto-shod, platinum-wigged drummer in an all-girl band that toured Vietnam during the war. She was also brilliant and well-educated. When she returned to be my midwife she was with a new girlfriend, Gayle, who was more interested in Oma than life on the Rio Grande or the impending birth.

Within a few days after the visit from our would-be rescuers, the flood receded somewhat, but it was generally agreed that the water was still too high to evacuate me safely in case of a birth complication. The question became: Where can I have my home birth on the highway side of the river? As Oma and Gayle were loudly discussing this at the local café, the owner overheard them and kindly offered me a room near the café that he sometimes rented out. The midwives proudly informed me that they had solved my problem. I had a place to have the baby! However, since they were having relationship problems that were hard to work out in the tipi we had provided them, they were going to move into the room—but I still could have my baby there.

As my due date arrived, it became clear that Tom would not be welcome at the birth. Over the course of the spring the midwives' issues about men had become focused on Tom. Although an avowed feminist and kind host, he had nonetheless become their persona non grata. Perhaps they took too personally his frequent analysis of how one could most effectively do just about anything. Between the banishment of Tom, the addition of black velvet paintings of semi-nude women and the fact that both women came down with flu, it was pretty clear I would not be having my baby in that room.

You might think I would be quite upset about all this. Oddly enough, I was not. I sat there like an overfed Ho-tai Buddha, believing in the good luck of the young and naïve. Then, amazingly, I was offered a house in Taos where I could have my baby. It was the town house of The Llama Foundation, the mountain spiritual retreat center located north of Taos. It would be vacated for a whole week—the exact week I would be having my baby. What good luck! I moved our whole group to that house and set up housekeeping of a sort. The week passed . . . . . .but no baby.

People I did not know started moving back into the house. So I packed up, cleaned up, went grocery shopping and drove home. I waded through the icy swirling thigh high water with my youngest daughter on my hip and hoisted myself onto the cable chair and pulled us both across the river. As I walked up the path to the house, I realized I was in labor.

Tom escorted me back to the cable chair and we skimmed over the river holding our feet up so as not to drag them in the churning water only inches below. He assisted my wade back to the pick-up and off we went to Taos again. This time we went to the Holy Cross Hospital. There in the foyer of the delivery room, with her father at my side, I delivered our beautiful baby girl. A nurse-midwife who worked at the hospital competently assisted with the birth. It was not the home birth I had wanted, but fortunate beyond expectation.

We brought our new little girl home the next morning. We raised Elena Rosa and her two older sisters, Anna Sunshine and

Mila Grace, by the river under the great cottonwood trees for thirteen sweet and discordant summers. There, in a world which was isolated and idealized, we guided them toward self-confidence and integrity.

I believe a mother may forget the pain of labor, but she never forgets the circumstances of each of her children's birth. My three daughters' births are imbued with the uniqueness of that special time in the Seventies when we, the Flower Children, the Back-to-the-Land Hippies and the steady flow of unkempt youth, sought a new way of life in rural New Mexico. As we rebelled against the status quo, we created a revival of and revolution in organic farming, home birthing, alternative education and green building methods. Of course, our efforts did not always go well. Often we were guided through our folly and ignorance by patient Hispanic, Native and Anglo elders who so graciously shared their knowledge and wisdom with us, the displaced and sometimes drugged-out, idealistic young people fleeing a superficial, materialistic and tumultuous time in America

JEAN WESTLAND

Jean has always been interested in art and writing. She drew her first pictures on her mother's scratch pads at four, wrote and illustrated her first book at seven and worked as an artist for the Walt Disney Studio at eighteen. One of her themes throughout her career has been the Southwest, inspired in part by her spunky horse, "Indian," and her childhood friendship with an old cowboy named Shorty, and his tall tales of the West.

TAOS MOUNTAIN

I was called to come to Taos. Two intuitives told me to come to the mountain. One, an American Indian artist, who paints portraits of peoples' guides, told me to go to Taos. He said, "Can I give you a message from our guide?" I said, "Yes". Then he said, "Go to Sodona, but don't stay there. Go to the highest mountain in New Mexico." The second said basically the same thing, "Go to a sacred place, but only for a while. Then go to the highest mountain in New Mexico."

Two intuitives telling me the same thing got my attention. I looked at a map of New Mexico. I found the highest mountain, Wheeler Peak. Then I looked for the closest town; it was Taos. To Taos I would go. I was under a bit of stress at the time and a fresh beginning looked attractive.

I decided if I were to go and live someplace else I should at least check it out first. So I took a plane to Albuquerque, and then a three-hour trip in a rattling bus to Taos. The bus trip set the tone for my adventure. There were about six of us in the bus, including an older lady, a rough country person, who had a partly eaten carcass of a turkey in a large torn brown paper bag. She kept dropping it and losing it. "Where's my turkey?" she'd call out. She was delightful. I smiled. I felt good. I knew somehow I was getting into the spirit of the place.

When I got to Taos though, nothing seemed to go right. I couldn't find a rental agent, I couldn't find an apartment, and I kept getting lost in a town three miles wide. I was to be there only a week, and I was discouraged. In the evening, two days before I was to leave town, I was in my motel room feeling very weary. It was about eleven o'clock at night. I silently asked God, "Please God, I don't know where I'm supposed to be. I don't care whether it's California, Europe or Taos–just let me know where I can serve you." Then I went to bed.

At 3:00 a.m. I was awakened. I had the feeling I should write. Intuitively, I wrote down this message.

"The Blue Lake is my home. I am the mighty bear. I speak to you through our fathers."

"Come White Bear, join the brotherhood. Be at one with us, with All.

"Do not be misled by mankind. He is on a destructive path. He does not soar with the eagle. He is mired in the dung.

"Listen to the mountain. I am the spirit of the Blue Lake. I am large. I am powerful. I am peaceful when not provoked. I give strength to the tribe. I shall give strength to you. Come to the mountain."

The next day everything fell into place. I found a place to live and signed up for the utilities. The day after that I took the scheduled flight back to California. I moved to Taos less than a month later.

I have had many people tell me how the mountain has called them.

One woman told me she had recurrent dreams that she was to move to Taos. She told her husband of the dreams. After many dreams she, her husband and children moved to Taos. The dreams, she said, then stopped. She says she knows she's meant to be here.

After I had lived here several years, I wrote a short piece for the local newspaper entitled, "The Mountain Calls Us." The day the article appeared I attended a large function in Taos, a memorial for Eya Fechin, the daughter of the well-known local Russian artist, Nicolai Fechin. We were sitting at tables. I happened to mention the article. A number of people had read it that day. They agreed with the story. They had been called to Taos. One said she would keep it as a reference to read to her friends. She had a hard time explaining to them why she was here. The article put her experience into words. She had been called to Taos like many spiritual people, sometimes called “New Agers”, who have come since the Seventies.

I met a woman here, a writer and intuitive, who doesn’t want people to know she gets spiritual inspiration. I may be the only person she has told. She can also see spirits, and since I’ve never seen spirits I find that interesting.

Once I was with her and she channeled about Taos. She said, “It is a very special place. One looks around and sees desert, but it is really a beautiful garden. Once, during Earth’s history, it was an actual garden. It is now a spiritual garden. Many spirits wish to be here, they enter the plants and flowers.”

One day after I had been in Taos for some months I felt spirit about me. I get the feeling in the back of my neck. Feeling “high” is about the only way I can describe it. I had the “high” feeling, and felt I should write. I wrote about two pages. I typed it up right away for some reason. It was about going into the mountain. Someone was going to lead us into the mountain.

Later, I found out that a number of people know about “going into the mountain.” I’d never heard of it. Some feel they are to enter the mountain physically. Others say it will be a spiritual experience.

Anyway, that afternoon after channeling about the mountain I went to a local Taos art fair. I met an artist there I hadn't met before. After talking to him for five or ten minutes I told him, “Oh, I channeled something this morning. It is for you.” I went to the car, got it, and brought it to the young man. He read it and smiled. “Yes”, he said, “I know. I am to lead people into the mountain.” He took the piece. That’s Taos. It is a magical, spiritual place.

People say the mountain either embraces you or it spits you

out. I've only met the embraced. Guess the others leave before I can meet them.

ROY, NEW MEXICO

RUDY GONZALES

Rudy Gonzales was born in Roy, New Mexico on January 1, 1934. After graduating from Roy High School, he moved to Pueblo, Colorado to study telegraphy at a commercial college. He moved to Tucumcari in 1953. There he was drafted into the Navy and served two years. Subsequently, he attended the University of New Mexico and the College of Albuquerque with the intention of teaching art. Government funds were cut and Rudy began working for several prominent New Mexico sign painters. In 1980, he went into business for himself. Rudy painted signs as far away as Dallas, Lordsburg, Gallop and Raton. He was an oil painter and amateur violin maker. Rudy passed away in 2024

CHICHO

When I was in the second grade, I was walking home accompanied by my brother, Gilbert, and my friend, Christy Gonzales, when suddenly we were aware of two kids across the street shouting insults at us. My friend, Christy, had a short temper and quickly accepted their challenge. He squared off with Chicho and I took on the other one, who we learned later was called Sonny. Somchow we changed partners once or twice. Christy and I were better scrappers and were getting the best of them when Chicho's mother came out of her house and shooed us away with a broom! This was my introduction to Chicho.

For a brief period when I was in the second grade, Chicho and I got along. However, there was a dark side to his personality that emerged when he had the upper hand. Since he had many brothers, he would constantly start trouble, knowing that he had backing. He also cultivated friendships with the bigger and tougher kids. He had a gift of sweet-talking people.

In response to these circumstances, my friends and I banded together. There were brief skirmishes and periods of quiet. Chicho mostly challenged my cousin Christy. I can't fathom why, because Christy was very strong and could handle him. On one occasion, Chicho went so far as to knock on Christy's door, accompanied by an entourage of friends. He was carrying boxing gloves and challenged Christy to come out and fight. I supposed he thought he could handle Christy and show off to his friends. Christy handled him easily, since all my friends and I sparred frequently with gloves.

This was a period when, like Banty roosters, we kids made indirect, veiled challenges to one another, posturing and strutting. Occasionally a fight broke out, but mostly there was an uneasy feeling, like an undercurrent of things to come. My friends and I weren't the only focus of Chicho's attention. He became famous throughout the area. Since those early years, I have talked with others who had stories similar to mine!

My best friend, Joe Maestas, was known as the best boxer in Roy, New Mexico. I constantly sparred with him. He bloodied my nose constantly, but I came back for more until I could almost hold my own with him. This made us a formidable pair. People hesitated to challenge him, but they might be persuaded to challenge me.

During my senior year I was enrolled in a P.E. class where the coach taught boxing. The individuals boxing at the moment were Chicho and a very good boxer by the name of Ralph

Romero. Being that he was Chicho's friend, Ralph was taking it easy on Chicho. Chicho was emboldened by his supposed prowess and stopped boxing and addressed the coach. Pointing at me he said, "I WANT HIM!" The coach asked me if I wanted to box Chicho. I couldn't refuse since the whole P.E. class was witness.

The coach proceeded to put the gloves on me. They were sixteen-ounce gloves and had no laces, thus being easy to remove. The gloves were so big it was almost impossible to hurt anyone. Chicho and I squared off. He was shifty on his feet and made a very fast shift with his right foot and landed a very hard right just behind my ear. I quickly figured his move. I had been in a southpaw stance, which means boxing left-handed with your right in front and your left in back. Right-handers have their left hand in front. I was capable of boxing left or right-handed.

I made a mental calculation and hoped he would try this maneuver again. He did! I timed this move and shifted to a right-hand stance. He ran into a hard left hook, which I quickly followed with right-left combinations. His eyeballs rolled, the snot flew and he staggered back and starred at me. He placed the gloves between his legs and pulled them off. The coach stepped between us. I don't like to tell this story for fear it might sound like bragging, but I did get an immense satisfaction from the fight! It might have been the straw that broke the camel's back.

For a short period after this encounter Chicho behaved. I even started getting along with his best friend, Willy. Willy was tall and more formidable than Chicho. A short time later, there was a dance, and I was enjoying myself watching the couples. Several of my friends were with me.

Chicho, accompanied by several friends, approached me at the dance hall. I greeted him in a friendly manner since it seemed there had been an armistice! He started making some remarks that I wasn't sure how to interpret; I didn't know if he was insulting or challenging me! I couldn't understand why all of a sudden he was being so cocky!

My friend Christy asked me, "Are you going to take that!?"

"Do you think he was challenging me?" I asked.

"YES!" he replied.

I then started after Chicho outside the dance hall. I challenged him and he started backing down! A large crowd gathered to observe the proceedings when out of the crowd burst Chicho's big brother, looking mean with a vicious scowl on his face! It was perfectly obvious why Chicho was acting so cocky: his big brother had been away in the Army and now was home on furlough!

"What's going on?" he asked.

Chicho replied, "Sharkey"—that was my nickname—"wants to whip me!" Chicho then attacked my friend, Joe Maestas, instead of me! I couldn't understand this since Joe was a better fighter than I was. We were standing on the edge of the cement platform with steps. Chicho pushed Joe down the steps, so I punched Chicho and sent him down. Someone hit me and down I went. I landed on my knees and felt a torrent of punches on my neck and head. Finally, someone must have intervened and taken my tormenter away.

As I stood up there were fights all around! The only ones not fighting were Willy, Chicho's best friend, and me. Our supposed treaty was broken! We started punching and somehow I landed a lucky left hook and Willy went down! I looked around and the fights were breaking up. Women also participated, and one was clobbering another with a high heel!

The conflict seemed to be over when loud drunks spilled out of the bar and started shouting, "What the hell is going on!" Since we were still full of testosterone and adrenaline we proceeded to shut them up!

This was my adios to Roy. Although I have visited Roy occasionally since then, and have had other slight altercations, I have had to walk on eggshells when I returned.

Chicho and I finally made peace and even have visited each other's ranches and laughed about the old times. I suppose that Chicho has mellowed out because his brothers are all dead. Today we are almost friends.

RUDY GONZALES

ERNESTO AND CHINO

Yesterday, after I commented about Roy and the brawls that sometimes occurred at the local dances, I slightly regretted having broached this subject. I have always been hesitant in discussing these street and barroom fights for fear of placing a negative image on the Hispanic community. I feared that we would be judged uncivilized. However, since I opened a Pandora's box, I might as well really tell how it was in that era!

Generally, people were peaceful, polite, and loyal to family and friends, and helped each other. They were also churchgoers and very devoted. However, there always seems to be a pair of individuals who love to create trouble, and sometimes resentments against some families broke into fights. Generally, since the local dances were the biggest social events, the fights occurred at the local bar, when people would be fortified with strong liquor. Mostly, these fights would occur among adults. The younger generation, however, would fight over the girls.

Another way for fights to get started was when out-of-towners would attend the Roy dances and try to "woo" the local girls.

Sometimes people were assaulted by bullies or bigger people. These assaults were seldom reported; people took their lumps and resorted to taking care of their own problems. In general, they didn't trust the law, unlike now in this litigious society when it seems everyone is suing everyone else.

Two families from Sabinoso moved to Roy. There were numerous brothers in both families. They were very rough characters and the local young men had to band together to keep from being attacked.

This is kind of a background for a story that became famous and almost a legend about two individuals. One was named Ernesto Lucero, the other Agustin Ulibarri (known as Chino, translated into Curly.)

In the beginning they were very good friends but became bitter enemies and resorted to fighting several times.

I was eight years old and in the evening I could hear the "a rat a tat tat" noise coming from a block away from my house. I quickly learned that the noise emanated from Chino punching the speed bag. Both Ernesto and Chino were boxers and evidently Chino was training for one definitive fight. At my age, I was unaware of what was happening. Evidently Ernesto and Chino decided that Roy was too small for the two of them, and that they would have one deciding fight, and the loser would leave town.

This part of the story was related to me by my father.

Chino worked at a local mercantile store as a cashier and when Ernesto happened to walk in. Chino confronted Ernesto saying, "Today is the day to settle our differences." They thought that they were being unobserved and started to the back of the store, and to the north, where there was a huge warehouse where lumber was stored.

In walking out of the store they had to pass by the barbershop. When my dad (who was a barber) saw them together, he realized that the fight was about to take place. He left a customer in the barber's chair with the barber's apron still on and maybe a little lather still on his face. He quickly walked into the pool hall and hollered to Panchito Romero, the caretaker of the pool hall, "Ernesto and Chino are about to get it on!" The pool hall quickly emptied and everyone followed the two contestants.

My dad told me that Chino was really prepared. He took his pants off. He was wearing boxing trunks under his clothes, ready for the occasion.

They proceeded to fight. My dad said that it was more of a boxing match than a street fight. They were sportsmen-like in their fighting. My dad said that they would score knockdowns but would allow their opponent to get up.

They fought for several minutes and it seemed that Chino was the better boxer, but Ernesto seemed to have a harder punch.

Dad says that Chino started getting cocky and after scoring some punches taunted Ernesto asking him, "How did you like that!" Ernesto answered by scoring punches to the ribs that Dad said sounded like boards breaking.

Then Ernesto started bleeding from the nose and didn't want to stain his dress pants. He asked Chino if he could remove his pants. Chino replied, "Take all the time you wish!" Ernesto took his time and folded his pants neatly and placed them on a pile of lumber.

The fight resumed and Ernesto scored a hard right that knocked Chino out! Ernesto proceeded to put his pants on and started to walk away when Chino started to come to. Still on the ground, he started waving to Ernesto, "Come back! I'm not through with you yet!" A brother of Chino's grabbed Ernesto and told him to go back! Ernesto just gave Tony, the brother, a quick punch and knocked him out also.

Many years later, I met Ernesto in Albuquerque, and in spite of the age difference we became friends. I asked him about the famous fight, and what he related was very close to what my dad had told me. However, he added some additional details. It seemed that when he asked Chino if he could remove his pants, he was in danger of losing the fight, so he took his time removing his pants in order to recuperate. Ernesto told me that Chino had a black birthmark on the point of his left jaw, a very vulnerable spot. Feeling that his stamina was diminishing, when the fight resumed he concentrated all his attention on this birthmark. When an opening occurred, he hit Chino as hard as he could with the remaining energy of his right hand, on the vital spot. This right put the conclusion to this fight.

I asked Ernesto how two friends became enemies. He said that they had been good friends and always watched each other's backs. But back in the Thirties, when work was hard to find, several jobs opened up in Conches, at the start of the Conches Dam construction. The two friends came to Conches and were hired. One night a big card game started in a tent. Somehow a fight ensued over cards, and Chino was hit over the head with an object and knocked out! Ernesto was also hit and knocked out! Chino, however, didn't believe Ernesto and accused him of running out on him. He never forgave Ernesto and they fought several times until the final conclusive fight.

Chino left town, and during the Second World War was killed—I believe in Guadalcanal. Ernesto died in 2001.

I should add that Ernesto became a marked man. He was famous in the local area and like a top gun in the Old West, there would be tough guys wanting to test him.

The old timers in Roy still recount the story of Chino and Ernesto's fight, but unfortunately they are too few. Ernesto was feared by some and a hero to others. I considered him a friend.

RUDY GONZALES

BOB WILLS IN ROY

I was raised in Roy, New Mexico where the events I will talk about took place and were related to me by my father.

My father was Diego Gonzales. He was a barber by trade, and very well known at that time in Harding County. Barber shops were kind of local meeting places.

My dad played the fiddle and usually had a fiddle handy in the barbershop. During this period there were a lot of local violinists who would drop in to play with my dad when he wasn't busy attending to a customer. Usually guitar players would accompany him.

On the day in question, my dad was playing his violin during a break from barbering. He was being accompanied by a well-known local man named Adolph Romero. I'm not certain whether Adolph was playing the banjo or the guitar. He could play both instruments. He was the only banjo player that I know of who lived in Harding County.

During the time my dad was playing, a stranger walked in. He was dressed in overalls and looked like a typical farmer. My father asked if he wanted a haircut. The stranger said he just wanted to listen to the playing. My dad continued to play and then a customer walked in. My dad placed the fiddle in the fiddle case and proceeded to attend to his customer. The stranger then addressed my dad. He said, "Mister, do you mind if I play your fiddlc?"

My dad replied, "You're welcome to."

My dad told me he thought to himself, "He's welcome to play my fiddle, but I've never seen a gringo farmer that could play worth a damn." The stranger then proceeded to play. My dad and

Adolph Romero were pleasantly shocked! The stranger was a great fiddler. His name was Bob Wills!

It seems he was traveling through small towns looking for work in a barbershop. He had recently graduated from barber school in Amarillo, I believe.

After the initial introductions, my dad and Adolph proceeded to plan a dance at the local dance hall. The owners were to rent or lend the dance hall free of charge. Dances were well attended and attracted a large clientele to the bar, thus benefiting everyone. The word was quickly passed on that there would be a dance and that a very good fiddler would play with the local musicians. During this period, there were many fiddlers in Roy and Harding County. It was the custom for fiddlers to take turns playing, allowing the contracted musicians to have a brief respite.

Bob Wills was introduced to the local musicians and played regularly during his stay in Roy. Some of the musicians he played with were Abram Vargas, a locally renowned fiddler, and his two brothers, Juan and Mark Tafoya, names now probably known only to very old people. I am fortunate enough to have known these gentlemen. Unfortunately, I met them several years after Bob Wills left Roy. Another fiddler, probably alot younger at the time, was Abenicio Salazar, known as “Abe.” Abe had very fond memories of the events I am relating and filled some of the gaps that my dad hadn’t told me.

I am not exactly sure of the time these events took place or how long he resided in Roy. But it was probably in the Thirties. It is known that he composed the music to “San Antonio Rose” in Roy, but had titled it “Mexican Two Step.” He later changed it to “San Antonio Rose” when he auditioned to play on a radio station somewhere in Texas. His prospective employer liked the tune but said that he needed lyrics to go with the tune. Supposedly, Bob and his accompanist retired to his home and in one afternoon wrote the lyrics that became famous. When Bob Wills decided to leave Roy, he asked my dad to accompany him. He had plans of starting a band.

My dad told me that Bob Wills really liked my dad's violin and attempted to buy it from him. My dad was very attached to his fiddle and wouldn't sell it. My dad said Bob invited him to a local bar and proceeded to try and intoxicate him and convince him to sell it. My dad refused and accompanied Bob to the train depot. Years later, my dad learned that Bob had become famous.

My dad's fiddle had a very good tone, although the top didn't have the best grain. This I learned years later when I began to study fiddles and did a lot of research. The sides and back did have excellent maple wood. The back had the name of the maker stamped on the back, not a sticker on paper as is common. The maker's name was Paganini, not to be confused with Paganini the great fiddler.

Years later I learned to make and repair fiddles in order to repair my dad's, which had been severely damaged. When I made my first fiddle I visited Abe Salazar in Las Vegas, New Mexico to show him my fiddle. It was then that he filled me in on the details of Bob Wills' attempt to buy my dad's fiddle. He told me that after my dad refused to sell his fiddle, Bob said that if he wouldn't sell him the whole fiddle, would he sell him only the neck. That he would pay for a new neck to replace my dad's. My dad refused. Abe then asked me what was so special about that neck. This question bothered me for some time, and I came to the conclusion that this neck was thinner than that of most fiddles. Several fiddlers who have played this fiddle have commented on the ease of the fingering due to its narrow neck. Many fiddles I have repaired have too thick a neck. I guess the preferences for a thinner or thicker neck might be due to the size of the fiddlers' hands. This leads me to speculate that Bob Wills must have had small hands.

NARA VISA, AMISTAD & LOGAN

Introduction

Nara Visa, Logan, and Amistad are located in the heart of 1930s Dust Bowl country, a region which encompasses adjacent areas of Oklahoma, Texas, New Mexico and Colorado. The calamity that struck this region was caused in part by years of drought, but in greater part by homesteaders who expected bumper crops of wheat year after year from a land without topsoil. In the early 1900s the lands surrounding Nara Visa, Logan, and Amistad were filled with homesteaders who had come in search of 160 acres, their portion of the Promised Land. But inevitably the Promised Land, this land without topsoil, turned out to be a land of broken promises. The homesteaders plowed up sod and the land blew away. For years the great dust storms swept in, week after week, and for years the people left, family by family. Now Nara Visa has practically emptied out and Amistad has just two citizens—new arrivals. Logan, thanks to a lake and dam project that brings in summer tourists, hangs on.

In consequence of this gross abuse of the land, the federal government bought up millions of acres in New Mexico and Texas, which are now permanent grasslands. But these federal lands are not contiguous, and the corporations and individuals that own adjacent sections are repeating the mistake of 100 years ago by ripping up the sod. Some ranchers plant wheat for winter silage, and vertically integrated corporations operate processing plants and/or feed lots for finishing operations.

The three towns of this section—Logan, Nara Visa, and Amistad— are situated in the northeast quadrant of the state, south of Clayton.

Renée Rinestine, who lives outside Nara Visa, wrote, "A man told me recently that Nara Visa was founded in 1901. It was the location of a railroad terminal between Tucumcari and Dalhart. No one really knows the origin of the name. . . " The Homestead Act, she wrote, "brought most of the people to the area. At one time it had several hotels, three newspapers, and several churches; it was really a thriving town. A fire broke out in 1910 and burned most of the business section. It never recovered from that loss. Then, as the drought of the 1930s hit, more and more moved away. During the 1950s-1970s there were truck stops, several cafeés, but one by one they closed." So did the school, which now houses Nara Visa's Community Center.

Barbara Copeland, who with her husband ranches outside of Amistad, tells us, "In 1906 a Congregational Minister from Yale Divinity School by the name of H. S. Wannamaker had formed a group of supporters who were interested in developing a new town in New Mexico. He and his group took a train to Middlewater, Texas, rented a buggy and started looking for a likely spot. They at first thought the land in and around old Emberson, six miles south of Amistad, would be the place. However, they finally decided on the land where Amistad is now located.

"Wanting to establish a religious community, Wannamaker advertised in religious periodicals of churches in the East. He told of the free and fertile land, and the healthful climate. He organized immigrant trains for the hopeful homesteaders from Pennsylvania, Massachusetts, Michigan, Indiana, Ohio, Illinois, and possibly other states who answered the ad and came west seeking the free 160 acres the U.S. government was offering to homesteaders. The immigrants came with all their worldly goods including livestock, household goods, wagons, plows, canned food, and pets. . .

"The town took shape and eventually grew to have a couple of hotels, a lumber yard, a hardware store, a drug store, a fresh meats market, and Macy's Hardware & Furniture and Paints & Oil Store. . . . There was an attorney, a barber, a general repair shop, a well-drilling business, a milliner, and a seamstress."

Logan, like Nara Visa, is situated along the railroad. In 1910, a Logan bank owned by the McFarland Brothers issued an advertisement or prospectus to attract more settlers. The Donald and Bob Harrold family website reprints the prospectus. "Logan's first house was built in 1901, and the town has a gradual but slow growth, until now it has a population of about 300.

"Our main crops planted are corn—not doing much good in the last 2 years, Maize, Kaffa Corn, Beans, Peas, and other garden crops—fair to good, but the last 2 years are dryer and less crops than any year in 5.

"There is some land to be filed on 8 to 15 miles from town and relinquishments and deeded land can be bought reasonably close in. Stop off and take a look at our country when out looking for land."

Today this area and the contiguous areas in West Texas are once again cattle country. Until a few years ago, every September Nara Visa hosted the Nara Visa Gathering, a convocation of ranchers, cowboys and their wives for three days of visiting, with fiddles and guitars, a chuck wagon, and a crafts show. It was a genuine, unaffected celebration of a vanishing heritage.

FRED KELLY

Fred Kelly was born in northern New Mexico in 1916, delivered by a country doctor fourteen miles west of Nara Visa. He ranched about fifteen years with 4000 - 5000 mother cows. In 1977 he moved to Colorado and had 15,000 laying hens and 200 cows. He never bought a place but always leased. At age ninety he was still riding and was bucked off May 20, a week before he was interviewed for this story. Fred died in 2009. This article is based on an interview.

THE DEPRESSION AND DROUGHT IN NORTHERN NEW MEXICO

The Twenties was really good. The rain, the moisture, was good. They raised good crops. Anyway, in '29 here come the Depression. Oh, terrible. Depression and the drouth [drought], both. And the settlers, it really did hurt 'em. Of course it hurt everybody. I seen as many as twenty-five to thirty men a-walking down the Highway 54.

Well, here come the panhandle of Oklahoma! It was terrible, it was sad. Anyway, those Oklahoma people was going to California to get work. They just dried out. Gosh, in all kinds of Model T's [and] Model A's, their bed springs, their mattress, maybe a few cooking pans. Terrible sad to look at. And the men riding both ways on the Rock Island Railroad. Both ways. Ever box car was full of men. And the men on top looked like a bunch of blackbirds. They was all settin' on top of the train, trying to get some kind of work, or something to eat. They'd go east, they'd come back. They'd go to people's houses and ask for something to eat. The woman would say, "You go out to the chicken house. The sand has blowed up around that house. If you shovel the sand away from that door or you haul an ole tree and chop it up for wood, I'll give you something to eat." When the lady got through [feeding them] they'd get down on their hands and knees and thank her and thank her. That's how bad they was a needin' food.

I seen it. It's still in my heart how pitiful it was. I was just a big kid. My dad would pick 'em up and give 'em a ride as far as he went, just to find out how bad it was. They couldn't find no work, until the WPA come along and had those little projects.

I seen a young boy, he wasn't over eighteen, nineteen years old. My dad picked him up and hauled him about forty miles. That boy, when he let him out, big tears was runnin' down his cheeks for that ride. He said, "I cannot find no work. I got a wife and a little boy." He was vicious for somethin' to do. I had a big memory over that.

The gov'mint couldn't take care of them [the hungry people]. There was plenty of meat, plenty of grain—wheat, barley, things could of got brought in. They just didn't have no place like a fridge, an icebox, to keep 'em in. That [situation] lasted all through the Thirties, the Dust Bowl. Big clouds of dust. It would just roll in. It just blackened everything, [made everything] black and dark, just like at night.

Wind, wind, southwest wind just blowed. It seemed like every day. The ranchers finally run out of grass and everything. The gov'mint in '34 they went to buyin' livestock. Gave ten dollars for a yearling, sixteen dollars for a sound cow, eight dollars for a calf. But the old cows that had a broken hoof or was kinda lame, they drove them up in the corner and they had a gov'mint man kill 'em, the old cows. The gov'mint was buying the cattle. How sad it was seein' them drive as many as forty and fifty up in a corner and just kill 'em. And those people was beggin for food, just somethin to eat. This was on these bigger ranches. They had three, four thousand cows. All over Texas, Oklahoma, all over the West and Southwest, Kansas, Nebraska, ever place.

No rain, just like it is now. It just kept [up]. Ever year it seemed like it got a little worse, a little worse. Lasted a good eight to nine years and the wind blowed and those dust storms, gosh, they just rolled in and really turned things black, dark and black and dusty. Just choked you down. [It was] sticky like. Run your finger on it, black, just ole dry stuff. You just touch anything like metal—tie the windmill off— it was just like a spark plug. It would just shock you. Or anything had metal in it. Just combin' your hair—if it was kind of dark, if you didn't have lights—you could see that little spark. We didn't have electricity. We had kerosene lamps. The cows had electricity in their hair, the horses had electricity in their manes, in their tails. Ever'thing was so dry.

And when it did go to rain, course it was shortage of cattle and the prices got up. People began to buy these settlers' places, or from the loan company. Just like the bank had a mortgage on their place, they would take it over. The bankers didn't want their land, they wanted their money. But the ranchers who could stay bought up the land. Some put up ten sections together, maybe some more than that.

So, the Depression it always stuck in my mind how sad it was, how they begged for work and ever'thing through the Depression. The gov'mint finally [created] what they called the WPA work, like buildin' this gymnasium or building a road. In some parts of the state they built parks and things like that. The time come along when there was work, a little more work, like the shipyards, military. It [the Depression] just eventually went away.

My dad was a ranchin'. We had about twenty-two hundred head of mother cows and anyway we didn't have no grass. Tryin to save a few for seed but the gov'mint took [bought] the best cows and calves, of course, and yearling cattle. But the old toothless cows they would kill them. That was the govmint helpin' the rancher out. After the drouth [drought] broke, the cattle brought a pretty good price.

I was born in 1916 and when it [the Depression] started, I guess I was about thirteen, fourteen. [I have a] lot of memories of how we lived. We just lived like all the rest. Our house wasn't any better than the rest. We didn't eat no better than our neighbors. Our clothes wasn't no better than the other kids and we had as good a schoolin' as we could expect, you know. But we didn't have the money to go to college, or go away from home.

We didn't never go hungry. My mother always had a garden. We had a good well and storage. She had a good garden where she raised beans, okry, tomatoes and sev'ral other things, and she canned all of her food. She canned ever bit of it, so when the pressure cookers was a coming out, she got to cannin' meat, like chicken, like pork, like beef. Canned lots of that and like if she did have a little corn she could can it and tomatoes and sev'ral other things. We didn't go hungry, no.

We didn't have nothin but a wood stove. Most of the people didn't have no wood in this country. Picked up cow chips. They would pick up several loads of cow chips and burn 'em in the cook stove, burn them in their heat stove. Them that could afford coal would buy enough to get em through the winter. If they went far away to Cedar Breaks, they'd gather wood.

We had neighbors would allow us to pick up cow chips [after our cows were sold]. On Saturday and Sunday us kids would take the team, and the wagon had a box on it, and [we'd] get two or three loads of cow chips to burn for fuel. A wagon box of chips would last about a week, just about a week. It [the Depression] affected me. I still have the memories of what they went through. Another thing, it just alerted me how to save, not destroy anything.

BOB WHITE

Bob White was eighty-four years old when this interview was conducted. He worked in the live-stock business his entire life, ever since World War II, when he served in the Navy in the Pacific. He owned his own irrigation farm and grassland. Bob was married to his wife, Stella, for over sixty years. They had three children, ten grandchildren and four great-grandchildren, all girls.

LIVING IN NARA VISA IN THE 1930S

Moving

We lived at Happy, Texas when I was a small boy. Happy is approximately fifteen to twenty miles east of Nara Visa. My daddy came to New Mexico and leased a place at Rosebud, New Mexico, which is approximately twenty-five miles northwest of Nara Visa. This was in 1929.

We had horses and wagons and had just bought our first automobile when we decided to move to New Mexico. We had two mules on each wagon. We had two separate wagons. One wagon had bows, and we put a tarpaulin up over the bows to cover our goods and furniture. My dad drove the automobile. We came across the Canadian River, which was approximately ankle deep, as I remember, and it was more water than I had ever seen. My daddy said we should get out and walk because the wagon might sink with the extra weight,

It took us approximately five days to make the run from Happy to Rosebud. We had camping gear with us and cooked and ate along the way. Slept on the wagon and under the wagon in bedrolls. When we got to Rosebud my oldest brother started school, but I was too young. There was many more Hispanics than Anglos in that school. That was probably in 1930.

It was a big world to me. I had never been anywhere besides Happy, Texas. It was very adventurous, it was a big land.

School and Chores

In 1931 we moved from Rosebud halfway back to Nara Visa on a place that my father had purchased. I started school in Nara Visa in 1931, rode a school bus. The ride was approximately twenty-five miles the way the bus circled around the ranches and back to school. When we got home from school we had cows to milk and chores to do, by the light of a kerosene lantern. The next morning we'd have to get up early enough to do the chores, also by the light of a kerosene lantern.

We had to haul our drinking water from a half mile away from home. We used our wagon with the mules, hauled it in fifty-five gallon barrels and turned washtubs over to cover the barrels.

My mother would send me on horseback after the mail, which was one mile from our home at Rosebud. I couldn't get off on the ground because I couldn't remount my horse, so she taught me to get off on top of the mailbox, set on it, and open the mailbox door, put the mail on my saddle (the horse would be standing by), then I would remount and take it home. I was about five then.

Quilting

After we moved to Nara Visa, my mother went to club meetings and rode horseback, and I had one brother that was too young to go to school, and he would ride behind her on the horse. They would attend club for about four hours and then return home a-horseback. And in later years my sister was born and before she went to school mother would take her to the club with my sister behind her on the horse. During this time the ladies built a friendship quilt and embroidered every lady's name on it. The ladies had frames and they would put the lining in the quilt and then they would make blocks and in the middle of each block the lady who had built that block would embroider her name on it and then the blocks would be sewed together. My mother and my sister's names were both on this quilt from 1943. Just last year, which was 2004, the friendship quilt showed up at the Nara Visa reunion. One of the mothers had it stored, and the son brought it to the reunion, and this time I talked him into donating it to the Nara Visa museum.

The school at Nara Visa went from 500 students in 1931 to 125 when I graduated in 1944. One hundred twenty-five. Total school. The homesteaders had moved out, and the population had dwindled that much in that many years.

Homesteaders and the Dust Bowl

Homesteaders were before my time. Most of the homesteading was done before we got here, but the homesteaders would homestead on 160 acres and had to live three years on their homestead before they had their title. So most of them built dugouts with sod roofs to prove up on their claim. Lot of them left here and would come back but a lot of them sold their claim to other ranchers or neighbors.

The homesteading, most of it, took place in the early 1900s, from 1900 to 1925, in that era. The place we moved onto in Nara Visa was a homestead.

They couldn't make a living on such small acreage. It got such a hard times they had to find work elsewhere. Later years they developed what they called WPA projects to help keep some of the people on the land. That was through the 1930s, up till the '40s, the WPA projects was in effect.

The homesteaders couldn't make it, couldn't produce on account of dry weather and drought in the 1930s. In their words, this was the Dust Bowl days. We had big storms come in from the north. It would be full sunshine, and they would roll in just like clouds and make it complete dark, so much dust in the air. Mothers would wet tea towels and such to put over their children's mouths so they could breathe, there was such dust in the homes.

The dust storms usually wouldn't last very long, but was very frequent, maybe once a week or several weeks, seemed like a week apart. It would have been in April or May in the mid-thirties, '34, '35, when the dust storms were real prevalent. We had a real hard time breathing, but mother would put a tea towel over our noses and you could breathe kind of normal. She would dampen them in water and tie them over our noses and faces, around behind our heads.

Dust would get a fourth to a half inch thick, settle on the ground and everywhere. That's one reason they [the government] originated the WPA, to help people through this crisis.

My father was trying to farm, but even the fields would blow away. We had a few head of livestock, but it was very hard to raise the feed to feed a few head.

The government came in and made a deal with ranchers and farmers to shoot some of their animals because therre wasn't enough food to go around. We're talking about seven to eight dollars apiece. They shot 'em to have one animal, but the others was to be destroyed.

I heard my daddy ask why the neighbors couldn't have the beef to can. They said the program wasn't designed for that. They would stay and watch until the beef would spoil. They would leave a guard.

TRAVIS NELSON

Born in 1919, Travis Nelson grew up in Nara Visa and received her bachelor's degree in Home Economics. She taught school for one year, then worked as a home demonstration agent before marrying Jack Nelson in 1957 and moving to Illinois. There she became mother to his three sons. She received a masters degree in special education at New Mexico State University, Las Cruces. After Jack's death in 2001 she returned to Nara Visa where she taught special education in Tucumcari. She was extension agent for Quay County and the county's first female county commissioner. Every

January, when the New Mexico legislature was in session, Travis traveled to Santa Fe to lobby on behalf of Nara Visa.Travis pased away in 2010.

FALL ROUND-UP

My family's small ranch and farm was three miles outside of Nara Visa on a section line that runs east and west. It was surrounded by other ranches, one of the largest being the DeBaca Ranch. The DeBaca Ranch was probably a land grant, going back several hundred years.

Growing up I always looked forward to the cattle being shipped to market in the fall. Cowboys would sort and round up the cattle while winds began to blow from the north and frosted leaves began to yellow and carpet the surrounding creeks and hillsides. Rounding up the white- faced Herefords in small clumps and sending them along the fenced dirt and gravel roads to ship to market from Nara Visa was a necessary task. Cowboys always looked exhausted as they kept their small bunches in place. Usually one cowboy had several to keep in place. If one group, in the hundreds being driven, became spooked, it took a dedicated cowboy to keep the cattle from spreading alarm.

It was fun to listen to the bawling cattle, the calls of the cowboys keeping them quiet, the rustling of their spurs and chaps, and the sounds as they got the herd to stop and water at appropriate times (with the owner's permission), where the windmills happened to be. It was a terrible task to drive those cattle fifty miles, all the way to market.

My dad would get together with other small ranchers and order a few rail cars to come into the Nara Visa stop. The cars had to be in place for at least a day so that word could spread to the cattle ranchers that they were there to load. The men usually had the cattle ready to sell, so the herd didn't have to be run into the corrals on the ranch and be divided. Instead they would round up the cattle and head them for the train.

Growing up I always looked forward to ranchers in the area moving their cattle down the lane to the Nara Visa railroad stop where the cattle were loaded on cattle cars and moved to Kansas City, with several of the owners and others to care for them en route. Sometimes they would first put them in the pens overnight and load all at once in the early morning when the train would pull them off the switch cars and proceed to Kansas City. There they were sold at auction, and the ranchers returned home, paid off their debt to banks and others, and started again on a new loan. It was hoped that next year's cattle prices would be high enough to pay off the new debt.

BEULAH BRANNAN

Beulah Brennan was born in Texas and raised on a ranch. She and her husband lived in California for over a decade and moved to Nara Visa in 1970 when they leased the truck stop and café. After her husband's death in 1975, Beulah continued to run the café until 1985. She died on September 7, 2008. This article was based on an interview.

GREAT LITTLE PLACE IN THE WORLD TO LIVE

I grew up between Wheeler and Shamrock, Texas, in the Panhandle. I grew up on a ranch. My dad bought a farm in that area and they drilled oil wells on it. Magic City was a little town that sprouted up around the oil wells, and we had money. We moved to Plainview, Texas from there, and that was when the market crashed, in 1929.

After we lost our money, we just kind of existed, like everybody else. The Ford Motor Company manager was a friend of my dad's, and his bookkeeper had married and moved away and I had studied bookkeeping and he asked Dad if I wanted a job, and I said, "Yes!" Of course I did, it was $30.00 a month. Many years later I realized that that money would have supported a family, but back then I was just thinking about myself.

I married in 1939. My husband and I had a prenuptial agreement: you go to the ballet and theater with me, and I'll go hunting and fishing with you. He kept the agreement. Well, we went to Amarillo. They had pretty good shows there. Granted that [even though] he slept through most of the ballet, he was a wonderful person. A friend told me one time, "Say, if you ever decide to get rid of him, let me know."

We moved to California in the 1950s and that's when I started going to the theater and ballet. I worked in a drug store and he did construction work. We were there until 1967 when he had a heart attack and developed respiratory problems. And that's when we came back to this area.

We came here because his cardiologist suggested that he go where it was high and dry. My sister, who died ten years ago in 1995, lived in Logan. That's why we moved nearby in Nara Visa.

My husband knew the cafe´ business and the truck stop in Nara Visa was for lease. We leased it in 1970. He died in 1975, but I stayed and ran it until 1985.

The cafe″s closed now. Steve Garcia was the last one that had it. I want to cry every time I go down that street. No, I won't cry. Because some day, when I write a book, I'll call it *I'll Never Cry.* Because it doesn't do anything besides make red eyes and runny noses.

I learned to cook. I knew absolutely nothing about a cafe′, but I learned the hard way by doing it. I think there was one time three weeks running that I had a full crew and I didn't have to work two shifts. That was heavenly. We had three shifts—11:00 p.m. to 7:00 a.m., 7:00 a.m. to 3:00 pm.., and 3:00 p.m. to 11:00 p.m. And the only time I ever closed was on Christmas day. I always gave everybody a free meal on Thanksgiving. A lot of people showed up, including the long haul truck drivers, but they stopped there anyway.

You kind of get accustomed to working two shifts. Well, not exactly. It's just something you have to do. I had to do all the buying. Swift out of Amarillo brought my beef and usually some of the other meat. Borden delivered milk and ice cream, and I usually bought the other stuff at a grocery store in Tucumcari. They usually gave me a discount.

The help was being paid $2.75 an hour and the waitresses were being paid $2.75 an hour, plus tips. And they weren't reporting them. So I raised the cooks to $5.00 an hour. I told them that if someone helps me to make money, they're entitled to part of it. And I still feel that way.

I got calls from Logan and Tucumcari and Dalhart and Clayton. "What are you trying to do, run us out of business?" And my stock answer was, "Anyone who helps me make money is entitled to some of it."

The worst day I ever had came during the time we had the problem with the colored people. They thought they were being mistreated. I was waiting tables and the café was full and this African-American came in and I came by him and spoke to him and said, "I'll be with you in a moment." I had both hands full of food and was taking it to a table, and he didn't say anything right then. But I had to go back and get more food for the same table and that made him angry and he said, "I'm going to report you for not waiting on me." And he called NAACP in Albuquerque and reported me. And they called me and I told them the circumstances and that I had said that I would wait on him as quickly as I could.

They asked, "Do you have witnesses to this effect?"

I said, "Yes, I do."

I wondered who was in there who would stand up for me. My lawyer took depositions from some who were there and others who were there wrote letters and he sent them to the NAACP. I never heard another thing.

And another bad day was when we had hippies. They had on jeans, no underwear, dirty T-shirts, long shaggy hair, and I believe they both had beards. They were *dirty*. One of them had a hole right in the seat of his pants and he had on no underwear and he got up and shook his hinnie in front of a couple that was sitting in the front booth. He left twenty dollars on the table and I called him and gave him his money back.

But I was to blame for that because I didn't have a sign that said, "We reserve the right to refuse service to anyone." Needless to say I got that sign in short order.

I used three cans of Lysol spray where they had been.

Other hippies poured the salt shaker out and poured sugar in it, and they dumped the pepper. I don't remember them putting anything in the pepper shaker. I found out because a customer sprinkled sugar on his eggs and complained about it.

Another time a drunk woman fell down outside. There are three steps at one end of the cafe'. She fell down. It was concrete and she fell. She was pretty drunk. I offered to call an ambulance, I offered to help her anyway I could and she refused. She wanted to sue. I contacted my insurance company and they sent a representative to obtain all the details and to verify that I had offered to provide her services if she wanted them. The insurance company's lawyer took a deposition from me on what transpired and then they notified me that the woman had dropped the suit. She did have her legs bandaged and they paid for that. I'm a firm believer in insurance.

There were truck drivers who stopped on a regular basis—company and independent drivers. They were a different breed from what we have now. Most of them were gentlemen. They were polite and clean and cooperative. Now the drivers are spoiled brats. They act like jerks. That's true, I don't know why. I don't know what happened.

I have a niece who wanted to work in the summertime when she got out of school. I told her okay. I stayed with her to show her what to do and how to do it. But one day I had to go to Tucumcari for supplies. I told her, "I think you can do it. I'll be back as quick as I can."

When I came back I asked how she did.

She said, "Oh fine. We had a vendor while you were gone."

I said, "Who was it?"

"The Tom's salesman," she said. "I wrote him a check."

"But Cary the bank doesn't have your signature."

"But that's okay. I signed your name."

I called the bank and told them to let the check go through.

That's one nice thing about a small place where everybody knows everybody else. All I had to do was call the bank, and they accepted the check. Cary thought she had done a good deed.

I bought coffee and tea and maybe spices from the Kane's Coffee salesman. Anyway, I'm pretty observant and I thought I was being charged for merchandise I didn't get. He would check what I had on hand, write the order, and put the merchandise in my storage area. So I watched for two weeks. He came once a week, and once I was charged for three bags of coffee I didn't get and once I was charged for two bags of coffee I didn't get.

So I waited until Saturday morning when I thought no salesmen would be at Kane's Coffee. Sure enough, the manager was there. I told him the salesman had been charging me for merchandise he hadn't left. The manager was very indignant and said, "I don't believe that!"

I told him, "From now on I will check the merchandise as he leaves it."

About two hours later he called. "You were right. I called him in and asked him how many people he was cheating besides the truck stop at Nara Visa and he answered, 'Three.'"

They didn't fire the man. He had a charge who was ill and required a lot of medical services. That was before companies carried insurance on their employees and he needed the money for that. The salesman asked, would I be agreeable if he would not charge me for merchandise he had shorted me before?

And the first thing he did when he came in the next week, he had a bouquet of roses and the most beautiful apology I ever heard. And I was so glad that when the manager said, "Do you want me to fire him?" that I said, "No. We all make mistakes and bad choices but we have to live with them."

*

Next Wednesday I'll be 91. I have atrial fibrillation, the top of my heart, instead of beating, it quivers. I take two medications to keep that under control. I have macular degeneration. I am profoundly deaf. There is something wrong with my esophagus. I have arthritis and just recently was diagnosed with osteoporosis. I can't see or hear but my mind still works.

Nara Visa has been very good to me. Some of the most beautiful people in the world live there. I lost my hearing in 1989, and that wasn't too much of a problem but in 1999 I lost my sight, and that was horrible. I couldn't drive any more. Nara Visa is fifty miles from a doctor, a dentist or a grocery store, but I've never missed a doctor's appointment or gone hungry. Somebody always takes me. Travis takes me to walk every afternoon at four o'clock. Somebody picks me up and takes me to church and my doctor's appointments.

Karen Bell was probably not more than twenty when I came over here and she and her mother both worked for me. And I stayed with Jonnie, her mother, just before she died. But today I live in her mother's house, the big house, and Karen lives in the small house, and she won't take any rent. I pay the utilities, that's all.

And then there's Joanne Hughes, who reads a Sunday school lesson to me every week, and writes the checks to pay my bills. I can still sign checks. That's all I can do, I can still sign my name but I can't write checks. And so far the bank's not turned one down. So Nara Visa's a wonderful place to live.

But the main thing is the Lord took care of me then,and he still does. My favorite Bible verse is in Proverbs 3:5: "Trust in the Lord with all your heart and lean not into your own understanding. In all thy ways acknowledge Him and He will direct thy path."

I have Talking Book service, and I have Newsline. The *Albuquerque Journal* reads the paper to me every day, and now I'm getting *Newsweek* and *Reader's Digest* through the Talking Book Program.

When your family is gone you make a new one. I am alone, but I am not lonely. Friends you can pick, relatives you're stuck with. This is a wonderful place to live.

When a door closes, look for an open window. But remember it may take a while to feel the breeze.

PEGGY CLAY

Peggy Clay was born in the Texas Panhandle where she was reared on a farm. She and her farmer/rancher husband, James, moved from Texas to New Mexico, near Amistad with their three girls and three boys. The children are now grown and James has passed away, but Peggy lives on the same land. One of her sons now takes care of her cattle. She is forty-five miles from the nearest gas station and grocery store and 100 miles from the closest Walmart.

THE MOVE

The big change in my life came when I moved to Amistad. I was thirty-one at the time and had been raised in the house where I was born. Even after I was married, I lived within twenty miles of my home. Home was the rural community of Hart, in the middle of the Texas Panhandle. There was a farmhouse every half mile or so.

The economy of farming was changing rapidly. The small farmers were having a hard time. Land owners who had a section or more began to realize the wave of the future was to get bigger, the sooner the better.

My husband, James, and I had six small kids. James had always rented land. Suddenly what had worked for years began to fall apart. The land owners discovered they could buy a small acreage and lease it for about what they had bought it for. It's hard to turn loose that amount of money, knowing that in one year you will have to pay the same amount again. It was sort of like a downward spiral, leading to nowhere. My husband gave up the farm he had rented for ten years. Now he was searching for another piece of ground.

He found one in Bovina, Texas about forty miles from where

we lived. The farm was twenty-eight miles from town and did not have a house. We rented one in town. For the first time in my life I had to live in a strange place. I had three children in school and three at home. We lived there for one whole year. Let me tell you it was a year from hell!

I did not know that code of small town living. I thought that all people who came into your home were to be treated like guests. Even children. The block we moved on had nine children of assorted ages, all under twelve. Some had a mother and dad. Some were being raised only by their mother. All the mothers worked except me. Very soon I found myself being den mother, referee, policeman, nursemaid and cook. I finally figured out that you had to make them go home. As I pushed some out the front door, others would come in the back. I had a drawer with candy for my children's afternoon snack and boy, oh boy, I had to guard that candy with my life!

The block had six houses and one laundry. None of the yards had a fence. It was like open range where cattle run together in one large area. When it is time to brand or sell, the owners sort them and take care of their own. Like I say, it was open range on our block. At night about supper time most of the children would go home.

I learned something new every day. Some of the more horrific things I remember very plainly after forty-one years are backyard fights using sky rockets aimed at each other and the bicycle races between the bigger boys and the smaller children running for their lives. If one fell down, he came in crying with tire marks across his back and legs.

Everyone had cats and dogs. One day as I was taking clothes off the line, I noticed little black hopping things on my white sheets. To my horror my clean clothes were covered with fleas. I had taken in two armfuls. I ran into the house and sure enough fleas were hopping everywhere! There was a bitch dog under the trailer house near my clothesline that had a dozen flea bitten pups under it. What a mess!

This was the year my seven-year-old daughter was introduced to horse trading, except it was Barbie doll clothes. Twila was my oldest daughter, so I would let her go play with Lisa. Lisa lived on the corner opposite our house. She was the only child. Twila would take her little suitcase of dolls and clothes and wind her way through the other yards. Twila had received several new sets of Ken and Barbie clothes for Christmas. I didn't realize it until later that Twila had traded her nice sets of clothes for very crude homemade things that the girls had cut from scraps. Needless to say I sure did not appreciate her trading efforts.

Now back to the move that changed my life. Not knowing anything about my past you could not appreciate my life in the wonderful, remote area of Amistad, New Mexico.

After James turned our rented farm back to the owner I was scared and happy and worried. For the first time in my life I didn't know where I would soon be living. I remember so well coming back to Bovina from spending Christmas with my mom and dad. Even now I can smell the cold, fresh winter air. James and I were silent. There was no need for talk. We had discussed our plight and discussed it over again until there was nothing useful, or even useless or comforting, worth saying. There was nothing to occupy my mind but our troubles and so the drab scenery slipped past. I dwelled on it until I felt as though my safe world were leaking away. I knew after living in town for a year I could not repeat that nightmare, so I began to pray for God to help us find a safe, remote place to call home and raise our children.

Suddenly James broke the silence. "Your dad and I had a talk today."

I jumped because we had been riding in complete silence for

miles. My heart jumped too. Now the two favorite men in my life were beginning to make decisions. I cautiously asked, "Oh?"

I knew I didn't want to press too hard or I might not find out what they had talked about. You know how guys are. James and my dad had a really special relationship. They truly respected each other.

"We're leaving tomorrow to try to find a place to buy."

Immediately my whole being relaxed, and I began to feel safe. Nothing had really changed. The night was still dark, the air was still cold but all my uncertainty left. My guys would fix everything. They always had. The children were still quiet, hugging the toys from their grandparents. By now the spice smell from the pumpkin pie was filling the car. I was drawing strength from my two youngest, one on my lap and the other wrapped in my winter coat with the fur collar. How could I doubt when these precious ones depended on us? I knew James didn't need a response. His mind was already running ahead to what tomorrow and the next few days would bring. This was all a new concept to him. He had never owned his own place. I prayed, "Thank you, God."

The next day dawned cold and clear. Dad got to our house early. I wanted to thank him for what he was doing but that seemed a little premature. I would have loved to have gone with them, but I knew my place was to stay home and care for the children. This was their quest. They didn't need me.

They were back late the next day. I could tell by the look on their faces they were well pleased. "We did it!" James exclaimed. "We bought a farm and ranch at Amistad, New Mexico."

My first thought was New Mexico? I'm a Texan! My mind was whirling. I was trying to look happy and excited so as not to disappoint them. They looked like small boys who had just discovered a new playground. In the excitement the big question in my mind was, "Where is Amistad, New Mexico?"

"When are we leaving?" I asked.

"Just as soon as we can pack up!" James said. He was ready to get on with things. I, too, knew the sooner the better.

The next day as I began the preparation to leave, I told my neighbor we were moving. She had been a good friend to me for that year. She and her husband did not have children,and they were fascinated with our six.

"We're moving to Amistad, New Mexico," I said it in a loud voice, trying to sound like I wasn't in the least bit concerned. I didn't expect her startled reaction.

"I know exactly where that is! There is nothing there except rattlesnakes and cactus!"

I felt like she had slapped me! I was doing my best to convince myself things were great and wham! I was right back drowning in my doubts.

In just seven short days we were packed. We had our entire household goods in two old grain trucks and the back of James' pickup. Dad and mom had their pickup loaded too. They were not about to miss out on such an adventure. We must have looked like a band of gypsies! Luke, our Negro hired hand, was pulling a small camper-trailer. James had just hired him a few months before, but he was willing to follow us to wherever we were taking him. He didn't have a family, and he and James had worked closely the past months. I could feel some of Luke's uncertainty. I was thirty-one years old and, except for the year in Bovina, had lived in the same community all my life. We were moving 150 miles north. I needed to just keep telling myself. "It's going to be okay, it's going to be okay, it's going to be okay . . . ."

Lynn and Joe, the two oldest boys, were with James. The three girls and Jimmy and two cats were riding with me. Before long we were traveling mile after mile through endless wheat fields. Winter wheat becomes dormant in the winter months, so the fields look almost naked.

When we reached the cap rock near San Jon, we slowly wound our way down the steep grade. We were driving through a different type of landscape now, miles of endless grassland. Every few miles there was an old weather-beaten tree near a broken cement foundation, but most of these deserted homesteads had a windmill still pumping water from the breeze that blew. The busted cement tanks had been replaced by steel ones. There were not any trees for lumber. Every now and then I would glimpse a house and barn off in the distance. I could see from the dirt road leading off the highway that someone lived there.

As the miles rolled away, taking me further into this new, remote land, I could feel the peacefulness and quietness settle around me. Isn't that what I yearned for in my prayer?

Finally James pulled off the road to check his load. "We're almost there," he exclaimed. Six excited pairs of eyes looked out the windows, anxious to see where home would be.

We turned onto a rough dirt road. Our house sat by the side of the road. A good place to keep our horses. The pens were strong enough to hold cattle while we branded. I had to remind myself, "This is New Mexico where the cattle have to have a brand. It's the law."

The house had several large elm trees, naked in the winter cold. It was totally hidden behind a wild growth of salt cedar. I could tell that it was two stories tall. The kids ran ahead of me, anxious to explore the inside. The doors were not locked and forty-one years later they still are not locked. The doors did not have keys, and I felt so safe. I just never had any made.

The rooms were pretty big, with large windows. Lots of windows. Mother explained that when the pioneers began to move out of the dugouts, the women were all adamant about having plenty of light. We had lots of light, but the old windows also let in lots of cold and dirt!

In the next few weeks James and Luke finished moving all the farm equipment and tools that James had accumulated over the last fifteen years, plus a mountain of stuff his dad had farmed with for the past thirty years. They made many trips. The equipment had been collected over the years by lots of blood, sweat, very hard work and money. To James it was like part of his family.

The kids and I settled into our new life quickly. We had to. Two days later the four oldest kids started school. Soon they were involved in everything. When I say "everything," you have to know about a small school. There were 120 students from the first through twelfth grades. Each class had eight to ten students. I couldn't wait for the bus to bring them home. For the next twelve years they would all hit the door talking at the same time. Snacks would be ready. I thrilled at the excitement and joy in their voices. I heard stories about what they had learned, but also the gossip that comes along when the student body is small and everyone knows everyone.

I was relieved that more of the homegrown kids made my newcomers pay the price of showing what they were made of. I loved the peace and safety more than anything. That was the one thing I yearned for. Without being able to identify it, that was my quest.

The years rolled by fast. Happy years. The boys helped their dad farm. During the fall and spring they would get off the bus and get on the tractor, plow until dark and come in to do chores and homework. The girls helped me in the house and yard. It was a busy time with lots of cooking and washing clothes. But it wasn't all work. The kids got me involved in sports, 4-H club, school plays, cheerleading, newspaper and annuals.

But the most important thing was our church. I told myself before I moved that I did not care what church we attended, it would have to be the one closest to school and home. The first time I went to Amistad, there stood a little white church with a steeple and a cross right across from the school. It didn't take long to get acquainted with the town. It had one school, one garage (with one gas pump), one grocery store (with the post office in the back) and six houses. I loved it! There sure were not any town brats running loose. Well, there were five town kids. They all belonged to one family. So if there was any corralling needed, their mom got the job. The school and the church were the hub of the community.

The area was massive. I soon found that out when my oldest daughter became fast friends with Cindy Shepherd. She lived thirty-five miles to the west. Rhonda and Barbara's best friends lived in Nara Visa fourteen miles south of us. The school district reached over into Texas, ten miles east and twenty-five miles north. I never have figured out how many square miles that is, but in no time I knew where all the roads went and the faces and names of all the great people who lived there. Just like it was back in Texas where I grew up. In all that large area there was not a stop light, a doctor, a movie theater or policeman.

I thought I would miss mama. I did, but I soon discovered this wonderful group of gray-haired ladies with work-worn hands and smiling eyes. They all had large families of their own and led busy lives. They just spread their arms wide open and welcomed this greenhorn from Texas.

Their knowledge amazed me. In northeastern New Mexico, the Anglos and Hispanics have mixed and mingled since pioneer days. The best of two cultures. They were very eager to open up their homes. My quest was over. I had found my safe place.

Forty years have passed. The kids have all grown and gone. They have kids of their own. We have twelve grandchildren. The excitement of going to the sandy creek and catching lizards has been passed on to them.

This is home now and forever. The old farm equipment sets on the hill like forgotten dinosaurs. The grass is getting thin and short from several years of drought but water is still available. It is our life blood. I think back often about the unexpected move in my life that has defined who I am and who my children are.

RENÉE ROCK RINESTINE

Renée Rock Rinestine is very involved in community and civic activities. She started playing the piano as a small child and continues to play for community programs and church. She ran a custom drapery shop from her home for twenty years. Renée and her husband, James, own and operate a cattle ranch outside Nara Visa on land which was homesteaded by their families in the early 1900s. They have one son, one daughter and five grandchildren.

DANCING

Living on a ranch ten miles from town was often lonely for me, so when it was time for a dance in town I became really excited. Dances were the main source of fun and entertainment as I grew up, as it was for my brother and sister and my parents many years ago.

I can remember my parents talking about going to neighbors' homes on Saturday nights, moving furniture from one room to another to make room to dance. Those who could play an instrument entertained as the others danced. My dad, Roderick

Rock, played the guitar; my future grandparents-in-law, Webb and Lucille Wilson, played the fiddle and the piano. There were others who played the harmonica, banjo or whatever they could, and all of them played by ear and were self-taught. The music consisted of old-time country tunes such as "Red River Valley" and "Red Wing."

In 1937 a gymnasium was built in Nara Visa, which provided a spacious floor on which to dance. Some of the band members from that time were Bertha Yessler, who beat the drums, with Lester Whitaker, Keith Wise and Wanda Dale adding to the group. Since there were no electric instruments, the band set up in the center of the floor and couples danced around them.

During the 1950s, square dancing was popular and dad was a caller. Four couples formed a square, and the caller sang directions as they would "promenade left" or "do-si-do" to the sounds of "Turkey in the Straw" or "Texas Star." The melodies were fast and the couples had to pay attention to the call to make the correct moves. If you got mixed up, someone would give you a shove in the right direction to keep it all going to the beat of the music. Many couples came regularly, and often went to neighboring towns such as Tucumcari or San Jon to dance. The women dressed in very full skirts with lots of rick-rack trim, and some of the men had matching shirts. It was a matter of pride for the women to sew those elaborate costumes. Each wanted to outdo the other. There was a lot of hand clapping and shouting, adding to the fun.

Some of my best memories are of the dances in Nara Visa and Amistad, where I attended high school. There were many dances throughout the year. Couples came with their children, who learned to dance at an early age. As the kids got sleepy, they would be laid down on the gym bleachers to sleep; everyone else danced on until it was over. My dad did not play guitar at these dances, just at house parties. He was not a good dancer, as he had only one dance step, no matter what the beat of the music; however, no one enjoyed it more than him. Dad danced to every song, no matter how long the dance lasted into the early morning hours.

Nara Visa always held the Thanksgiving and Christmas dances. The New Year's dance was at Amistad. The gyms were usually decorated with lights and appropriate items pertaining to the occasion. Christmas and New Year's were the best. A large Christmas tree, usually a piñon, would be decorated with glass balls, homemade ornaments from tin cans, lights, and icicles, which were hung just so. Strings of multicolored lights were strung from the center of the gym ceiling to the walls. For the New Year's dance, the gym would also be decorated with strings of colored lights, and in the center of the ceiling, hung a large net container. Everyone could hardly wait until the seconds counted down to midnight, as the string from the net would be pulled and the confetti, necklaces and noisemakers would fly down in a flurry. People sang "Auld Lang Syne," and hopefully someone you liked might even give you a New Year's kiss!

Through the later years dances were held as fund raisers for the school or community center, but fewer and fewer people came, and it became difficult to pay the bands, so for a while they ceased to be held. However, a few years ago a friend and I began hosting an annual invitational dance. Those invited pay prior to the dance, which allows it to be private, so people can bring their own bottle of spirits. Everyone brings snacks, which are shared in the gym kitchen. The money collected pays for the band and decorations, with any remaining money donated to the Nara Visa Community Center for building repairs. Each year a different theme is chosen and the gym and kitchen are decorated with Hawaiian, Western, or Mardi Gras motifs.

Many neighboring towns host annual celebrations to commemorate area special events. These bring in local residents and visitors from miles around and are held during the summer when the weather is warm. These usually conclude with a dance, and often these dances are held outdoors. Some are street dances. A block is cordoned off from automobile traffic, allowing a large area for the dancers. Other towns have a cement slab, sometimes behind the roping arena, for their dance. The band is located atop a flatbed trailer, playing the latest country songs. The crowd stands around the edges of the "dance floor" visiting or people watching. All ages come and enjoy the festivities, from babies—who soon fall asleep in their car seats—to great-grandparents.

Dances have always been an integral part of the culture of the area and evolve with the times, and the opportunity to enjoy music, dancing and friends remains just as it was long ago.

RENÉE ROCK RINESTINE

SMALL TOWN TRIBULATIONS

"First Rate Roofing. We cannot come to the phone right now. Please leave a message and we will get back to you as soon as possible."

Beep

"This is Renee Rinestine from Nara Visa. You put a new roof on the gymnasium last summer and it is leaking very badly in several places. We really need you to come back and make the repairs. Please call me or Mary Brown." No return on my call.

A few days later Mary had reason to go to the city where the contractor is located. She went to his business and explained the situation to him and he said it couldn't possibly be the roof. He had fixed it. The water had to be coming through the walls.

"Please come and inspect the roof. If it is not the roof, then please give us advice on whom to contact."

"Okay. We'll be there in three or four days."

Three or four days pass. I call again.

"First Rate Roofing. We cannot come to the phone . . . etc. etc."

"This is Renee Rinestine from Nara Visa. Before you come to inspect the roof, please let us know when you will be here so someone can let you into the building and show you the places that are leaking. One corner of the ceramic room is crumbling. The far corner of the gym is too. Muddy water comes down the walls on the outside and inside of the ceramic room. Please call before you make the trip here so someone can point out the problem areas." Weeks have gone by and still not one word from First Rate Roofing.

This is what faces small communities that are somewhat isolated and have few resources. Local residents can do only so much. Even when there is money to do some refurbishing, it cannot start until other jobs are finished properly. The buildings in my hometown are designated on the State and National Historic Registry and must not be left to deteriorate.

Frustration soon sets in and turns to despair. The community center is the only meeting and entertainment facility in the area, so keeping the buildings intact is important to everyone. When those who have been trusted to do a job fail to do it properly and refuse to accept responsibility, you feel betrayed and helpless. Why does everything have to be so difficult when you are trying to do good things that will benefit your town and neighbors?

TUCUMCARI

PAT SPEUDA

Pat Speulda has enjoyed the rugged beauty of New Mexico for the last fifteen years. She enjoys nineteenth-century novels and now has the time to read them. She lives with various local cats in Tucumcari, in a small adobe home that is slowly listing to the north.

HARD LANDING

Like many Americans, I was swept from my comfortable existence by the 2008 economic tsunami and cast ashore in a new world. In my case the new world was the small town of Tucumcari, on the edge of the Great Plains, in eastern New Mexico.

Forced to give up our home, not by a dust storm, but by economic necessity, we packed some dishes, clothes, books, a few pieces of furniture and four cats and headed away from California, an Okie and a New Mexican, migrating back in the direction we came from.

We arrived on a cold, rainy night, unpacked our bed, and the next morning woke up to our new reality: an old trailer with no heat or electricity, lacking major appliances, and covered in hideous wall-to-wall carpeting at the beginning of the worst winter in a decade. This was followed by a record-breaking summer, complete with twisters. I saw a funnel cloud from our front yard one evening. Our property seemed to grow only dirt, weeds and some Chinese elms that, happily, turned green in spring. The harsh climate and prickly landscape seemed to reflect my own state of mind as I tried to recover from my personal upheaval.

I quickly learned not to walk barefoot in the yard (or in the house!) because of goatheads and biting ants. I learned where to get free rice and beans and how to salvage and barter for building materials and household items. I learned that half my husband's family didn't talk to the other half. I learned that the clerks in the convenience store knew everything that happened in town, and that half the town saw the shoes that fell off the hood of my car when I turned onto Route 66, called the Boulevard. ("They must have been run over five or six times by the time I saw them," someone said. "Better just buy some new ones!")

I learned that there are wonderful people in Episcopal churches and that people will appear and help when your car gets stuck in snow-melted mud. I slowly grew accustomed to doing without a daily paper—even *USA Today* is no longer delivered to stands here—or a coffee shop with real coffee. Though it wasn't easy, with help from my in-laws we managed to get along until things got a little easier. I enrolled in the local community college, joined the new food co-op and the arts council, and attended bluegrass concerts and quilt shows.

I now have a home with major appliances, rugs covering much of the carpet, my own paintings on the walls, and handmade shelves filled with books. My husband's experiments with weed-based mulch paid off—we now have more vegetables than we can eat. And we are happy patrons of the new espresso bar on Route 66. Our cats have a hangout under an old travel trailer, and I have all the time in the world to catch up on my reading, sitting in my little pool in the backyard, under the trees.

I can't do anything about the weather.

NICK ARAGON

Nick Aragon lived in Tucumcari until age ten when he moved to San Francisco where he went to school, worked, and raised a family. He is now retired and has moved back to Tucumcari.

MR. CHAVEZ AND THE RATTLY TRUCK

My eye opened and I peeked from under the blanket to see a dark room with hints of the closet door, the chest of drawers and the light switch. Slowly, I saw images of miniature soldiers, a truck, pictures, string, rocks and clothing laid out for the morning. I closed my eye, content that it was still dark and I was home in bed.

TICK pause TICK pause TICK pause. The old nightstand wind-up clock marked off the seconds till it was time to explode with CLANGA-CLANGA! Just as I started thinking, "It's still the middle of the night," it went off. Time to get the day started.

"Wait a minute, it's Saturday. Oh well, I have stuff to do. Let's get it over with then. The rest of the day is mine." I heard the door to my sisters' room squeak open, followed by the thunk of the bathroom door closing. The race is on.

I hit the floor running, bolting out of my room and slamming into my other sister, Rosie, in the hallway. She careened off the wall and knocked off one of the pictures as I bounced off of her and land back in my room. We just looked at each other, ignoring the damage done. The race was on again. "KNOCK IT OFF!!!" came from the room at the end of the hall, thundering through the house. It sounded like the gods had spoken.

Arriving in the kitchen and seeing the box of oatmeal on the counter, not the new box of cereal, was a disappointment. The race to get the prize in the box was a race that didn't have to happen.

BB, the oldest of us four, was the one who would light the old coal/wood-burner stove, even though we all knew how. "Get me half a can," she said. "Half a can" meant half a coffee can of coal from the bin outside the back door. "AND the oil."

Meanwhile, Rosie was put to the task of filling a pot with water and getting out the bowls and spoons. BB got the stove lit and was heating the water. She would heat it almost to boiling, then move it aside to another part of the stove where she would stir in the oats and return it to the heated end and take out the tortillas. While all this was taking place, Rosie and I were getting dressed.

Everything was set, and we were sitting down for the second-best breakfast on earth, second only to cold cereal because cold cereal was a lot less work.

More commands bellowed from the back room: "BB, FEED THE BABY! ROSIE, GO GET THE EGGS! ROBBER (Ma never pronounced the "t" in my name) LET THE CHICKENS OUT! FEED THE DOG! WATER THE GARDEN! CLEAN THE COOP, AND PUT ON YOUR OVERALLS!"

My day was going to be one of the good ones, I thought. Putting on my overalls meant I was going someplace with six of my cousins.

Riding fence? Moving livestock? Repairing a barn? Picking crops? I didn't care. It was fun. I enjoyed all the strange things that happened and the critters that showed up with a surprised look when things were moved, like the barn that fell down last year and jackrabbits scattered in all directions when we lifted the pile of lumber.

Yes, it was going to be an interesting day for me, and I could hardly wait.

Just as I was finishing up, dad came out and went next door to talk to old man Chavez. He was a thin, old cowboy who lived by himself for two months during the winter and was only seen on Sunday mornings all cleaned up with "Sunday-going-to-meeting" duds, from the white Stetson hat to the Tony Lama boots. Then he would disappear until the next Sunday morning.

This was the first time I had seen him on a Saturday and for a moment it seemed kind of strange.

Dad called me over and said I was going with old Mister Chavez to help him and do whatever he said.

"Okay!"

Even though I did not know what was in store for me, still I knew it was going to be a real interesting day. I ran back into the house as quickly as I could and grabbed a small box of matches and my fencing tool. When you were going to work somewhere, you automatically took a box of matches and a fencing tool.

As quickly as I ran in, I ran back out, forgetting to close the screen door quietly. When it slammed I thought, "Oh man, I'm going to hear about that when I get back!"

Dad just looked at me with the expression that everyone knew as: "What the hell's the matter with you?" Then he pointed to the old truck and with just a look told me to do whatever I was told. "Don't bring home any problems!"

Old man Chavez started for the truck. I ran around to the passenger side and grabbed the door handle. I cranked it to the left. The handle turned too easily and the door didn't open, so I figured a turn to the right would do the trick. Nothing. Looking inside I saw the door was locked. Not only was it missing all its glass, but also all the guts that made it work. The door was held shut with pieces of metal and baling wire.

"Get in," Mister Chavez said, pointing to the back of the truck. That was fine with me because the seat was nothing but old springs and wire, without padding, seat cover, or backrest. Without hesitating, I climbed in the flatbed and sat on a wooden crate, with one foot going through a hole I could have climbed through.

"Perro!" Mister Chavez yelled. Out of nowhere an old mangy dog came running with a kind of sideward gait and in one leap jumped into the cab, passing through the window that wasn't there. We were ready to go.

Errr Errr er er…the truck didn't start. "AH LA VERGA!" He pounded on the steering wheel. Old mister Chavez got out, opened the hood, propped it up with a stick, and grabbed the hammer he kept next to the battery and started banging on everything.

Tink, kank, kank, BANG, BANG, BANG, tink, tink, thunk. "UN DIA VOY A CAMBIAR PARA UNA NUEVA!" he yelled. Then, taking out the stick and slamming the hood shut, he got back in and pushed the start button and "Er-VROOM!" As if the truck understood what he said (and didn't want to go to the dead truck end of town) gave Mister Chavez no more trouble all that day.

With a small cloud of exhaust, a short jerk and a whurrr from the transmission in need of oil, we were on our way.

It was kind of a good thing we lived on Seventh Street, the last road on the west end of town. It made it easy to get out to Main Street and head in any direction out of town. Seventh Street was a dirt road, and I think it was a smoother washboard path than the sand-tar paved streets around town, with their potholes big enough and deep enough to plant a telephone pole. During winter the ground froze eight-inches deep and the tar along the edges of the streets broke off. This action was balanced out every summer with the 105 degree heat that melted them back together.

So we were on our way, heading north on Seventh Street. I figured we would be stopping at my Uncle Juan's house to pick up *some* of my cousins, because I didn't think all ELEVEN would fit in the little truck, even if some stood on the running board and a couple rode on the old truck's beat-up, bulbous fenders.

Rattle, rattle, rattle. We went right past my cousins' pink house and, without even slowing down for the stop sign, made a right turn onto State Highway 54, which changed to Main Street as it went through the three blocks of downtown.

Still not knowing where Mister Chavez was headed made no difference to me. I was still happy that today was going to be a very interesting adventure.

Oh man, a sharp left turn onto Hwy 104 threw me off the wooden crate and nearly stuck me head first into the hole in the truck bed. When we drove past the poorest end of town, I knew we were heading to one of the large farms or vast ranches out past the bridge where the divided highway stopped.

Rattling on down the road, leaving the town behind us at a steady fifteen miles below the speed limit, Mister Chavez didn't seem to be in any hurry. Then I realized that Mister Chavez had his foot to the floor and that the old truck was doing her top speed. Then came a long uphill grade, and the truck slowly lost her pace and (with a bang from its Swiss cheese exhaust pipe) he shifted to a lower gear and resumed a steady pace, passing the last farm out of town.

We had pulled off the road to a ranch gate made of gnarly limbs of mesquite and barbed wire that ran in different angles and twists. I knew there wasn't a single nail holding that thing together.

Perro suddenly sat up, putting half his body through the door, ready to exit the cab and get to work. Perro knew where he was. Mister Chavez looked at me,and I knew that meant, "Get out and open the gate," which I did, dragging it inward along the ground.

Mister Chavez drove through the opening and up the slight grade, rattling all the way. I closed the gate, hooking the wire loop over the fence post and kicking the bottom of the gate to close it completely.

I turned and headed for the truck, which was still in motion, running as fast as I could to catch up. He stopped, and just as I took hold of the old truck's tailgate, Mr. Chavez started moving again. As I hung on for dear life, he hit a pothole. The sudden jerk ripped me off the ground and hurled me into the bed of the truck and halfway into that damn hole in the floor. Traveling on down the rutted dirt road, rattling and squeaking, with the frequent WHONK of a rock hitting the bottom of the old truck, I was afraid I would be beaten and broken from being tossed and bounced like a pinball in a cement mixer.

We arrived at a small, one-room adobe ranch house with a small corral connected to a three-walled stall. I couldn't see them, but judging from the noise and the thick burning scent, I knew that beyond the stall had to be the world's biggest herd of pigs. Flies wouldn't go near that pigpen.

Parking the old truck under the biggest bare tree, we got out and walked over to the water tank. At the same time three cows came from behind the hovel with the same idea—a nice clean drink of water.

Perro, walking alongside Mister Chavez, adjusted his gait to head off the cattle, yet keeping them in the area until we had had our drink and wet down.

"VAMOS!" said Mister Chavez, and Perro turned away from guard duty and, with his tongue hanging to just an inch above ground, took three big leaps and splash! into the tank he went. He swam a couple of laps and drank as he swam, then leaped out and went into a water-shedding shake, showering everything within ten feet.

"Well, let's get started." Mister Chavez said, making a motion that said we were heading for the pigpen.

Bracing myself to see the band of pigs that made the aroma from hell, I laughed when I saw only a sow and three little piglets. Mister Chavez, using Spanglish, spoke in an "I'm only going to say thisONCE" tone of voice, "Yo tengo much too acer and you are going to plow all that asta la fence aya y de la tree asta los rocks aya."

"Okay," I said, while thinking to myself, "I've done this before and it looks like an all-day-and-half-the-night chore." We walked over to a large shed that had collapsed on one side. That is where the tractor was kept.

Looking the tractor over, I read the manufacturer's plate: 1938 FERGUSON MULTI-FUEL 2 SPEED. She was newer than the truck. I smiled and felt relieved, knowing that I wasn't going to be driving an ox team with a single blade.

Mister Chavez climbed on up and, turning knobs, moving levers, and stomping all the pedals a few times, finally pressed the start button: ER-ER-er-er. It was a repeat of the old truck this morning. The difference this time was that he just reached into the metal box welded to the fender and took out the twin to the hammer used on the truck.

KANG! KANG! on the left side. KANG! KANG! KANG! on the right side. All in a long smooth Keystone Kops routine. Then he reached over and pressed the start button. The old engine started to turn. I counted every time the bent fan blade turned. It took six full turns when the first chug came out of the exhaust stack, then another and another. Chuger-chuger-chuger-chug-chug-chug, faster and faster until the black, choking smoke billowing out turned to a nice light blue choking straight-up column.

Mister Chavez looked at me and nodded just once, placed the hammer back in the greasy dirt-encrusted box and walked out.

I climbed up and stepped on the clutch, put her in low gear and took off. It took all of twenty minutes to make the first run, as I did my best to keep her in a straight line. The first one is the hardest.

Taking a full three minutes to raise the plow, turn around and drop the left front wheel into the furrow, I knew it would take twenty minutes to get back.

Moving back into the seat, I placed my feet on the crossbars of the steering wheel and just went along for the ride.

On approaching the end of the line, I thought up a detailed plan on how to get a drink of water and a cool splash at the water tank. The only problem would be if the cows were still there.

Squinting my eyes, I saw I had the all-clear. I smiled. I knew this was going to be easy. I thought out loud and set the plan in motion. "End of the line, raise the blade, hard right turn, realign and drop the right front wheel into the furrow and drop the blade. Okay, go." I jumped off and ran to the tank, knowing that the tractor was in low gear, and that I would have just enough time to stick my head in the tank and drink and wipe my face while running back to the Furgie. It worked perfectly. I repeated this routine all the rest of the day until the signal came to pack it up.

Perro came to the tractor and stood in front and gave me four barks, then went back to the house. I knew to take Furgie back to the shed and turn all the levers, knobs, and switches to OFF.

Old Man Chavez came to me and said I did a good job and gave me a basket with fire-roasted chicken and a Mason jar of sun tea and said, "Let's go." Just taking my grips, I got back into the bed of the truck and fell asleep.

LAS CRUCES, NEW MEXICO

DONNA PADILLA

A life-long resident of New Mexico, Donna Padilla moved to Santa Fe in 1953 where she lived with her husband Tony, whose family has been in Santa Fe since the 1690s. Donna passed away in 20XX.

BOOMTOWN, NEW MEXICO

It was the early Sixties and the beat generation was hanging out in coffee houses, listening to bongo drums and incomprehensible poetry. Before the decade was out, teens would be dropping out, forming a counter culture, riding freedom buses, passing out flowers, and burning draft cards. I dropped out of college after two years, loaded all my worldly possessions in my beat-up, old Buick and headed for a boomtown in southern New Mexico to stay with my sister until I could figure out my next move.

New Mexico was having an extractive heyday and boomtowns were springing up all over the state. This once quiet ranching town was now surrounded by trailer parks. Grazing land was dotted with pump jacks bobbing up and down, sucking oil from underground basins. Skeletal drilling rigs towered over scrubby desert plant life. Miles and miles of new natural gas pipelines were being laid. Every other day pipes and industrial equipment were unloaded from flatcars, and gondolas were loaded with tons of potash. Mud trucks and water trucks paraded up and down main street, and parking spaces were filled with cars and pickups bearing out-of-state license plates.

Extractive industries usually run three shifts a day, so there is always one shift working, one shift sleeping, and one shift eating and drinking. Hotels, motels, bars, and restaurants are the real gold mines in any boomtown.

Work is always easy to find in a boomtown, and having had some bar experience while working my way through college, I set out to canvas the bars in town. Every bar was fully staffed, but each wanted a backup person to call when they needed an extra hand, or when a bartender or waitress failed to show up. Within no time I found myself working almost every bar in town. It wasn't unusual for me to work the day shift in one bar and the night shift in another.

In the hotel bar one encountered company executives, local bigwigs, tourists, and the railroad crew that stayed over every other night. One night a bus carrying a college basketball team (mostly black) on its way home from a tournament stopped at the hotel. I was waiting tables and was very embarrassed when the bartender refused to serve the team. Martin Luther King was very far away in the South.

Red Adair and his crew headquartered in the hotel while working at extinguishing the well fire that turned night into day. I am proud to say that I have met Red Adair, the world renowned oil well firefighter. Whenever the classic movie channel airs the film with John Wayne portraying Red Adair, I watch.

All the local good old boys hung out at the country-western dance hall and rode herd on the local good old girls. Women are always in short supply in a boomtown. Stetson hats and Wrangler jeans were the accepted dress. On weekends the parking lot was always filled with Ford and Chevy pickups, and it was not unusual for a rebel yell to rise above the amplified guitars.

A couple of bars catered to the boomers. Money changed hands over the pool tables, liar's poker was played at the bar, and everybody always knew where the real poker games were. City and county coffers were strained, law enforcement officers worked overtime, and gambling laws were not high on the enforcement priority list.

It took me a while to figure out that there were at least three different kinds of poker games going on. One was the typical spontaneous game that people play on payday. Another was a twenty-four-hour-a-day, seven-day-a-week game in one of the motel rooms. The players changed as the work shifts changed. Finally, I discovered that there was a group of professional gamblers working around town. They never played two days in a row, never used the same location twice, and the games were by invitation only. There were spotters working for the professional gamblers in some of the bars, keeping their eyes open for people flashing wads and looking for action. These spotters had to have a sixth sense for personality because they could not afford to invite an undercover cop or a poor loser.

The one pro who played in every private game was the Midget, who seemed to have stepped off the page of a Damon Runyon short story. He was just a tad over five feet tall and always wore a white Stetson to hide his baldness. A diamond ring flashed on his left hand, and he called it his insurance policy. There was always a buck or two tucked into his custom-made boots because he never knew when he might need bail money. He had a construction job which took him to boomtowns, and he was a member of his trade union.

Eventually I managed to land a full-time bartending job. The clientele was a mixture of local blue collar and farm workers, documented and undocumented aliens. What held them together in common bond was the Spanish language. The bar was a drafty, unadorned barn-like structure with generic chairs and tables, a couple of pool tables, and a jukebox that blasted Mexican music. The bar ran halfway across one side of the room and was constructed of rough, unfinished lumber. The only access to the back bar was through the store room, and the only door in the store room led to the parking lot.

Bill, the owner/manager, had sustained a back injury while trying to break up a bar brawl and had very strict rules for his bartenders. They were never, never, never to cross to the other side of the bar. If something started going down, they were to go into the store room and lock the door behind them. They would then lock the front door from the outside and call the cops. Forget the bar. Take care of yourself.

One night I was pulling some draft beers and looked up to see about eight or nine cowboy hats coming through the front door. Knowing that this particular crowd usually drank Seagrams VO, I went to the store room to get a full bottle. Bill was there with his feet propped up, and when I reached for the VO he came to immediate attention and muttered, "Oh, shit." Knowing that the two groups now occupying the bar might not be an amicable mix, we discussed a couple of possible impending scenarios, then both went back into the bar. All the cowboy hats were lined up at the bar waiting for their drinks. There was nobody else in sight.

On Saturday nights we usually served a standing-room-only crowd, so I was backed up by a bouncer and a waitress. One particular Saturday night, about half way through the shift, I realized that the bouncer had given up and joined the crowd, and that the waitress was about half crocked. I was pulling drafts, opening beer bottles, and ringing the cash register as fast as I could, but not fast enough for one man standing at the end of the bar. He started by yelling, "Cerveza, *cerveza!*" Shortly, he began punctuating his yells by banging his empty bottle on the bar. Finally, in total frustration, in an attempt to get my attention, he hurled the bottle in my direction. It missed. All activity in the bar came to an abrupt halt. Nobody knew what my reaction was going to be. I marched to the store room, grabbed a broom, poked the offender in the chest with the broom handle and roared, "You broke it, you clean it up!" I never crossed to the other side of the bar. He did.

ADA, OKLAHOMA

PAT SPEUDA

PORTRAIT OF MOM

My favorite picture of my mother is an old black-and-white photograph. She's standing in front of the old red brick "House on the Hill" in Ada, Oklahoma that we kids only knew about from the painting she did of it when young. She's standing with her hands on her hips, shirtless, wearing only her cowboy boots, a pair of shorts, and her gun belt, with a gun on each hip. She's squinting defiantly at the camera. She's about six years old. Eventually, when she was eleven or twelve, her mother made her come in and put on a shirt.

Mom never really outgrew this attitude, even when she was grown and raising four children of her own. She grew up on "the Hill" in Ada, surrounded by the showy homes of the rich kids. These were the days of the Oklahoma oil boom.

Her family was not one of the rich ones. She had her chores every day. My grandparents raised their own hogs and had a cow and a goat for milk. Mom's well-off friends begged to come over to the Suggs and help with their outside chores, which seemed very exotic and fun to them.

Mom's parents were old-fashioned Southerners, loving but fairly strict, at least with their three older children. My mom, as the youngest, and a girl, was cut the most slack, and she took full advantage. She cared about nothing but her horse and her dog, and later joined the local Round-up Club. Once she borrowed the family car and promptly drove it into a ditch. My grandfather uttered not a word of reproach, but a look from him was sufficient. She worshiped her big brothers, Jim and Hob, and followed them around whenever they would let her.

Mom would get to talking about her early years after a shot or two of tequila (or "tea") and her pal Jean could be persuaded, after a few beers, to spin stories about their "wild" younger days. Mom would climb out her second-story bedroom window, saddle up her horse, and meet Jean. They sometimes rode out to cowboy bars on the edge of town, where Jean, over-developed and under-experienced, would occasionally have to be rescued from an amorous cowboy who was buying her drinks and paying her compliments. Mom would drag her out to the horses as Jean complained, "But, Dod, he was so NICE!"

They both joined the Round-up Club, and avidly attended rodeos. We still have some glossies of Mom and her pals participating in these events, roping calves or posing in their satin cowgirl shirts. Their heroes really *were* cowboys. Eventually Jean accepted a marriage proposal from her boyfriend, but refused to go on a honeymoon with this "old boy" she barely knew without my mother coming along. Along she went, along with her boyfriend, an Indian cowboy. The result was that the wrong girl got pregnant. A girlfriend made arrangements for Mom to live in Arizona while waiting for her baby and giving it up for adoption. She had told everyone back home that she was visiting a friend. This was a common solution to unwed motherhood in those days, not so very long ago. She didn't think her parents ever found out.

After returning to Oklahoma, she went to college where she especially loved her courses in geology and Spanish (I still have her book of Spanish poetry), and learned to identify aircraft. When her brother Jim came home from San Diego, where he was working as an engineer in an aircraft factory after the war, she returned with him and got a job there. When she met his friend Lloyd, they began dating, then married. Like many couples after the war they moved into a Quonset hut where they started their family. They then moved to Norman, Oklahoma, where my dad went to school at Oklahoma University on the GI Bill and they had three more kids. I have pictures of the six of us all dressed up for Easter services, complete with patent-leather shoes, but generally our upbringing was more relaxed, as Mom's inner cowgirl re-emerged, and she sought the freedom of earlier days by finding friends with horses, and then acquiring her own.

We generally lived in town and boarded the horses. She would tell us, "We're going out to the horses!" and we would pile into the car, head out of town and breathe the free air of open country, where we would ride through pastures and along creek beds, pick unripe persimmons from horseback, and play house in haystacks. We learned how to stay in the saddle, or how to get right back on, and never to complain. Mom showed us how to find plant fossils in old creek beds and how to hike through the woods without making a sound, "like an Indian."

Whenever I think of my mom, I picture her on a horse. Some years ago, she made the great sacrifice of selling her last horse and moving to northern California to be near her kids, who'd been pretty well scattered for many years. When she got cancer, we spent her last year spending as much time with her as possible, sharing secrets and stories we'd never told each other, and holding her hand when she wept for the friends she had to leave behind. After she died, we divided up some of her ashes and mailed them out in leather pouches (Indian bags) to a long list of her friends across several states. Her friend, Bitsy, told me she had put her share of Mom's ashes into a little pair of cowboy boots and flung them into the branches of a tree, high in the Colorado mountains Mom used to hike and ride in.

Mom made many friends and had plenty of adventures in her life, but her true home was always in the saddle, where she seemed supremely comfortable and in command.

SUE EMORY

THE DIRTY THIRTIES

The Depression went on for years and years. Men worked for a dollar a day. The saying was, "Another day, another dollar." Another saying was, "We work from can 'til can't." In other words, people worked from daylight until dark, and longer if possible. Jobs were scarce as hens' teeth. Young boys often worked for fifty cents a day, *if* they could find one. They learned to *work*! . . . No coffee breaks, no benefits. *Work* they did. If they didn't, someone else would. It was a struggle to feed and clothe the family and keep a place to live. Whatever they bought had to last as long as possible. People have ways to cope, and they did as best they could, under the circumstances.

They often had dances on Saturday nights. Gather at someone's house. Get two or three musicians. Pass a hat around for money to pay them. Dance all night, get home in time to go to work on Sunday, if their job required it—most jobs did. But it was a break to get together and socialize with friends and neighbors.

We had to walk everywhere we went. Walk to school—back home for lunch—back to school again—home again—then back to the store and/or Post office. Shoes for school kids was a problem that couldn't be ignored. When one got a new pair of shoes, we all had to see them and admire them. We really appreciated new shoes. We didn't get them until it was an absolute necessity. We didn't have to decide what shoes to wear. We had one pair—for school, church, whatever, and lucky to have one pair. Coats were also a prize possession for growing children. We were lucky to have one. Occasionally, we might get a "hand-me-down" from someone who had outgrown their coat. Most of the women sewed and made most of our clothes. They rarely had money to spare for patterns, but they were creative and made some stylish clothes. They made quilts from scraps left over. They "made do with what they had."

There were lots of hobos on the freight trains. If the train stopped to take on water, and knew it would be there for a while, the hobos would scatter through town and ask for something to eat. We usually gave them whatever we had. Most of them were polite, and we were never afraid of them. We felt we were all in about the same situation, so we gave them what we could.

A bunch of us were playing together. We heard a train whistle. One boy said, "Let's go to the depot and count the hobos." The train wasn't stopping for very long. The boys counted ninety-six men and one woman. It really disturbed the boys about the one lady. They were shocked.

Strange as it may seem we played all over town. We were never afraid —nor did our parents seem to worry. We always felt safe wherever we were. The whole town was our playground. The town folks knew us and our dogs by name. All of us grew up together. We knew we had to be polite and mind the adults. If we didn't they would tell our folks and we would be in *trouble*!

If we thought the Depression was bad, we found we didn't know the half of it. We were in the Dust Bowl, without warning. We never referred to it as the Dust Bowl; we called it the Dirty Thirties! The first dust storm I remember came when I was four or five years old. We lived in a house that faced an unpaved highway.

My sister looked out to see a woman across the highway trying to thumb a ride. A big sandstorm was headed our way from the northwest. She told my brother to go ask her to come in. He came back to say she was gone. Mother sent him to look for her. He found her in a nearby vacant house, piling up newspapers, trying to make a bed with them. He brought her home with him. We sat down for supper. My sister asked the woman if she wanted to say grace. That prayer went on and on. I was seated right by a vinegar pie. Head bowed, I would open one eye and peep at the pie. The prayer finally ended with all of us saying amen! The woman was a traveling evangelist. She spent the night with us. When I awoke the next morning she was gone. The sandstorm has blown out. A nice sunny day for a change!

Another sandstorm I remember, I was at a friend's house on a farm in the country. We saw the storm boiling toward us. The mother ran to the chicken house to gather the eggs. She wanted my friend and me to help her get a hen with baby chicks into the chicken house. The sun was still shining and the hen and chickens didn't want to go in that early. It took some time and effort, but we barely got it done in time. We headed to the house. The father drove up and went to the windmill. Windmills in those days didn't have an automatic cut-off. He went to turn off the windmill. The storm hit before he got to the house. The mother put a lamp in the window. He got lost in very familiar territory. It was pitch-black. He groped and stumbled, sand stinging his face. He finally saw the faint glimmer of the lamp and got into the house. Sand piled up on east-west fences so high you could walk over fences, with no problem at all. You might see the very top of the fence posts.

Most people remember Black Sunday, which was on Easter Sunday. One of my brothers was working out in the country. Some people came to visit. They heard lots of birds—very noisy, and unusual. They went out to look. He said it looked like thousands of birds desperately trying to get away from the huge black clouds rolling toward them. He had never seen so many birds—all kinds—all sizes—all together—all in flight, racing with all their strength to get away. The clouds were black, as black as coal. It was always remembered as the worst of the worse.

Another sandstorm on a farm. The mother was coming in on the train. The father went to meet her. There were several of us there at the house. A storm of high wind and *dust*. We had been told to cover our faces with wet cloths to avoid dust pneumonia. A little two-year-old boy wanted no part of that. He was not about to sit still, let alone have a wet cloth over his face. The next day they brought big number-three size tubs and shovels in the house to carry the sand out. They tried putting tin over the north windows and painting the windows shut. None of it helped.

The Dirty Thirties have never been forgotten by anyone who went through it. The Depression, The Dust Bowl . We thought that was bad enough. Then we had an invasion of grasshoppers. All of these plagues seemed to stay with us. Most of us wondered why we stayed in it.

EL PASO

CARMEN CHAVEZ LUJAN

Carmen Chavez-Lujan is a second generation Chicana, born and raised in El Paso, Texas. She is the proud mother of four children, Chacho, Andrea, Daniel and Alfonso and has a beautiful three-year old granddaughter, Lilliana. She got her Bachelor's Degree in English with an Extended Major in Spanish from Stanford Unity in 1982. She now resides with her children in Santa Fe.

"TIO"

Tío was not actually my tío. He was an old Chinese man who owned the Shanghai Grocery Store on Missouri Street in Sunset Heights in El Paso, Texas. The store has since been torn down to make way for the freeway. But all the neighborhood children called him Tío. His son, Buck, and Buck's wife, Sylvia, helped him run the store.

My mother would send me to the store for a loaf of bread or a pound of *carne molida* (ground meat) or whatever. Buck would grind the meat right in front of me. The store was across the street from where we lived. The house has been torn down too. Mom would always say, "Be sure to ask Tío for *pilon*." That meant to try to get something free, not to be mistaken for a five-finger discount. So I would run across the street and into the store.

Tío would be sitting behind the counter on his stool, usually falling asleep. Tío was fluent in Chinese and Spanish. He pretended to be a mean old man, and he would glare at you when you came in. But the kids knew better. He would get me what I was sent for and put it on the counter. I would ask him to put it on our *cuent*a (account) like my mom would say.

"Cuenta?" Tío would say. "What cuenta? You a clazy kid. When your momma gonna pay?"

Then I would say, "Tío, pilon?"

"Pilon? What pilon?" And then he would mutter something in Chinese, turn around and give me a loaf of day-old bread or a bunch of overripe bananas, and then he would tell me to go away.

I remember one day I did a very shameful thing, and I have not confessed it until today. It was right before school started. Tío had all the school supplies behind the counter. He would let the kids go behind the counter and select their supplies. I grabbed some paper that day, and I hid one and only paid for one. It cost a whole nickel. I got away with it, but I felt so guilty. I went back later and snuck the paper back on the shelf. I'm glad my mother never found out, because she would have spanked me for sure.

I was very sad when Tío died. He was a good man.

CARMEN CHAVEZ-LUJAN

MY BROTHER LUIS

Besides my mother, my brother Luis is the only other person in the family who has been constant in my life since the day I was born. I was born exactly two years to the day of my brother's birthday, December 1. I've heard it said that he was having a birthday party when I decided it was time to come into this world. I have been a burr on his side ever since.

Since my mother divorced my dad when we were so young, my brother took on the role of the man of the house. My mother catered to him and, consequently, so did his sisters, to some degree anyway.

He was a very independent kid. He didn't like school much and every chance he'd get, he'd sneak away to the movies in downtown El Paso. Back then, the Plaza Theater on El Paso Street was the state of the art theater with a beautiful two-sided staircase that led to the balcony, covered with lustrous, red carpeting throughout. The staircase reminded me of the one in *Gone with the Wind*" when Rhett Butler tells Scarlet O'Hara, "Frankly my dear, I don't give a damn." Anyway, my brother didn't much give a damn about school either, and he saw a lot of movies. He went to see Charlton Heston in *The Ten Commandments* about twelve times. He knew the dialogue by heart. It is still his favorite movie to this day.

One day, on one of his outings, he decided to go get his haircut. He could do this because at a young age he got a newspaper route and earned his own money to pay for things like haircuts. Anyway, he went to the barber shop in South El Paso. When he came home that afternoon he was wearing a cap on his head, which was very unusual for him. He took great pride in his hair, which was black and thick. When he took off his hat, we were shocked to see he didn't have any more hair.

"What happened to your hair?" I asked him.

"The barber said something about "Butch," he said. "I thought he asked me if he could call me 'Butch'. When he got done cutting my hair, I looked in the mirror. I couldn't believe it. I asked the guy, 'What did you do to my hair?' He said he asked me if I wanted a butch haircut and he said I said sure."

We laughed so hard; even my mom couldn't control her laughter; we fell down on the floor laughing. Needless to say, this only served to make my brother angry, and he stomped out of the room.

Talking about my brother's newspaper route, one day Luis came up with a brilliant idea.

"Carmen," he said. "How about going with me to deliver papers; that way, if I get sick, you can help me out?"

"Hey," I said. "That's a great idea! Mom will be sure to let me go as long as I'm with you." My mother never let the girls go out of the neighborhood by ourselves. This would give me a chance to venture out just like one of the guys.

My brother then proceeded to put an apron-like garment on me. It had a lot of pockets. We then rolled up all the newspapers and stuffed them into all the pockets. I waddled behind him carrying all the newspapers. He carried nothing. We walked from house to house, not to mention apartment buildings, up and down stairs, so many stairs.

"Hurry up, Carmen. I ain't got all day!" he yelled from the top of the stairs.

I looked at him, sweat dripping from my brow, my shoulders hurting from the weight of the newspapers.

"I'm hurrying as fast as I can, okay!" I yelled back I didn't dare say anything else; for fear that I would lose the opportunity to tag along with him.

At one of the houses there lived an elderly man and his sister, who was a couple of years younger than her brother. I wondered even way back then if my brother and I would be like this couple. They were a sweet pair who offered us milk and cookies every time we went to deliver their newspaper. One day, before we left their home, they gave my brother and me an embroidered cloth of the Santo Niño de Atocha, adored with sequins and beautiful threads. They wanted us to have it.

"No, thank you," my brother said. My eyes were glued to the piece of fabric I thought it was the most beautiful thing I had ever seen. I wanted it so badly.

"Yes," they insisted and put it in my hand. I looked at my brother, and he nodded that it was okay to take it.

"Thank you," I said, and we left.

"I don't know why you want that thing. It's just a rag." Luis said.

I became the caretaker of this beautiful needlework and I kept it with me up until ten years ago when I gave it to my brother for Christmas. Times were hard that year and I had nothing else to give.

"Thank you," Luis said, and I could see in his eyes that his thoughts went back to that day when this "rag" was given to us. He took it home to El Paso, had it framed in a special frame. It now hangs displayed on a wall in his home.

Getting back to “my brother’s” newspaper route, I learned his route and from that day forward, Luis often got sick, and I was left to deliver "his” newspapers. He was very healthy, though, when it came time to collect the money. I can’t really recall getting paid for my help. Maybe that’s why he is now a very successful businessman and I am not.

Luis was very protective of me, even at a young age. We lived on Oregon Street and later on we moved to another house where the Texas Employment Commission is now located. But my mother sent us to Holy Family Elementary School in Sunset Heights. The school was quite a distance from where we lived and we did not have a car. It was my brother’s responsibility to walk with me to school and make sure I got home. He was in second grade and I was in kindergarten. The problem was I got out of school at 11:30 and he did not get out until 2:30. So, I sat on the steps of the kindergarten school and waited for three hours until he came for me. I imagined seeing my brother playing with his friends at recess and during the lunch break as I waited. Thank goodness my Mom decided to move closer to the school. I don’t think I could have handled waiting for three hours for a full year.

Luis and I were very close, and I don’t think it was of his choosing. I just decided to tag along everywhere he went. Needless to say, I was a real tomboy and would join my brother and his friends at the corner lot and play baseball and football. He taught me to be a champion top spinner. We played marbles, and we dug holes and tunnels in the backyard for our little cars and trucks.

One winter, we got so much snow we got to stay home from school. I remember we had this great snowball fight against all the other kids in the neighborhood. We did not have any gloves, so we put extra socks on our hands. The snowball fight lasted all day. There was this kid named Domingo who kept hitting me with snowballs. I think he had a crush on me. My brother bombarded him with snowballs and he never came around again, at least not when my brother was around. By the time we got in the house, our hands and feet were frozen. My mom ran a tubful of hot water and stuck our feet in the tub until we got warm.

As the years went by, Luis and I kind of grew apart. He had his friends, and I discovered other interests. But even in our grown up years, he continued to keep an eye on me. When I was eighteen and started to date another young man named Luis, who later became my boyfriend and then my husband, my brother Luis went around asking questions about Luis Luján. He wanted to make sure he was a good guy, good enough for his little sister. I found this out years later. It goes without saying, "Once a big brother, always a big brother!"

CARMEN CHÁVEZ LUJAN

THE PRODIGAL MOM

To say my mother was always a prodigal mom would be untrue. She took good care of us when she was at home. When she was not at home, she made sure that there would be an adult to take care of us. Sometimes it was a live-in housekeeper, or a relative. But it was always someone who she thought she could trust.

I have vivid memories of my mother in the kitchen, always in the kitchen. She has always loved cooking and would try different foods with us, as the guinea pigs. When we lived in Sunset Heights, our meals consisted of lots of soups and stews. *Caldo de res* (beef broth) was a staple in our home. The aroma of beef bones simmering with cabbage, turnips, corn-on- the-cob and potatoes could be smelled from a block away. Although I did not appreciate this dish back then, I sure miss it now. My mom's fried chicken was and still is the best, and Colonel Sanders' fried chicken cannot hold a candle to hers. The chicken pieces were perfectly floured with succulent spices and fried to a deep golden brown. My brother, Luis, still goes over to my mother's house when he knows she has made her famous fried chicken.

There were a few dishes that mom just couldn't get quite right, however, try as she might. With the Yees having their grocery store across the street, they introduced their delicious Chinese foods to us. It was then that I acquired an affinity for Asian foods. My mom would make her rendition of chop suey and, quite frankly, it was an affront to my taste buds. I couldn't tell my mom that because she was very proud of her concoction that she called chop suey. Just looking at the chicken swirling around in a tan colored sauce surrounded by over cooked bean sprouts was enough to make me want to excuse myself. But if that was the meal, that is what we would eat or go hungry until the next day. Mom would always say, "*No es restaurante!*" (It's not a restaurant).

When my mom would make *tortillas de harina* (flour tortillas), I would stand next to her, waiting for the opportunity to cut the dough with cookie cutters which she would then cook for us to eat. Memories of tortilla giraffes, elephants, horses and, for the holidays, camels, stars, and angels still linger in my mind. Then, with the last few pieces of tortilla dough, she would cut the rolled out dough in sixes, fry them in hot, deep lard, which would result in *sopaipillas*. She would then take these delicacies and roll them in sugar and cinnamon and give one to each of us to snack on before dinner. It was heaven. It didn't take much to make me happy.

Every so often, though, my mom would get a hankering to go to California, to visit her cousin Elodia. So, one day we would get home from school and her clothes would be packed in boxes, ready to go to the train depot to catch the next train to Los Angeles. She would take us with her every summer, but some trips she would go alone. She would arrange for Lupe, the maid, to stay with us, or my Aunt Mary. Then we would walk her to the depot, which was only a couple of blocks away, dragging her boxes behind us, running, always running to catch the last train that evening. Even after we all grew up and could afford to fly to Los Angeles, we were always running to catch our flight just minutes before they closed the door. Once I was on my own, I decided that this would not be my *modus operandi*—that I would leave with plenty of time to get to the bus depot or the airport and even have time to go to the gift shop and buy a magazine. This was unheard of when I was a kid.

She would say, *"Ya me voy. Se portan bien. Les llamo cuando llego a Los Angeles!"(*"I'm going now. Behave yourselves I'll call when I get to Los Angeles.")_

"Adios, mama!" we would yell, running alongside the train until she was out of sight. "When is mom coming back?" my little sister, Cecilia, would ask. "She'll be back soon!" my brother Luis would say. I would say nothing. Then we would cross the tracks and go back home, anxiously waiting for her to call us and for her to get back.

The next day, mom would call. *"Que estan haciendo?" (*What are the doing?)_

"Nothing, we're just watching television." Milton Berle would be on our black and white television set. No one in our neighborhood had a color television. I don't think anyone in the world had one back then, except our next door neighbor. Maria's TV had a piece of colored cellophane covering the tv screen. I could see George and Armando, Maria's nephews, through their porch window, watching tv through strips of red, blue and green cellophane. Milton and George Gobel sure looked funny with blue faces. During the early morning hours we would watch Mighty Mouse, Little Lulu or the three black birds. (I can't even remember the name of that cartoon).

"Here he comes to save the day! Mighty Mouse is on his way!" We would sing while my brother Luis spoke to mom on the phone. Lupe would yell from the kitchen to lower the volume.

Lupe yelled, *"Su hermano esta hablando con su mama. Cállense*!" "(Your brother is talking to his mom! Shut up!)

Lupe or my Aunt Mary would prepare meals for us, but it was nothing compared to mom's cooking. A week would go by and mom would call again.

"When are you coming home, mom?" we would all ask.

"I'll be home this Saturday," she would say.

So on Saturday, Luis, Ceci and I would walk to the train depot to meet mom. The train would arrive, and the conductor, who knew us by sight, would allow us to go past the gate and wait for our mom. We would wait until all the passengers would de-board and there was no one else in sight. We continued to wait until the conductor would say, "There's no one else on the train, kids." We would walk home. Once home, we would call her and ask her what had happened.

"I missed the train. I will be there tomorrow."

On Sunday, we walked to the train depot and waited again until all the passengers had left and the conductor would say, "That's it kids. No one else on this train." We would walk home.

She would call that night and say, "I missed the train again. I promise I will be there tomorrow."

This same scenario went on a couple of times until one day she would call and say, "Where are you kids?"

"We're home watching cartoons on the television," my brother Luis would say. "Where are you?"

"I'm at the train depot! Why aren't you kids here?'

"How were we supposed to know you would get here today? We thought you had missed the train again," Luis said.

Then we would hurry and put on our shoes and jackets and run the two blocks to the train depot and run to our mom who was waiting, sitting on a bench with her boxes full of clothes. I would wrap my arms around her and say, "I missed you mom!"

Then we would walk home together, talking and laughing all the way home, anxious to eat our mom's cooking and see what she had brought us from California.

DOUGLAS, ARIZONA

Introduction

Located on the Rio Grande directly opposite the Mexican city of Agua Prieta, Douglas, like other Arizona border towns, is sustained by mining. And like other mining towns throughout the old West, in its early days Douglas attracted plenty of rough customers. Late in his life, Arizona Ranger Burton Mossman said he had been to plenty of rough towns, including Deadwood and Tombstone, but that Douglas was the roughest of them all.

Douglas, however, remained unknown to the rest of the country until 2010 when Douglas rancher, Robert Krentz, was murdered by a Mexican illegal crossing Kentz's land transporting drugs. That killing made national headlines, in large part because Douglas was a hotspot for illegal trafficking of drugs and people. The following year, I visited Douglas hoping for an interview with Robert Krentz's widow, and with others who had first-hand experience of the border problem .

I did interview Sue Krentz, the widow of Robert Krentz, but her family declined to have the interview published. Among the other interviews I conducted, the most informative, was the one published here. Eddie Valdez, the man interviewed, had spent his working life in law enforcement. I found Eddie by chance at a MacDonald's that was within sight of the port of entry. I had arrived in Douglas the night before, and the next morning drove to the border, near the port of entry, intuiting that there I would find someone willing to talk. Eddie was sitting by himself, and I decided I would approach him. I sat at a nearby table and waited until enough time had passed to make my approach less intrusive. As I found out the next day, the MacDonald's was a hangout for Border Patrol agents. One of them, a big burly man with tattoos up and down his arms was friendly, but could not be interviewed without permission from the Tucson section. I called Tucson, and they passed me on to another headquarters, that passed me on to Burbank, California, which handed requests for filmed interviews. So much for an interview with Border Patrol.

When I think of Douglas today, I see a town bleached by the sun, whose only bright spot is the Gadsden Hotel, a building on the National Historic Register. In 1962 Thornton Wilder, seeking a respite from the East Coast literary scene, headed west in his Thunderbird. The car broke down outside of Douglas, and Wilder stayed for the night, then for another,, and finally settled in Douglas for a year and a half, where he wrote his novel, *The Eighth Day*.

EDDIE VALDEZ

Eddie Valdez spent seventeen years in law enforcement, both in the Cochise County Sheriff's Department and the Douglas police force. Esddie passed away in 2013.

MEXICAN DRUGS AND A CULT

RW: How safe is it over there in Mexico?

EV: There have been some shootings, and one of the Chiefs of Police got shot there maybe three years ago. Another lieutenant for the State Police got shot and killed. There's been some, but not as many as I would think there would be, and I know for a fact that the Chief of Police [in Aqua Prieta] was a dirty guy, you know. I had known him for a long time, and unfortunately, I had to deal with him on stolen vehicles, and he would move around a lot in the State of Sonora, and he ended up getting shot.

Coincidentally, his brother, after he got shot, was also suspected of being not a clean cop, turned himself in, or he got caught with twenty pounds at the port of entry, and I think he's still in the United States, probably. The reason I suspect that happened is [so] that he wouldn't get killed. His whole family happened to be in the car. They had twenty pounds of marijuana in it. That was pretty coincidental, I guess, like a couple of days after his brother got killed.

He was not let go, and I think probably he might have talked. He might have said something to the federal agents on this side, and they arrested him. And I think a lot of it is something he intentionally did just so they wouldn't kill him, go after him, because him and his brother were really tight . . ..

RW: So, it was intentional. They drove over with the marijuana so he'd get picked up?

EV: Yes. It was something that was planned.

RW: Going back over the history of police work, what was the most dangerous episode that you encountered?

EV: Probably the most dangerous one were the drug smugglers. It's always been around, and for a long, long time, Douglas was, you know, really, really hit hard by the drug trade to the United States, and we got hit with a pretty bad reputation. Everybody knew Douglas because it was always a big smuggling community, when in fact, it was all over the place. And so if you were a cop and you went somewhere and [and you said] you're from Douglas, [they would say] "Oh, yeah, I smuggled out of Douglas," and stuff like that. Maybe so, but the drugs very rarely stayed in Douglas. They went from Douglas to Tucson, and then Tucson is where they would stay [temporarily], whether they were smuggling them back East, or wherever they were going to go. The biggest thing was probably, of course, you had the drug smugglers, and then illegal immigrants coming through. For a while there they were sending illegal immigrants first and then the drugs right behind them, just to deploy Border Patrol to start chasing them [the illegals]. They're very smart. They're very smart. Then the fence [between Doulas and Aqua Prieta] started coming up, so everything was moved out towards the outskirts of town. There wasn't that much illegal immigrants [or] illegal smuggling entering the United States through the city limits. It would actually move them out from the city limits out to the county.

RW: What was your most dangerous assignment?

EV: Well, realistically, they're all dangerous, but after twenty-seven years of law enforcement, probably going out on 80E toward New Mexico. You would lose all radio contact. We had walkie talkies. They were okay for a short distance. The further out east you got, the worse it would get because you had no radio contact. Up in the mountains, the same thing. So it's interesting. I'd do it again. It was fun.

RW: Pick one assignment.

EV: One incident, probably…this didn't have anything to do with drug smugglers. There was a group of people that came from Mississippi, a group of Black people, church people, that were hiding behind the religious constitution, and they came and they started terrorizing this place called Miracle Valley, which is outside of Bisbee, to the point where they were attacking law enforcement.

They did not believe in healing. They did not believe in doctors. The whole thing was prayer. What brought this all out was that they took a child into the Emergency Room at the hospital in Bisbee and come to find out that the child died of a hernia rupture. It was obvious neglect because they had prayed and prayed and prayed for this child, and of course, he passed away. So then DPS got involved. It determined that it happened in the county, so they called another deputy out. They determined it was Bisbee's jurisdiction, so they called me out, and that's the way the whole thing started.

There was a Ms. Mary Thomas, and then there was the father, Reverend Thomas, and there was a son, also Thomas. He had a lot of military experience, so they would go out and do military-type tactics. They were involved with explosives. They were running around with the bombs and a bomb blew up in their van. We were called and sure enough, there was one person dead with a big hole in the stomach. He had been holding onto the bomb. It was actually activated by a paper clip. This guy was messing around with it and, boom, it blew up.

They were chasing the news people out, throwing rocks, throwing hammers at 'em. They would trap utility people, that's the APS public service people up on the poles. The APS was gonna shut down their electricity because they weren't paying their bill. They were not a religious group. They were hiding behind their religious constitution. Their people are very well programmed, very well programmed. They would stop an APS guy, about eight or nine would get out of a car and start circling the car and singing verses from the Bible.

The final incident was that we had an agreement with the Governor [Bruce Babbitt] and DPS. The sheriff called the Governor and told him that we were going to go in at 6 o'clock in the morning the following day. It was on a Saturday. I remember that very well. And apparently, Babbitt called the DPS Director, and the DPS Director called Captain Hurt, a Black man. Captain Hurt called Mr. Thomas and told him that we were going to go in. When we went in, they were waiting for us. Basically, our job was to find out what was going on and to take pictures. Sure enough, I went to a house. The ones we were looking for weren't there. We went to a second house. Then went to a third house. And then the Blacks started coming out of the houses with sticks and bats, and they kind of like surrounded us, and we asked for two more units to be sent in. Things got a little bit nastier. They sent two more units, boom, sent everybody in. There was only 36 of us and again, maybe 300 of them. So we were very, very outnumbered.

They had weapons, they had long gun firearms, they had bats, they had rebars, they had twigs, they had bottles. The women were pretty tough, let me tell you. They were maybe about 5'2", 5'4" about 260, 280 [pounds]. They put the children first, then the women. The men were always in the back row. That was their style. And seriously, we took a beating, a bad beating. Like I said, Thomas, Jr. got shot and he died, and there was a son-in-law who also got shot, and he died. And then the Sheriff got shot in the face. Dave Jones, the deputy, got shot in the face and had two broken arms from rebar. And another deputy—I forgot his name, actually is the one who did the shootings. We pulled out and we left. We pulled out, then Pima County, which is Tucson, they sent a SWAT team, and they helped us clear [them] out…we went back in with them and cleared it to make sure none of our people were left behind .

They sued us for $75M, and I think they got like $70K, and all the attorneys were fighting for that $70K, and they all moved back, back to Chicago and Mississippi, but they sold everything. Some of these people actually had money, and they sold everything and gave it to Mrs. Thomas because she controlled everything financial.

EDDIE VALDEZ

DRUG TUNNEL

EV. I was commenting on a drug load that was found here in Douglas, which was started in Mexico, in Agua Prieta, Sonora. The interesting part about that was that they had a very sophisticated tunnel built by Chinese. Afterwards they were all put on a bus and taken somewhere, and the information, that we weren't really able to confirm, was that they were all shot and killed. We were never able to confirm that, but that was one of the interesting parts about that, because it all happened in Mexico. We were very limited as to what intelligence we got out of Mexico. But it was a very cooperative operation with them [the Mexican police]. What happened is there's a warehouse on this side that we were collecting on, and we went in, and we were able to find traces to a place called Queen Creeks in Phoenix. I think it was about 600 pounds of cocaine that came out of that warehouse. We brought some machinery, Customs did. I was assigned to Customs Office of Enforcement at that time. These particular machines we brought in are used to measure if there's any hollow earth underneath the ground. We were using them in one section of town. Finally, we found something hollow underneath. When we went ahead, we hit the warehouse around this side in Douglas, at the border. We were able to find a tunnel, and we contacted our Mexican counterparts, and sure enough there was a house on the other [Mexican] side with a very sophisticated tunnel. They had lights. They had a little railroad system, railroad tracks for a cart, and they would pull it to the United States.

On the Mexican side, it was a nice house [with a] big den.

But we had a heck of a time figuring out how this thing operated. Our chief of police—we're all looking—turned on a valve outside, and sure enough, there was a pool table and probably two hydraulics like you use at the gas station, but big ones, lifted the pool table and lifted some cement out. Underneath there was actually a room, probably about thirty-eight by thirty, and there were some drugs there. That's where we were able to find the tunnel on the Mexican side.

RW. How did you locate that house?

EV. Well, we looked at the house because we got into the tunnel on this side, and then we walked over there, so we were able to figure out more or less where it was, and you [could] actually see [from it] to the other side. We couldn't get into the Mexican side, of course, because it's Mexico, so we had to work with them.

RW. They were cooperative?

EV. Oh, yeah, they were cooperative.

RW. What I seem to be hearing is that there was a lot of corruption in Mexico.

EV. Yes, definitely. There's a lot of corruption in Mexico. You have to be very, very, very careful who you work with and what you say. But, unfortunately, you have to work with these people. You have to. If someone in Mexico is wanted here, you can't go into Mexico and bring him back home. If you do that, you've just kidnapped somebody. That's what happened with the DEA [Drug Enforcement Agency] with [DEA agent] Camarena, when he got killed. They [DEA] went into Mexico, and they brought back a doctor that had actually tortured Camarena. So then there were two warrants out for the DEA agents [who had gone into Mexico]. One of them was assigned here in Douglas, and up to this day there's still a warrant for this DEA agent, who is retired. The U.S. would not arrest him or anything. You just can't go in there and bring somebody back across.

RW. Which is what these two DEA agents did, right?

EV. Yes. They went over and found out where he was in Mexico, and they brought him back, so that's kidnapping. Without any paperwork. They didn't go through the legal system. They wanted him so bad over here, that they brought him back.

REW. And where is that guy now? Is he in jail, prison?

EV. I don't even know if he had to get released or if he's in prison.

RW. He was a dealer?

EV. Oh, he was the one that ordered the DEA agent killed in Mexico

RW. Okay..

EV. So yeah, they did that, and as a matter of fact, I know that particular agent who kidnapped the doctor now has a big, big private investigation business and he does really well. I know him really well. For a while, we had eight to ten DEA agents assigned to the Douglas area—Border Patrol, Customs, DEA. FBI had never really had an office in Douglas. They had one up in Chula Vista, but they were doing a lot of work in Douglas. There's a lot of law enforcement in Douglas. Over on my side of town where I live, every other house is either a cop, Border Patrol, or something.

RW. Is the DEA agent living here?

EV. No, no. Actually, he had already moved out of his house when this happened. I think he was assigned to Mexico City, and that's when they found out that this guy [the doctor] was over there, and they just set him up and brought him back. There's a lot of, I guess, uneasiness between law enforcement at that time in general. I'm talking about city, county, and feds with the Mexican authorities because of what was done, but everybody on this side, as far as law enforcement is concerned, were happy it happened. It was like we finally got this guy, but in reality, it was against the Mexican law, and it really is kidnapping.

Afterword

Readers will note that the stories in *Coyotes and Stars* illustrate the impact that family and community had on the lives of its writers. My friend, Tom St. Clair, after reading the manuscript, thought this was one of the book's important lessons. "Family and community," he noted, "have been seriously degraded. Losing them has meant losing a sense of personal purpose and role." Their formative roles are amply illustrated in two of the book's sections, "Hispanic Villages" and "The Pueblo of Pojoaque."

The stories in "Hispanic Villages" describe a culture woven out of a common religion that gave meaning to human existence. But beyond religious lessons there was something else. Perhaps it was the necessity of relying upon one's neighbors in a time before the diffusion of technology made us believe ourselves to be self-reliant islands. Need—necessity—created community by forcing cooperation and ethical behavior.

Delores Griego's essay, "La Escuela," makes clear the role of the family in fostering virtue. She begins: "My parents were our first teachers. Our learning center was a solid, rectangular wooden table . . . . It was around this solid, polished kitchen table that my two brothers and I were fed—body, soul, and mind. We were taught responsibility, honesty, commitment and integrity." This modest essay was written to remind us what we have passed over.

The stories in "The Pueblo of Pojoaque" describe tribal members working consciously to build links to their tribe's heritage, which not only creates a role for them but helps propel their community into the future. Mary Ann Fiero's story, "Traditional Bread Making," illustrates the cultural significance that hand made bread, baked by the family in the horno, has for Native Americans.

She and her family had been buying their feast day bread from Santa Clara Pueblo until they realized that making their own was one way to link themselves to their heritage. Anna Sanchez' story, "The Dance," illustrates yet another way the pueblo is reviving its culture —by encouraging the young to participate in sacred dances. And yet a third way, Francine Maestas tells us, is by reviving traditional gardening methods. Lucy Tafoya and Daniel Moya found their roles in the pueblo through their traditional art. Learning Tewa, their tribe's traditional language is yet a fifth way.

Coyotes and Stars enables us to realize that in New Mexico the three cultures—Hispanic, Pueblo, and Anglo— co-existed and collaborated peacefully for centuries. In isolated areas, necessity initiated cooperation. Moving from Texas to a ranch in rural New Mexico, Peggy Clay found help and assurance from neighboring Hispanics and Anglos. "Their knowledge amazed me," she writes, "In northeast New Mexico, the Hispanics and Anglos have mixed and mingled since pioneer days. . . . They were very eager to open up their homes. My quest was over. I had found my place."

A great part of my appreciation for the Southwest derives from the vibrancy of the three cultures that created this unique region. But our collective toleration for difference is strained, perhaps broken, in recent decades by the waves of immigrants crossing our southern border. Many factors have united to create virulent opposition to the immigrants. It is like the impetuous flow of white settlers into Native American territories that spanned two centuries. We don't know what lasting effects may come from the disruption, but we can hope that given time they, too, will find themselves with jobs, homes and growing families. The forces that seek to divide us are formidable but not absolute.

www.ingramcontent.com/pod-product-compliance
Lightning Source LLC
LaVergne TN
LVHW010051110826
845155LV00028B/286

* 9 7 8 1 8 7 8 7 8 1 2 0 8 *